LONG DARK ROAD

JASPER, TEXAS, WATER TOWER

LONG

DARK

ROAD

Bill King and Murder in Jasper, Texas

Ricardo C. Ainslie
Photographs by Sarah Wilson

UNIVERSITY OF TEXAS PRESS, AUSTIN

*The publication of this book was assisted by a University
Cooperative Society Subvention Grant awarded by The
University of Texas at Austin.*

Requests for permission to reproduce material
from this work should be sent to Permissions,
University of Texas Press, P.O. Box 7819,
Austin, TX 78713–7819.

∞ The paper used in this book meets the minimum
requirements of ANSI/NISO Z39.48–1992 (R1997)
(Permanence of Paper).

Library of Congress Cataloging-in-Publication Data

Ainslie, Ricardo C.
    Long dark road : Bill King and murder in Jasper, Texas / Ricardo C. Ainslie ;
photographs by Sarah Wilson.—1st ed.
        p.   cm.
    ISBN 0-292-70574-3 (cloth : alk. paper)
    1. King, Bill, 1974–   2. Murderers—Texas—Jasper—Biography.
    3. Murder—Texas—Jasper.   4. Hate crimes—Texas—Jasper.
    5. Byrd, James, D. 1998.   6. African American men—Crimes against—
    Texas—Jasper.   7. Racism—Texas—Jasper.   8. Jasper (Tex.)—Race relations.
    I. Title.
    HV6534.J36A37   2004
    364.152′3′092—dc22

                                                            2004009575

For Gemma, Roberto, and Gabriella

FOR WE ALL OF US,

GRAVE OR LIGHT,

GET OUR THOUGHTS

ENTANGLED IN METAPHORS, AND

ACT FATALLY ON THE STRENGTH OF THEM.

—GEORGE ELIOT, *Middlemarch*

Contents

Preface

FROM THE START OF THIS PROJECT I have found the discrepancy between the savage murder of James Byrd and Bill King's demeanor deeply troubling. Jasper County sheriff Billy Rowles once told me that following his arrest on June 7, 1998, Bill King was "a perfect gentleman." In the three years that I have known King, spending many hours visiting him on Texas's death row and via an extended correspondence, there has been little in our interactions to dispute the sheriff's characterization. King has consistently been a man of his word, sending me requested documents and responding to specific inquiries. King did once accuse me of being naive in my presumed acceptance of the state's view of him, and he once said that he doubted that I had the fortitude to tell the world the "truth" about his situation and to go against the grain of conventional thought and safe prescriptions in order to proclaim his innocence. But these were relatively measured confrontations, given that the stakes for King are so high.

It is difficult to reconcile the charming, amiable Bill King with a crime propelled by such raw sadism. The incongruity is disturbing, even haunting. When I've attempted to describe this tension to others, the typical response has been to simply label King as "psychopathic" or "sociopathic," diagnostic terms commonly invoked to describe individuals with a history of antisocial behavior who are capable of charm but who are incapable of genuine care and concern for others. Such individuals are prone, instead, toward manipulating other people, coercing them in overt and subtle ways to extract what they want from them, but otherwise are devoid of feeling for others. To be sure, I did occasionally recognize King's attempts to manipulate me. For example, though it had been clear from the outset that ours was not a professional relationship, King attempted to manipulate me—by threatening to remove me from his visitor list—into providing psychological testing that could conceivably be used in his appeals process. When I refused, however, he did not terminate our visits. King's friends and family have also provided many illustrations of his capacity for manipulation. Yet I remain convinced that King is a man capable of caring for others, such as his son, to whom he is deeply attached, and his father. I have also witnessed in King a capacity for an unusual degree of loyalty toward specific individuals, including Russell Brewer, his comrade in arms, a quality that does not readily fit the stereotype of the psychopathic personality. Bill King, in other words, is not easily reducible to handy psychiatric formulations.

Something that has been particularly difficult for me in writing this book is the fact that over the years I have come to feel attached to King, notwithstanding what he has done. Finding the humanity in a man who has committed a barbarous act raises myriad questions, and for the longest time I think I found it difficult to admit the presence of these feelings, as if they might somehow suggest tolerance or acceptance for what happened to James Byrd. As a psychologist, I am accustomed to hearing about thoughts, feelings, and actions that the world might find morally reprehensible but in relation to which I am entrusted to adopt a less judgmental stance in order to further another's self-understanding. But this situation seems different, both because I have not been in the role of psychologist in my dealings with King and because of the nature of his crime.

Without removing the burden of responsibility that King bears for his actions and for the manner in which his life has unfolded, I believe that King's failures, in the end, are our collective failures. Bill King is now locked up in a little cubicle with its lone shaft of light, safely contained. To many, the fact that he is in line to be executed is reassuring. However, his sins cannot be contained within the walls of death row. Instead, they seep out and rejoin the great chaos of the human condition, finding new forms, new identities, new victims, and new reprisals. The forces that may have worked to create Bill King's life will continue to exist among us and will continue to pose a challenge to society. We may be able to extinguish the life, but we can never erase the fact that Bill King is, ultimately, one of us.

Acknowledgments

OVER THE COURSE OF THE THREE YEARS I spent working on this project, numerous people have been invaluable for their support. I am especially indebted to Helen Thorpe and Steve Harrigan for their close reading of the manuscript and for their generosity of time and ideas. Jan Reid and John Works also offered many excellent suggestions for the manuscript. In addition, other friends and colleagues read portions of the manuscript or contributed to my thinking about the book through discussions and conversation, including Jim Magnuson, Larry Wright, Greg Curtis, Bill Crawford, and John Burnett. Their support, too, has been extremely valuable and much appreciated.

At the University of Texas Press, Bill Bishel, my editor, has been very helpful and insightful in his suggestions, while the marketing director, Dave Hamrick, has been very enthusiastic about this book from the outset, which meant a great deal to me.

David Anderson and Tim Herman have been exceedingly generous with their time in sharing their expertise regarding legal documents and legal processes.

Sarah Wilson's photography has added a great deal to the book, and I am grateful to her for her collaboration on this and the related exhibit, "Jasper, Texas: The Healing of a Community in Crisis."

I also want to thank the Texas Department of Criminal Justice for permitting interviews, for providing input on the workings of death row, and for giving me the opportunity to visit its facilities. In particular, I wish to thank Michelle Lyons, Larry Todd, and Larry Fitzgerald of the TDCJ Public Information Office; Neal Webb, the warden of George Beto I Unit; Terry Foster, the warden of Ramsey I Unit; and Sammy Bonatello and John Moriarty of the TDCJ Gang Intelligence Unit.

I am appreciative of the following people for their various forms of assistance and their conversation: Sharon Bates, Gary Cohen, Dick Holland, Kat Jones, Jerry and Jaynie Lehman, John Magner, Jan McInroy, Valerie Primus, Alice Tucker, and Tom Zigal. Brian Junker helped me gain access to the Shawn Berry trial, a defining experience in the evolution of this book.

The following students and assistants have been great supporters of and contributors to my work over the years, and while many were involved in my academic studies of Jasper as a community in crisis rather than this project, their input, ideas, and effort have contributed, either directly or indirectly, to this work as well: Kalina Braebeck, Angelic Chaison, Mary Choi, Anna Dematatis, Emily Hall, Melissa Holt, Paul LePhuoc, Stella Nellms, and Ashley Senior.

Pat and Dave of the Belle Jim Bed and Breakfast; the Catholic Diocese of Jasper, which on numerous occasions permitted me to use its lake house; and Billy's Barbecue all provided a home away from home during my many stays in Jasper.

The people in Jasper were extremely kind and open as I pursued a story of which they had grown quite tired, having been overrun by the national and international media for extended periods of time. Their generosity is all the more impressive when one considers that the community itself often seemed to be on trial, as if this murder was somehow of their making, which it was not.

Vern Elizabeth and B. G. Harris, the "magnificent ones," provided me with a summer writing refuge that was idyllic.

Finally, I am grateful for my family's love and support and their willingness to endure my obsession with this story, as they have with others, for numerous years: my wife, Gemma Ainslie, and my children, Roberto Ainslie and Gabriella Ainslie.

LONG DARK ROAD

The Row

THE FIRST TIME I MET BILL KING, I was struck by his size; at five foot nine he appeared incongruously small in relation to the enormity of the crime for which he was convicted. On February 25, 1999, a Jasper, Texas, jury sentenced John William King to die by lethal injection for his role in the killing of James Byrd Jr., a black man who had been assaulted and dragged to death the previous summer while chained by his ankles to the back of a pickup truck. Byrd's torn and dismembered remains had been dumped unceremoniously in front of a rural African American church. Since the slaying occurred after midnight on a Saturday night, the presumed intent was that horrified worshipers would discover him on their way to services the next morning. Two other men were also subsequently convicted for having taken part in the sadistic murder, which many would later characterize as a modern-day lynching.

I felt fortunate to be visiting Bill King given that inmates are permitted to have only ten people on their visitation list (names may be added or deleted from the list every six months). King was escorted from his cell by two corrections officers, hands cuffed behind his back, to one of several three-foot-by-three-foot cells in the visitation area. Once safely locked inside the "box," as prisoners refer to these cells, King extended his hands through a slot in the door so that his handcuffs could be removed, freeing him to talk on the telephone that connected him to the other side of a window—to the outside world. All visits, including attorney and clergy meetings, take place under these circumstances, with prisoners and visitors separated by thick bulletproof glass.

King's prison-issue white jumpsuit was unbuttoned at the top, revealing a crew-neck T-shirt that had turned a dull gray from countless washings. "DR," for "death row," was stenciled in large block letters on the right pant leg and across the back of the jumpsuit. Most often, even in winter, King preferred short-sleeved jumpsuits so that he could sport the "full-sleeve" tattoos whose racist and satanic content had become infamous during his trial. A prison artist called "Dirtball," with whom King had previously been incarcerated, had rendered most of them. His tattoos start at the wrist line and extend all the way up each of his arms in an unbroken, seamless pattern of blue images (prison tattoo artists don't often have access to other colors). The only portion of his arms that has escaped Dirtball's artful eye is his right elbow, which King refers to as his "virgin patch."

Despite the tattoos, I found that there was something disarming about being in the presence of King, a man whom most of the world had come to view as a monster, the very embodiment of evil. His demeanor was not what I had expected from a man on death row, let alone from someone guilty of a barbarous crime that had drawn both national and international attention. He was baby-faced, and his expression readily conveyed geniality. There was actually something soft about him, a quality that might explain the steady flow of letters that he receives from female admirers from all over the country. King's manner was matter-of-fact; he was direct but not brusque. He was also a man of obvious intelligence. A high school dropout, King nevertheless has an impressive command of the English language, and he articulates his ideas with ease. I would later learn that he has the habit of searching the dictionary for unfamiliar words that he finds interesting and then incorporating them into conversation and correspondence, a strategy for improving his vocabulary that he learned from his tenth-grade English teacher.

King was twenty-five years old at the time of that first meeting, in August 2000, and his short brown hair was thinning prematurely. He told me that he preferred to cut his own hair with a razor in his cell rather than

JOHN WILLIAM KING

going to the prison barbers, whom he accused of not being particularly fastidious about disinfecting their barbering tools. He also described his "house"—as prisoners refer to their cells—as impeccably clean and organized, with his correspondence arranged according to source or subject matter and filed chronologically. King liked to make his bed with smart forty-five-degree folds, military style, as he learned to do at the age of seventeen, when he was first sent away to "boot camp" for participating in a burglary. This individual, now so notorious for having committed such a brutal crime, has a penchant for orderliness.

THE POLUNSKY UNIT, formerly named the Terrell Unit, houses the male prisoners on Texas's death row. The Texas Department of Criminal Justice prefers to be discreet about the prison; about a mile west of Livingston, on U.S. Highway 190, a modest green sign with white lettering simply announces, "TDCJ Polunsky Unit," with an arrow pointing left. It is the only indication that suggests the presence of the prison, and the sign's understated character might easily lead one to think that the Polunsky Unit is a facility for first-time offenders rather than the state's premier maximum-security prison. Death row inmates remain at the unit until the day of their execution, when they are transported in a three-vehicle caravan to Huntsville's Death House, some forty-five miles to the west.

A winding two-lane country road cuts through piney woods and thick underbrush—the typical terrain of East Texas—past weathered houses with sagging roofs and dilapidated trailer homes, until a final turn offers the first glimpse of the prison. From afar the Polunsky Unit does not evoke the kind of foreboding feelings that one's imagination might conjure when thinking about an institution that houses condemned men. By way of comparison, the Walls Unit in Huntsville, which includes the Death House (where Texas carries out the death penalty via lethal injection), is instantly disturbing, with its sheer 125-year-old blood-red brick walls dotted with guard towers. Shotgun-toting officers are visible as they walk the perimeter of the unit, atop the imposing parapet that encircles the prison. The gravity of what takes place within is immediately evoked.

The Polunsky Unit, on the other hand, is almost attractive at first glance. For one thing, it is relatively new; the first inmates arrived there in 1993, and it was not until 1998 that Texas moved its death row inmates out of Huntsville's Ellis Unit to this location. Most of its buildings are but two stories high, so the prison lies low on the horizon in an otherwise pastoral landscape cut out of the surrounding pine forest. The buildings are constructed of cement, reinforced by ribbons of blue-gray steel that form distinctive markings at intervals between the two floors. Two parallel twenty-foot-high chain-link fences surround the vast complex, each topped with concertina wire. In the morning, the sun glistening off the wire creates a bright sliver of light that runs across the very heart of the prison, its sparkle almost adorning the buildings, as if they were whimsically wrapped packages. The entire complex has a strangely contemporary character, as if designed for a high-tech industrial park. It is only as one drives closer to the prison, and the features of the various compounds become evident, that the illusion of smart aesthetics dissolves into the reality of razor-sharp wire and four strategically placed guard towers.

These prisoners on death row are modern-day untouchables; regulations prohibit them from having direct physical contact with loved ones, not even on the eve of their executions. Those who are in good standing are allowed one two-hour visit per week, not counting attorneys and clergy—although the reality is that few have friends or relatives who make the trip to Livingston with any regularity.

BILL KING SMILED COMFORTABLY as we talked, snacking on a sandwich, soda, and candy bar that I had purchased for him. Behind him, through the metal latticework of the door to the "box" and across a hallway where corrections officers were escorting prisoners to and from their visits, I could see another set of windows, and through them a green field of grass. Farther still, I could see the walls of the death row compound. The intense sunlight of a Texas summer morning poured in through those farthest windows, backlighting Bill King as he sat there. It was as if King were framed by glass, and I had the unsettling sensation of looking into a diorama.

Nothing about Bill King's demeanor suggested that he was capable of the murder of James Byrd on a dark and lonely East Texas summer night. Even in a place like the Polunsky Unit, there are a small number of individuals whose crimes have been of such infamy that they hold a peculiar celebrity status—prisoners whose notoriety as evil sadists sets them apart even from the unusually cruel cohort of men whose crimes made them eligible for the death penalty. Certainly the character of James Byrd's murder qualified King for membership in this circle. It was an act so heinous, with the victim so brutally tortured, that it had shaken the emotional moorings of even veteran law enforcement officers. One could conjure scenarios that might render lethal acts comprehensible (say, moments of passion, or an attempt to cover one's tracks by leaving no witnesses), but the specific character of this murder defied such attempts at understanding or rationalization. There was nothing within the realm of logic to account for it. The atrocity had momentarily forced the nation to reflect on its comfortable and sleepy belief that race relations in America had somehow transcended their ugly past. It was as if the discovery of Byrd's mutilated body had momentarily thrust us back into some bygone era of Jim Crow racism, a time when Texas and the South were shaped by the agendas of the secretive network of the Ku Klux Klan and its sympathizers. It was this quality that made Byrd's murder feel uncanny, as though something familiar but ancient had been terribly mislocated into the present.

In addition to Bill King, Russell Brewer and Shawn Berry were later convicted of the murder in separate trials. King and Brewer had been in prison together in the past, and they were members of the same white supremacist gang, a small group calling itself the Confederate Knights of America, which was unknown even to most prison gang experts. Like King, Brewer also received the death penalty. Berry received a life sentence, spared the ultimate penalty largely because several African Americans testified that they did not believe him to be a racist and because he had no known white supremacist affiliations. Of the three men, Bill King was considered by most knowledgeable observers to have been the ringleader. They thought this because he was bright and had always exhibited a forceful personality, even an element of charisma. And they thought this because of his white supremacist ties. Nevertheless, King continued to profess his innocence, which is not surprising, for he was still appealing his conviction. However, by most accounts King appeared to be on what is termed a "fast track," having exhausted his state appeals in record time. Now, languishing on death row, he was awaiting the outcome of his federal appeals, the last steps before a Jasper judge would set his execution date.

A Dallas socialite has taken up King's cause, underwriting the services of a California attorney specializing in death penalty cases as well as an investigator who has scoured the evidence and interviewed everyone who would agree to meet with her. King's attorney has submitted an unusually lengthy and detailed federal habeas corpus brief, raising King's hopes of a possible retrial, but few outside of King's inner circle of family and friends believe that those efforts will spare King's life. In fact, Bill King's own views on the matter fluctuate significantly. At times he appears to feel hopeful and confident that his conviction will be overturned or, at the least, commuted to a life sentence; at other times he seems certain that his cause is hopeless.

The man believed by most to have been the central figure in the murder of James Byrd has done all he can to shore up his legal standing. Now there is little left for him to do but to spend his time reading and corresponding, waiting for the federal courts to determine his fate. I suspect that this situation, and the sheer boredom that must plague him, played some part in his decision to talk with me.

WHEN I MET RONALD KING, Bill's father, he was a brokenhearted man. The elder King is serving his own death sentence, dying from emphysema—a condition that, since his son's trial, has required that he be continuously tethered to an oxygen tank. Ronald King was living next to his daughter's house in Jasper, in a shed that is not much larger than the cell occupied by his son; it is a hovel, with no running water, no insulation, and only a bucket to serve him should he need to use the bathroom overnight. "Not fit for a dog" was the way one friend described it, and I couldn't help but concur when Ronald finally permitted me to see it.

I had known Ronald for six months or so when he asked me if I would be willing to meet with Bill. I asked him at the time what it was that he hoped might come from such a meeting, and his reply came without a moment's hesitation: "Understanding," he said in a firm but quiet voice laden with the nasality of a heavy Mississippi-Texas patois. He had looked at me with sad, pale blue eyes, drawing oxygen through the plastic tubes clipped to his nostrils. As always, he was wearing a navy-blue jumpsuit, his gray hair thinning severely at the temples and his face weathered, cracked, and stained with age spots. I assume that it was my background as a psychologist that made

Ronald hope that I might help him come to some greater understanding of
his son, or perhaps he hoped that his son might come to some greater understanding of himself, though Ronald never elaborated. I was intrigued with
the idea of talking to Bill King for other, albeit similar, reasons. I hoped that
I might come to some understanding of what would render a man capable of
committing such an unspeakable crime.

Accepting Ronald King's invitation, I was not sure what I would find
when I looked into the eyes of a man whom most of the world regards as a
monster. A few months later, when I went to the Polunsky Unit in Livingston for the first time, I was convinced of King's guilt and comfortable with
the state's decision to end his life. I have since spent in the neighborhood of
twenty hours talking face to face with Bill King while also maintaining an extensive, three-year correspondence with him. I have often left the Polunsky
Unit emotionally exhausted and physically depleted, at times uncertain of
the true facts behind the murder of James Byrd or the motives that played a
role in it. King's personality—intense, persuasive, and profoundly engaging—played no small part in precipitating such states.

During one of my early death row visits King volunteered that *The Silence
of the Lambs,* a novel by Thomas Harris, was one of his favorite books. I du-
tifully went home and read it. The book's plot revolves around the psychology of Hannibal Lecter, a primitive, monstrous creature (he is a serial killer
who has cannibalized his victims) whose collaboration the FBI desperately
seeks to enlist in order to solve the riddle of another serial killer's identity. As
was true of King, Lecter is confined under the highest security. It was evident
that King identified with Lecter, the novel's evil but ultimately human pro-
tagonist; that placed me in the role of Clarice Starling, the FBI agent sent to
obtain Lecter's insights and cooperation.

One interchange between Lecter and Starling, in particular, stood out
when I read the novel and seemed to signal Bill King's possible motives for
meeting with me. Starling has visited Lecter for the first time and asks him
to fill out a personality inventory, which Lecter mockingly refuses ("Do you
think you can dissect me with this blunt little tool?"). Starling continues to
press him, noting that he can shed light on the motives of other serial killers.
When Lecter asks her what possible reason he would have for complying
with such an endeavor, Starling replies, "Curiosity . . . About why you're
here. About what happened to you."

Perhaps, I thought, King, too, like his father, and like me, wanted understanding. But it was impossible to miss a different implication to which the novel lent itself, given that the story leans heavily on the tensions created by the possibility that Lecter will somehow manage to seduce and take control of the FBI agent. Lecter is already infamous for his hypnotic powers of persuasion. King, too, I would soon learn, possessed a powerful capacity to sway others, to bring them into his orbit, to alter their sense of what was real.

And so I found that "understanding" was hard to come by. It took many months for me to decide that I knew King well enough to begin to imagine what might have motivated him. I learned a lot about King by visiting him. At the same time, his personality was so mesmerizing and his interest in denying his guilt was so strong that it was often necessary to spend time away from him in order to learn more about him. The crime spoke volumes, of course, and from the law enforcement officials who solved the murder I learned a great deal about the alleged perpetrators. Friends and family were able to provide crucial information about the years leading up to the murder. Finally, the trial itself served as a forum in which the character of Bill King was debated.

Nobody but the men who were present that night knows what really happened out on the lonely logging road where Byrd was dragged to his death. The three trials yield contradictory narratives. What we do know is that three men—Bill King, Russell Brewer, and Shawn Berry—left their apartment in Berry's pickup truck after midnight on June 7, 1998. After failing to find a party on a country road to which some girls had invited them, they headed back to town, where they encountered Byrd walking along Martin Luther King Jr. Boulevard. Shawn Berry, who was driving the truck, made the fateful decision to give Byrd a ride. Up to this point, all stories converge. After it, they teeter and veer under the press of self-serving accounts and evidence that is by turns feeble and tenuous or conclusive and incontrovertible.

What most impresses me about what I have discovered is that though his crime was monstrous, Bill King, the man, is much more human than we would care to think. When the global news media descended upon his hometown of Jasper in a relentless hunt for sensational material, they constructed a perhaps comforting, but ultimately obscuring, myth about King's monstrous nature. The truth is that King is all too close, in kind and in temperament, to me or to you, and that is why so many people, especially those who knew him, are confounded by what transpired on that summer night in 1998. On the whole, the forces that shaped him were not particularly vile, and the flaws in his character, while clearly evident, were not such as to signal what was to come. He was, in many ways, an average young man gone astray until the night that Byrd met his death. Countless others like Bill King have lived ordinary enough lives. Although notable, the things that may have caused him to commit such a murder do not point to a foregone conclusion. They do not add up to the torture and murder of a middle-aged, intoxicated black man whom the three men happened to come upon as he was walking home late one night on a dark Jasper street. While it may make us feel safer to imagine that Bill King is a creature quite alien to ourselves, the uncomfortable truth is that he is more like the rest of us than we would like to believe. The propensities that might explain this act remained mostly latent, lurking beneath the surface, unrecognized even by those who thought they knew him well. And that means that Byrd's murder, however extraordinary, is perhaps more proximate, more in the realm of the possible, than we may want to acknowledge.

Huff Creek Road

EARLY ON THE MORNING of June 7, 1998, Cedric Green, a middle-aged African American man, was driving to town in an old orange Ford pickup truck. His six-year-old stepson, Marlon, accompanied him as they made their way down a narrow dirt road in a westerly direction through the logged-out piney woods into Jasper County. At the juncture where the dirt road gave way to the paved surface of a little country lane known as Huff Creek Road, in front of an old African American church, they discovered remains that were so severely mutilated that the dark form was almost unrecognizable as that of a human being. "We thought it was a deer at first," the little boy later recalled. In the ensuing moments, as the initial shock of what he was seeing dissipated, Green tried to shield his son from the horror of it. "Don't look," he said, hoping to protect the boy from what he instinctively knew would be a traumatizing experience.

The church where the body had been left was a few miles outside of Jasper. It was a small rectangular structure, with a roof line that sloped down on either side of a high center beam at a sharp forty-five-degree angle. The lines of the portico paralleled those of the roof, but on the portico's front, facing back down the paved road that ended at this very spot, there was affixed a simple cross. Like the church, the cross was painted white, and the white-on-whiteness of it gave it an aura of understatement. The church, resting up off the ground on short stilts, was nestled into the surrounding piney woods in a bucolic Southern rural setting. Immediately to its left was the dirt logging road on which the man and his son had been traveling before encountering the human remains, lying before the church like a dark and perverse offering.

The old Huff Creek Church wasn't used much for regular Sunday services anymore, but no one except the residents of the little African American community that lived along this road would have known that. The building and grounds were well maintained. People in the community tended to use the church almost exclusively for "home goings," as Southern African Americans often refer to funerals. The Huff Creek Cemetery was immediately adjacent to the church. Some of the headstones in the cemetery were made of fine cut stone and dated back to the nineteenth century, but there were many graves of people whose families had been too poor to buy headstones. Some, for example, were simply marked by the top half of an ironing board—an old custom among poor blacks in this region—protruding oddly out of the red clay soil, standing in rusty vigil over their plots. Other headstones were fashioned out of formed cement, their inscriptions scrawled by hand with a crude writing implement, sometimes decorated with a chip of a mirror or a brightly colored piece of ceramic tile.

Everything about the murder suggested a wish to defile. There was the mutilated condition of the victim, for example, as well as the specific placement of the body in front of the church, where the perpetrators no doubt believed it would be found by worshipers coming to services later that morning. Cedric Green and his son rushed to a nearby house and made a call to the Jasper County Sheriff's Department, thereby sounding the first alert to the world that something awful had occurred in this remote East Texas community. As the horrible details of the crime's racial hatred began to emerge in the ensuing hours and days, that shock would only deepen. That an act of such savagery could have taken place more than thirty years after the demise of the Jim Crow era seemed almost inconceivable.

That same morning Tommy Robinson and Joe Sterling were sitting in the dining room at Jasper's Ramada Inn drinking coffee. The Ramada Inn was

HUFF CREEK CHURCH

something of a hangout for local law enforcement officers as well as for business and civic leaders. Robinson and Sterling, officers with the Jasper Sheriff's Department, were about to head out to a community called Leesville, some fifty miles east of Jasper, just across the Louisiana line, where the local sheriff had apprehended a man attempting to sell stolen property. It was Robinson's day off, but he was the kind of officer who was always ready to set personal plans aside when something cropped up at the sheriff's office. The officers had finished their coffee and were about to leave the Ramada Inn when they received a call on the mobile phone from the dispatcher reporting that an agitated man had just called to say that he'd found a dead person out on Huff Creek Road.

Tommy Robinson looked like a stock character from a film depicting an Old South lawman. His gray hair was thin and cut burr short, as it had been all his life. He was potbellied and ruddy-cheeked, and he had a penchant for wearing jeans and Western shirts that showed signs of strain around his middle. Robinson was in his mid-fifties, but he looked decidedly older than his years. He had lived a hard life, a life reflected in the deep ruts that defined his face, and he was long past the days when he could run down suspects and wrestle them to the ground. His assignments these days tended toward interviewing suspects and collecting evidence. Unlike the stereotype of Southern justice, there was an easy geniality to the man, despite his intense, questioning blue eyes. There was also a reassuring steadfastness about him. Sterling and Robinson went back a long way. Sterling had spent many a day as an adolescent riding "shotgun" with Robinson, patrolling the lazy back roads of Jasper County. That experience had cemented Sterling's interest in becoming a law enforcement officer. So it was an appropriate turn of fate that the two officers would end up being together when the biggest case of their careers broke.

Robinson and Sterling headed in a northeasterly direction out of Jasper. It took them only a few minutes to travel the five or six miles to the community of Huff Creek. Huff Creek Road is short—a three-mile spur that branches off a farm-to-market road and comes to a dead end at the Huff Creek Church. Half a mile after turning off the farm-to-market road, one comes to a narrow wood bridge spanning the creek for which the community is named. It was just past this bridge that Deputy Robinson first saw strange marks on the paved road that morning, coming out of, or perhaps

DEPUTIES JOE STERLING AND TOMMY ROBINSON

going into, a dirt logging road that intersected Huff Creek Road on the left. Robinson did not initially make much of that observation. When a horse or a hog was hit by a car, or bitten by a snake, or died of some other cause, it was common for farmers to simply drag the carcass onto nearby logging company land in order for it to decompose away from their own property. It was a practice that Robinson had observed countless times over the years. For this reason, the road stains did not initially strike Robinson as more than a curiosity. Besides, Robinson and Sterling were concentrating on what they took to be a more pressing concern. They continued to follow the drag marks as they looked for a human body or something that would make a person believe that there was a human body. The officers had not discounted the possibility that what the caller had in fact observed was someone passed out by the side of the road, or perhaps a deer or a farm animal that had been struck by a car. It would not have been the first time in the officers' experience that a report of a dead person had turned out to be something far less dramatic.

The two officers proceeded in the direction of the Huff Creek Church, driving slowly as they followed the gently curving, narrow ribbon of asphalt; the road was barely wide enough to accommodate two cars side by side. They were surrounded on either side by tall, majestic stands of pine, elm, and hackberry as they continued on, occasionally passing small clearings of modest frame houses and broken-down trailer homes. As the two officers approached the end of Huff Creek Road, they saw what appeared to be a strange and out-of-place mound in the middle of the road. It was not until Tommy Robinson had gotten out of the patrol car to conduct a closer inspection and saw the victim's feet that he realized that the form was the badly mangled body of a human being. The victim had been decapitated, was missing one arm, and was severely lacerated. Robinson was unsettled and disoriented by the state of the victim. To Robinson the grisly sight was reminiscent of what one might encounter in a war zone.

As Robinson photographed the body, he ran the scenario through his mental filing system, reviewing decades of cases, trying to find a precedent, something that could suggest what might have taken place. He drew a blank. His initial hypothesis was that someone had tampered with one of the graves at the adjacent Huff Creek Cemetery. Robinson looked across the road to the cemetery, but there were no signs that a plot had been disturbed and a body exhumed. That's when it occurred to the officer that in all likelihood there was a link between the mutilated remains before him and the trail of blood that he and Sterling had followed on their way up Huff Creek Road, beginning at the logging road by the bridge.

Still, he found it difficult to wrap his mind around what had taken place. Robinson had seen the remains of pedestrians who had been hit by automobiles and those of motorcycle riders whose bodies had skidded across the pavement after an accident, tearing the victim's clothing and grinding the skin. But never in his twenty-five years as a law enforcement officer had he seen anything nearly as horrendous as this. The victim's pants, undershorts, and socks had been pulled down around his ankles, and there were deep cuts in his legs just above the ankles. In addition, Robinson could see that the flesh at the knees and elbows and along the back of the body looked as if someone had taken a large, coarse, grinding wheel and ground the skin off down to the bone.

The dragging marks along the road were the only thing that could explain the nature of the wounds. What might drive someone to do this to another person was another question altogether, one before which Robinson felt absolutely mute. He'd seen his share of vicious, hateful behavior over the years; he was intimately familiar with the consequences of passion and greed and discovered deceit. Yet his experience seemed to fail him in this moment. The veteran officer was as puzzled as he was horrified.

It was not long after coming upon the mutilated remains that Robinson and Sterling received another call from the dispatcher. A woman down the road had come out of her house to retrieve her Sunday newspaper and discovered a head and part of the upper torso of a body lying in a gully next to her driveway. The dispatcher indicated that the woman appeared to be in a state of shock. Robinson instructed the dispatcher to notify Sheriff Billy Rowles that there was indeed a dead person at the Huff Creek Road location. They would need additional units at the site, he told her, including a criminal investigator.

Curtis "C. C." Frame, a detective with the Jasper Police Department, was at home in bed that Sunday morning when he received a call from the police dispatcher indicating that "County" had a possible hit-and-run out on Huff Creek Road. He was instructed to go directly to the crime scene. Curtis Frame had been a law enforcement officer for more than twenty years, and he was the best-trained criminal investigator in the county. His credentials

included such specialized training as advanced fingerprint and evidence collection, taught by the FBI in Quantico, Virginia, a course on the recovery of
skeletal body remains, and training in blood splatter, stain, and interpretation. This background made Frame a valuable resource for Jasper County law
enforcement, which is why he was called in to help out the sheriff's department that Sunday morning, even though the crime in question appeared to
have been committed outside of the police department's jurisdiction.

Curtis Frame cut an imposing figure. Perhaps his most striking feature
was his clean-shaven head, which accentuated his inquisitive eyes. It gave
Frame a look of altered intensity and incipient wildness, a look that made
suspects uneasy. The officer was tall and trim, with the physique of an en-
durance athlete, and he had a penchant for wearing crisply pressed jeans with
starched, brightly striped, short-sleeved sport shirts. Like many Texas lawmen, Frame liked to wear his badge attached to his belt, which, deceptively,
gave his authority a casual flair. That same belt was also home to a hard-to-
miss 40-caliber Glock pistol, whose titanium sights ("they glow in the night")
and Hogue grips were a source of pride to Frame.

Detective Frame drove out to Huff Creek Road in his older-model, four-
door black Plymouth Diplomat, passing the officer who was now monitoring access to the area where Huff Creek Road intersected FM 1738. A mile or
so past the narrow wood bridge spanning the creek he came upon a gathering of law enforcement officers standing solemnly in a semicircle around the
victim's head, right shoulder, and right arm. It was here that the body had
struck a culvert and been torn apart. Sheriff Billy Rowles was among the
group. An avid golfer, the sheriff had been headed for the annual Police
Games in Dallas, where he was to compete, when the initial call came from
his dispatcher that morning. When Frame pulled up, Sheriff Rowles was still
dressed in golf shorts, a golf shirt, and a Calloway golf cap.

Notwithstanding the gory circumstances, Frame was all business. He had
been doing this kind of work long enough to learn how to detach himself
from the feelings he might ordinarily have experienced when confronted
with the vast array of violence that the human mind can conjure. His response was partly his professionalism, but also a manifestation of the mind's
protective mechanisms. Before Jasper, Frame had been employed in Brazo-
ria County, near Houston, an area with more than its share of major crime.
His attitude reflected not an absence of concern but rather an awareness that

to do otherwise would create an intolerable emotional strain that would in-
terfere with his ability to do his job.

Before Frame's arrival the other lawmen at the scene had been speculating
about the possibility of a less horrific crime. The sheriff, for example, having
spent many years as a Highway Patrol officer, initially suspected that the individual might be a hit-and-run victim. Frame dismissed that hypothesis out
of hand. "No way! This ain't a hit-and-run," he told the sheriff and the other
men. "You try and figure out how the guy got drug underneath the car all
that way. No way! It didn't happen! This is something way beyond that."

As he stood with the group of officers, Frame was perhaps the first to begin to see the broader, nightmarish possibilities reflected in this crime. He
left the group and drove up to the old church, where Robinson and Sterling
were still with the victim's torso. By now, it was midmorning, and the summer air was thick and heavy with humidity; the men out on Huff Creek Road
could feel the tightening grip of the sweltering East Texas heat. Frame's
hunch was confirmed when he inspected the remains and found that there
were ligature marks on the victim's ankles, which indicated to Frame that
someone had tied this person to the back of a vehicle. Frame also noted that
the pattern of the cuts around the victim's ankles indicated that a chain rather
than a rope had been used to secure him. *We've got a big problem,* he thought
to himself.

When the other officers joined Frame, they started to play out scenarios
and entertain speculations as to what had happened to this as-yet-nameless
man. Who might have murdered him and why? One of the Department of
Public Safety troopers present was an African American officer named Rodney Pearson. Pearson was from West Texas, but he had worked in Jasper almost ten years. He was married to a white woman, a fact that might have
once been a source of friction or controversy but that no longer seemed to
elicit much comment. Pearson was a respected officer in Jasper County and
Frame liked him. Frame turned to Pearson and said, "Rodney, a black man
is going to kill another black man, what are they going to do? Shoot him or
stab him or beat him. No black man is going to do this type of crime." In
Frame's view, the characteristics of this murder did not conform to the
informal profiles he had developed over his years of working as a criminal
investigator. To Frame, the murder had all the telltale signs of a calculated
crime of revenge.

HIGHWAY PATROLMAN RODNEY PEARSON

"I'm thinking the same thing you're thinking," Pearson replied. "We're probably looking for white people."

"I agree," was Frame's response. It was a grim conclusion that pointed the investigator toward unspeakable possibilities.

Even though Tommy Robinson had already photographed the victim's body, Frame meticulously took his own photographs of the torso, documenting his observations, and he measured the crime scene. He then put on rubber gloves and proceeded to carefully turn the victim's torn and shredded remains over in order to get full photographic documentation of the injuries. He removed the blue jeans and underwear, which were bunched up at the ankles, presumably to ensure that the chain did not slip off. He also removed the socks, making a mental note of the fact that the victim had been wearing no shoes and no shirt. All of the items of clothing were tagged and placed in individual evidence bags for subsequent analysis. When he was finished working around the victim, Frame placed a call to the dispatcher instructing her to send out "a body car." It was an old law enforcement term for the vehicle (typically from a funeral home) that retrieved a victim's remains once the relevant crime scene work was completed.

Frame now turned his attention to the broader area around the spot where the victim had been found. It appeared to the investigator that whoever was responsible for the murder had first pulled into a grassy dirt lane leading up to a low chain-link gate at the entrance to the cemetery that adjoined the church. They had then backed out hurriedly, looping around to the front of the church before stopping to unchain the victim some thirty yards from the church door, where the pavement ended. Frame found clear tire tracks at the fence, which he also photographed. He then retrieved from his car a plastic bag containing casting material, similar to that used for dental casts. When water was added, the casting material became a liquid substance that could readily be poured into the impressions left in the dirt by what Frame suspected was the vehicle that had been used. The liquid rapidly coagulated into a solid cast that could later be matched with the tires on that vehicle when it was located.

While Frame was covering the crime scene at the church, Robinson, along with Sheriff Rowles, Trooper Pearson, and some other officers, worked their way back toward the bridge from the location where the victim's head, shoulder, and arm had been found. As he went along, Sheriff Rowles marked the

locations of evidence as best he could. He needed to protect it from any
traffic that might be moving along Huff Creek Road. Jasper law enforcement
personnel had already sealed off access to the area, but an occasional patrol
car still might need to move from one location to another along the three
miles of the narrow country lane. When the sheriff encountered what appeared to be the victim's dentures, he took off his prized golf cap and laid it
next to them. A little farther on, he dragged a large limb from the roadside
and placed it next to a set of keys that were believed to belong to the victim.
In this manner, the sheriff fashioned a series of makeshift markers from
whatever he could find around him until his team could work up the crime
scene. As it was more than two miles from the logging trail near the wood
bridge to the Huff Creek Church, it was evident that the entire area would
have to be combed more thoroughly.

After his initial pass down Huff Creek Road, the sheriff gathered a team
to move up onto the logging road from which the bloody trail appeared to
have originated. In addition to the sheriff, the group included Tommy Robinson, Rodney Pearson, the sheriff from neighboring Newton County, and
some other lawmen. They hoped that the location of the initial assault, if
it could be found, might yield important clues as to what had transpired
and why.

The men were in a somber mood as they moved on foot into the thick underbrush. The vegetation was so dense that the logging road appeared to be
leading into a cavernous, emerald-green enclosure. A few feet beyond the
paved road, the officers came upon an area covered with the detritus of modern life: a rotting carpet, a rusted microwave, the broken cabinet of a late-
fifties-style television console, and an assortment of other trash and discarded
items. Thirty yards farther into the pine forest they were out of the area that
was easily accessible as a dumping site and moving into an almost pristine
area of stunning natural beauty. The vegetation was lush, and there was a
profusion of wildflowers and a multitude of singing birds. In many places
back here, the designation "road" was a generous characterization at best.
Rather, it appeared that they were following a creek bed whose sides sloped
at a rather precipitous angle down to a narrow channel no more than two
feet wide. The path was bordered by a canopy of tall trees that occasionally
blocked out the sun almost entirely, leaving only a gently shifting, dappled
light as a breeze blew through the leaves.

The sheriff and his men continued deeper and deeper into the woods, noticing scrapes and ruts in the ground that suggested that the victim had been dragged through the area. They followed these telltale marks, not knowing when, or even if, they would stumble upon the site of the initial assault. They had walked at least a third of a mile when they came upon an especially rugged section of terrain with deep ruts, as if a vehicle had strained to get through. The area appeared to be almost impassable, even for a vehicle with four-wheel drive.

For Robinson, the trek was quite arduous. He had a heart condition and suffered from early stages of emphysema, resulting in the removal of half of one lung. Both diseases were probably related to a three-pack-a-day nicotine habit: he'd been smoking unfiltered Pall Malls for nearly forty years and had only recently quit. It was a struggle for him to keep up with his fellow officers making their way up the logging trail.

An odd contradiction existed between the beauty of the logging road and the grim task upon which the team of law enforcement officers had embarked. When the lumber companies harvested pines, their practice was to leave some trees to re-seed. These were the most prominent trees in the landscape. The logging had also created spaces in the forest that were now dense with maples, elms, pecans, a variety of oaks, mulberries, and an occasional magnolia. The sweet, rich fragrance of the pines continued to dominate, but it was permeated by scents from these other trees as well. The underbrush was a combination of holly, yaupon, sumac, and wild grapevine. In the clearings and dells there were clusters of wild violets and daisies and other native wildflowers. Dewberries, blackberries, and strawberries grew in profusion. Here and there, there were red sassafras trees, whose root locals harvested to make a tea that tasted like root beer, and an abundance of hickory, whose wood many preferred to pecan for smoking meat. Nothing about the natural splendor reflected what had transpired earlier that morning.

About a hundred yards beyond the location with the deepest ruts, Robinson, Rowles, and the others came upon a Nike tennis shoe, a shirt with an NBA team logo, and another shirt. The shirts appeared to be soiled with fresh, moist dirt, indicating that they had not been at this location for long. The lawmen were certain that they belonged to the victim.

It was obvious that the victim had been dragged from farther on up the logging road, so Robinson stayed behind to begin photographing the evidence while the sheriff and his men moved on ahead. Not far away they found a second Nike tennis shoe and a place where it appeared that the vehicle had stopped. Here the lawmen found clear tire tracks and footprints in the sandy red soil. They hypothesized that the victim had slipped loose from his tether and that the perpetrators had stopped to re-tie him at this location. Near this same spot, the sheriff spied a wallet in the brush. It contained a Texas driver's license, a Social Security card, and a rent receipt, all of which bore the same name: "James Byrd Jr."

Although it was possible that the wallet belonged to whoever was responsible for the murder, there was little doubt in Rowles's mind that it was in fact the victim's. It was now around one o'clock in the afternoon. To avoid the civilians who made a habit of listening to law enforcement communications on their scanners, the sheriff used his mobile phone rather than the police radio to call Curtis Frame, who was still working the crime scene at the church. "Looks like we've got a probable," he told Frame. The sheriff instructed the criminal investigator to accompany the victim's remains to the funeral home and obtain fingerprints. James Byrd Jr. had been in and out of the local jail over the years, and Rowles and Frame both were familiar with him. However, his remains were so horrendously disfigured that neither lawman had recognized him. Even now, with a name to attach to the victim, neither could say with any confidence that it was, indeed, James Byrd. Frame was to attempt to make a positive identification by fingerprinting the body at the funeral home.

JAMES BYRD WAS FORTY-SIX years old, but years of heavy drinking and not infrequent drug use had taken their toll on him. In addition, Byrd had a seizure disorder, apparently caused by head trauma suffered years ago, as well as a back injury that made heavy lifting or prolonged standing problematic. But it was Byrd's extensive criminal history that had perhaps taken the biggest toll of all on his life. Beginning in 1968, when Byrd was sixteen years old, there were dozens of entries in Byrd's rap sheet, ranging from public intoxication to habitual theft. Some of these had resulted in brief incarcerations of several days or less, mostly in the Jasper County jail, although he had spent time in the jails of three other counties as well. Byrd had been in jail overnight six times for having crack pipes in his possession, and he also had two arrests for marijuana possession. More notably, on four occasions James Byrd had done time in state prison for theft and forgery.

This history of extensive criminal activity had also taken a toll on James Byrd's family life. Byrd had married Thelma Adams in 1970, and the couple had had three children before divorcing in 1994. However, their relationship had been quite turbulent throughout their marriage. Texas Department of Criminal Justice records indicate that James Byrd had an IQ of only 86, and a correctional counselor had recommended that Byrd be excluded from jobs requiring "understanding of complex instructions" in his Individual Activity Plan when he was being processed into the Bill Clements unit in 1992. Perhaps for similar reasons, James Byrd had been unable to hold down a job when he was out of prison. His longest period of employment appeared to be a two-year stint as a truck driver; otherwise, with the exception of the occasional job, he had been unemployed for most of his adult life.

Relationships were also often strained between James Byrd and his parents and six siblings, who at times grew tired of Byrd's antics but who did their best to maintain some sort of relationship with him. James Byrd was the one dim light in an otherwise accomplished, proud family. The Byrds were quite poor, and James Byrd Sr. had supported the family from meager earnings at a local dry cleaners. They were a deeply religious family and attended the Greater New Bethel Baptist Church, not far from their home, where Byrd's father was a deacon and his mother the lead Bible School teacher. There was a tremendous integrity to the Byrd family. Most of James Byrd's siblings, with the exception of James and one of his sisters, had gone on to make their lives elsewhere, moving to Houston or Dallas or Beaumont, and most had attended college. The family remained close, and the Byrd children made frequent trips back to Jasper, bringing their families home for visits.

James Byrd Jr. had not followed in his siblings' footsteps. Instead, his life consisted of one miscalculation after another. He was a familiar sight along Jasper's streets, frequently walking between a predominantly African American area of northeast Jasper known, since plantation days, as the Quarters, and his residence at the Pollard Street Apartments, public housing on the southeast corner of town. He was known to knock on friends' doors and volunteer to mow lawns or do other chores in exchange for a few dollars, a practice that sometimes made him something of a nuisance. Byrd mostly lived off of a disability check, his odd jobs, and whatever he could scrape together from a life of petty crime.

Byrd's reputation as a frequent drug user was well established. "Seems every time I arrested him, he had a crack pipe on him," one officer would later recall. Given Byrd's history of drug use, some would suggest early on that perhaps his murder was part of a drug deal gone awry. But Jasper law enforcement simply scoffed at such a notion. "No drug dealer would front him any drugs," one officer said. "They knew they couldn't trust him not to smoke the stuff up himself." Byrd was widely described in the media as something of a gentle loser with a gift for music—he was a talented vocalist and was adept at playing the piano and saxophone. However, perhaps leery of appearing to blame Byrd for the horrendous crime of which he was a victim or otherwise seeming to legitimize it, most accounts soft-pedaled James Byrd's real shortcomings.

NOT FAR FROM WHERE the search party found the wallet, the logging road abruptly opened into a wide, flat clearing. It was a crossroads of some sort; beyond it the road continued on to the north, but another spur intersected the clearing from the east in the direction of Newton County. It was immediately evident that some sort of struggle had taken place here. There were deep, angled indentations in the ground, the kind of marks that occur when individuals are exerting unusual effort to secure leverage or are pivoting abruptly. A volunteer oak whose trunk was only an inch and a half or so in diameter had been knocked over, and the grass and other vegetation in the clearing had been trampled down, as if an altercation involving a number of individuals had taken place at the site.

More important, the officers found a treasure trove of evidence at the clearing. This included a Zippo cigarette lighter with the name "Possum" written on its side with an indelible marker along with a strange emblem that at the time they found undecipherable. They also found a torque wrench and a nut driver, each with the name "Berry" crudely etched into the handle. A pack of Marlboro Lights cigarettes, a can of black spray paint, and a can of Fix-A-Flat for repairing tires had been left at the site, too. Other things were strewn about the area as well, including broken and unbroken beer bottles, cigarette butts, a woman's watch and another watch with a broken glass face, and a Kiss CD cover.

The search team was particularly interested in the lighter, the cigarettes, and the tools—things that more than likely would have been picked up if dropped by accident. They reinforced the perception that a significant scuffle had taken place here. In the early-morning dark, the scene illuminated only by the stars, the moon, and the twin shafts of light from a vehicle's vaporous headlights, it would have been difficult to spot such small items. And in the confusion of anxiety and rage and fear all clashing in the heat of the moment, it would have been easy to overlook the dropped items, an oversight that would later come back to haunt the perpetrators.

Two salient features of the crime made the officers view it as premeditated. First, it was obvious that the perpetrators knew where they were going and were intent on reaching this specific site. Between Huff Creek Road and the clearing, the logging road was nearly impassable in so many places that most people would have stopped long before reaching the clearing. Only someone who knew exactly where he was going would have persevered. Second, the location of the body was significant in the officers' scenario. There were countless places along the logging road where the perpetrators could have easily disposed of the victim's body in the dense underbrush and where, in all likelihood, James Byrd would have never been found. At best, perhaps in a year or two a hunter would have come upon his skeletal remains. Instead, Byrd had been dragged all the way down the logging trail and out to Huff Creek Road, where the culprits had turned east toward the church, which was, not coincidentally, the segment of Huff Creek Road most populated by African Americans. To the officers it suggested that the perpetrators intended to make a statement.

WHEN THE CAR ARRIVED from Coleman Funeral Home, a local African American mortuary, Frame helped load James Byrd's remains into the vehicle and then headed back into town behind it. He stopped by the police department to retrieve Byrd's fingerprint card and then went over to the funeral home to get prints off the body.

The scene at the funeral home was quite somber. Dorie Coleman, the mortician, and the others who were present were obviously affected by the condition of the body. In all their years in the funeral business, they had never seen anything remotely approaching this.

Taking fingerprints from a corpse is considerably more challenging than doing so from a living person. Frame had to print the one arm that was attached to the body. He then had to awkwardly work with the other arm, angling the wrist as best he could in order to be able to use the small semicircular tool called the print spoon that is used for the task. First it was necessary to ink the fingers. Then each of the inked fingers was pressed against the print spoon, which has a slot into which a narrow piece of paper is inserted. When Frame inspected the prints from the body and compared them with Byrd's fingerprint card, it was readily apparent to him that he had a definite match. On his way back out to Huff Creek Road, Frame called Sheriff Rowles to let him know that he had confirmed the victim's identity. He then joined Robinson, Rowles, and the others in processing the crime scene on the logging road.

It was Frame's responsibility to log and take possession of the evidence. By late afternoon, he had loaded it all into his car and transferred it to the Emergency Corps Building behind the sheriff's office. Here, kept under lock and key, it would be laid out on tables to be further examined and processed. Jasper law enforcement officers had collected well over a hundred pieces of evidence. Each piece had been photographed, placed into a paper bag, like those used in grocery stores to bag small items, and labeled. Paper bags had an advantage over plastic zipper bags in that they permitted items to dry whereas plastic bags tended to keep moisture trapped inside, which could destroy or otherwise compromise the integrity of some kinds of recovered evidence. The Jasper County law enforcement officers now had a monstrous crime on their hands and a mountain of evidence. Their next task was to begin to put together the pieces of a complex puzzle in the hope that it would lead them to the men who had murdered James Byrd Jr.

The Arrests

HAVING VERIFIED that the victim of the murder on Huff Creek Road was James Byrd Jr., Sheriff Billy Rowles now faced one of the most difficult tasks of his twenty-year career in law enforcement: notifying Byrd's parents. Rowles picked up one of his patrolmen, Sergeant James Carter, an African American with whom he had worked closely over the years and who also knew the Byrd family well. He wanted Carter along as a supportive presence, but he intended to do the talking himself. Another law enforcement officer might have delegated the job, but that wasn't the sheriff's style.

The Byrds lived in a modest frame home on Jasper's northeast side—not far, as it turned out, from where James Byrd had first encountered his assailants. The house was painted a chocolate brown, and on the porch there was a swing where James Byrd Sr. and his wife, Stella, liked to sit after supper and talk or wave at passersby. Though modest, their home was neatly kept, with a trimmed yard and old trees in front. Most of Jasper's African American churches were sprinkled within a half-mile radius.

James, Stella, and their daughter, Betty Boatner, who was also at the house, were already aware that someone's mutilated body had been found, al-

SERGEANT JAMES CARTER

though the identity of the victim had not yet been disclosed. The Byrds attended the Greater New Bethel Baptist Church, the same church as Dorie Coleman, the owner of the funeral home to which Byrd's body had been delivered. At church, rumors were rampant about the mutilation, but it wasn't until the sheriff arrived at their front door that the Byrds realized that in all likelihood it was James Jr. who was the victim. By the time the sheriff entered the house, the family was already quite distressed. In a very emotional exchange, Rowles started to tell James Byrd's parents that indeed it was their son who had been found dead out on Huff Creek Road, but halfway through his statement the sheriff burst into tears. "I promise you we'll find 'em," he said, looking James Byrd's father in the eyes. "We're not gonna quit till we do."

In addition to informing the family of their son's murder, the sheriff had a second purpose with his visit: to find out what they might know of their son's whereabouts over the previous twenty-four hours. While it was clearly awkward to make such inquiries at such an upsetting time, the need to reconstruct the events preceding the murder was urgent. The sheriff knew that most murders are solved within the first twenty-four hours or not at all.

The Byrds reported that James had spent part of the afternoon with the family. Some of his sisters had come into town from Houston. Later that evening James had attended a party hosted by a middle-aged couple and their son and daughter-in-law, who together were celebrating their joint wedding anniversaries in the front yard of a modest trailer home on Smith Street. The location was not far from the Byrd home. The sheriff's men later learned that James had not seemed himself all evening. James Byrd Jr. was typically a lively man who was likely to be dancing and singing at such an event. That night, however, he appeared unusually subdued. As the party began to break up, around two in the morning, Byrd asked several people for a lift home. For various reasons that they would no doubt forever regret, all had turned him down.

There were conflicting reports as to whether Byrd was intoxicated when he left the party. The Pollard Street Apartments, where he lived, were at the other end of town. With no ride, his only option was to walk home. Byrd left the trailer home on Smith Street and, a block later, turned east on Martin Luther King Jr. Boulevard.

Word spread quickly throughout Jasper's black community that a murder

REVEREND KENNETH LYONS

REVEREND BOBBY LEE HUDSON, PRESIDENT,
JASPER MINISTERIAL ALLIANCE

had taken place on Huff Creek Road and that James Byrd had been identified as the victim. Around the time that the sheriff was meeting with the Byrd family, an eighteen-year-old African American man named Steven Scott called the Jasper Police Department to report that he had seen James Byrd walking along Martin Luther King Jr. Boulevard between 2:15 and 2:30 a.m. Scott was driving home, having spent the evening at a Beaumont nightclub, an hour south of Jasper, when he spotted Byrd. Scott, who had given Byrd rides in the past, reported that he had slowed down and debated whether to offer Byrd a lift, but had decided not to because the man appeared quite drunk. Instead, he drove past Byrd and pulled into his driveway, got out of his car, and walked up the steps to his front door. When his mother opened the door to let him in, he happened to turn to see Byrd go by, riding in the bed of a pickup truck, his back against the cab. The truck was going at the speed limit, and there were no signs of protest or distress. Scott noticed that there were three white people in the cab, but there was nothing remarkable about that observation in Jasper. If anything, Scott was relieved that Byrd had found a ride home because he felt guilty about not picking him up. Scott entered his house and went to bed, unaware that he was the last known person to see James Byrd alive, other than the men who murdered him.

AROUND EIGHT O'CLOCK that Sunday evening Sheriff Rowles convened a meeting with most of the law enforcement personnel who had been working on the case. The meeting included representatives from the Jasper County Sheriff's Department, the Jasper Police Department, and the Texas Department of Public Safety. All told, there were some fifteen officers present, including Curtis Frame, Rodney Pearson, and Tommy Robinson. Because it was summer, it was still daylight when the officers gathered in the Emergency Corps Building, a tan-colored structure with aluminum siding behind the sheriff's department that housed a large meeting room on one side and two boats and an ambulance on the other. The building was used primarily for natural emergencies, drownings, and similar circumstances. The meeting room was presently serving as the evidence repository for everything that had been collected along the three-mile crime scene because no room in the sheriff's building was large enough to accommodate it. Curtis Frame had covered

an array of folding tables with white butcher paper, having meticulously arranged the evidence on top.

The purpose of the meeting was to review all the current leads. Sheriff
Rowles started by asking each officer in the room to speak to whatever piece
of evidence or information fell within his purview. The team had a number
of key pieces of information. One was the fact that they now knew the identity of the victim. This meant that they could begin to investigate how James
Byrd Jr. had spent his last hours, as well as who might have had conflicts with
him and therefore a motive for harming him. Second, the crime scene had
yielded what appeared to be important evidence about the identity of the
perpetrators (no one, by this point, believed that a lone individual could have
committed the crime). Lying on the butcher paper was the Zippo lighter
with the name "Possum" on it, as well as the two tools, a Craftsman nine-
millimeter nut driver and a torque wrench, each with the name "Berry" inscribed on it. Finally, a representative from the Jasper Police Department
summarized the phone call from Steven Scott in which he reported seeing
James Byrd Jr. driving by in a pickup truck with three whites riding in the
cab. He had also given a good description of the truck: it was an older-model
pickup, either a Ford or a Chevy with a "step side" body style, painted a dark
color or possibly primer gray. Scott also said that the truck was quite noisy,
suggesting a possible muffler problem.

The officers at the meeting were mostly local men, which, in a small town
like Jasper, translated into certain advantages when it came to tracking down
suspects. "Who do we know that drives a pickup like that?" Sheriff Rowles
asked the assembled officers after the description of Scott's phone call was
given. Curtis Frame had already described the tools with the name "Berry"
scratched on them, but at the time, the officers had been thinking that Berry
was a first name (they'd only heard the name, not seen it written out) and
they had drawn a blank. Things suddenly started falling into place with the
description of the truck, however. "Shawn Berry. Shawn Berry's got a truck
just like that," one of the Jasper Police Department officers volunteered.
"Yeah, he's got a roommate named Bill King that just got out of prison that's
a white supremacist," another said. The name rang a bell in the sheriff's head.

"Wait," he said. "We've had a complaint on a guy that's got a bunch of
pornographic pictures. I went and met with Bill King's girlfriend's mother.
She found these Polaroid pictures, some nasty pictures of Bill King with his

thing hanging out, with tattoos on his dick, tattoos all over his body, and shaved head with these satanic emblems. She wanted me to file on him. Her daughter had just turned seventeen and was probably sixteen when the pictures had been taken. But there was no date on the Polaroids, so it was difficult to prove that the girl was a minor at the time."

The discussion of the photographs was a digression, but Rowles could feel a certain quickening, as if the pieces of a complex puzzle were falling into place. These were solid leads, and the sheriff knew that they had to act on them quickly.

As the meeting broke up, the officers' assignment was to search the community for a vehicle fitting the description given by Scott. One of the officers who had attended the meeting at the Emergency Corps Building was a man named Larry Pulliam. Pulliam left the meeting and drove to the Jasper Twin Cinema, where he knew Shawn Berry was the manager. As the theater came into view, the officer spotted Berry in his truck, exiting the theater's parking lot. It had not been ten minutes since Pulliam had left the sheriff's meeting. As soon as Berry drove onto the street, Pulliam turned on his overhead lights and pulled him over. Berry was polite enough, but it was clear that he was quite nervous. Pulliam noticed that Berry's vehicle had an expired inspection sticker and also discovered that he was driving with no insurance. Using these infractions as a pretext, Pulliam arrested Berry on the spot. He called the sheriff's department to report Berry's arrest, and Curtis Frame was immediately dispatched to the scene to conduct a preliminary inspection of the truck.

Berry was already handcuffed and sitting in the backseat of Pulliam's patrol car when Frame pulled up. Frame remembers Berry watching him intently as he approached the truck. Berry appeared quite anxious and apprehensive, and Frame thought that the suspect seemed worried that he might find something as he conducted his inspection.

Plenty of dents, scrapes, and rust on Berry's pickup indicated that it had been worked hard over the years. The primer-gray paint job was apparently an attempt to spruce up the truck's down-at-the-heels look. Frame noted that the bed of the pickup was unusually clean, but when he leaned down to look at the front, across the bottom he saw fresh grass and mud. The differential and the suspension were similarly caked with a mix of vegetation and mud, all indicating that the vehicle had been run through rough terrain. The con-

trast between the clean exterior and the muddy underside was striking. *What's* *The*
wrong with this picture? Frame said to himself. The answer was obvious: *Arrests*
someone had gone through a great deal of trouble to clean up the truck but
had neglected its underside.

Frame ordered the truck towed to the sheriff's department, where he
could study it further. Once the vehicle was pulled into the sally port, Frame
crawled underneath the truck. From that vantage he could see that the soil
caked under the truck was red clay, appearing to match the soil he'd seen
out on the logging road earlier that day. As he inspected the underside of the
truck with a flashlight, Frame made another disturbing discovery: he saw
what he recognized to be blood spatter. A chemical applied to the stain with
a cotton swab turned green, indicating that the substance was human blood.
Frame also found a tool kit behind the truck's front seat that contained tools
matching the nut driver recovered at the crime scene. It was obvious that
the evidence was lining up perfectly: it was Berry's truck, his tools had been
found at the scene of the scuffle, the spatter on the underside of the truck
had been identified as human blood, and a witness had seen Byrd in a truck
whose description matched this one exactly. Frame and his fellow deputies
started exchanging high fives. It was only some twelve hours after the discovery of James Byrd's remains.

With Shawn Berry under arrest, Jasper law enforcement officers turned
their attention to the two ex-cons with whom Berry indicated he was living.
Bill King and Russell Brewer had served time together at a prison in Tennessee Colony, Texas. Having gleaned this minimal information, Curtis Frame
and his colleague, Officer Rich Ford, were running into a brick wall in their
efforts to get Berry to talk. However, there had already been reports suggesting that Bill King might be a white supremacist, and when Bill King's teenage girlfriend, Kylie Greeney, was questioned, she identified the Zippo lighter
that had been found at the crime scene as belonging to King. "Possum," she
told them, was King's prison nickname. She also revealed a disturbing detail
that supported the hypothesis that King had racist inclinations. Under King's
nickname, the lighter bore an insignia that had baffled Jasper law enforcement personnel: an equilateral triangle with each point of the triangle touch-
ing a short straight line. Greeney explained the meaning of the curious design. "That's a symbol for the Klan," she told them. The insignia was formed
by three *K* letters, rotated so that the branches of each formed the three sides

SHAWN BERRY'S TRUCK

of the equilateral triangle in the center. The officers also noticed that the
two *s* letters in the name Possum were actually lightning bolts, like those
used by the Nazi SS and popular among white supremacists. Such evidence
only served to reinforce the sheriff's fears that this was a racially motivated
murder. The sheriff ordered surveillance of the apartment where the three
men lived.

By ten o'clock that evening the stakeout was in place, with Stacey Chambers, a deputy with the sheriff's department, and Larry Ledbetter, a reserve
deputy, sitting in a blue Chevy pickup truck directly across from the Timbers Apartments. The Timbers was quite nice as apartment complexes in
Jasper go. Although the architecture was anything but distinctive—one
could have imagined such a complex in virtually any suburban neighborhood
in the country—it definitely had a middle-class patina. Tucked into the pine
trees on the west side of Jasper on Highway 190, the complex consisted of six
lime-green, wood-sided units, each with an apartment upstairs and another
downstairs. The apartments were conveniently situated, directly across the
highway from the local Wal-Mart.

Hearing about the goings-on at the apartment that King, Berry, and
Brewer shared during the weeks before the murder, one might have expected
something a bit more run down. For one thing, Berry was the only one of the
three with a steady job. For another, there were the late-night comings and
goings, not to mention the apartment's ever-shifting occupancy. The place
had initially been rented to Bill King, who lived there with his girlfriend,
Kylie, until she moved out following a quarrel. Shawn Berry had then moved
in, and his brother, Louis, stayed there on a regular basis as well. Two weeks
before the murder Russell Brewer had called Bill King from the bus station
in Beaumont announcing his arrival from Sulphur Springs. He, too, had
moved into the apartment. By that time, Louis had gone to stay with *his* girlfriend, but he was still around the apartment quite a bit. All of these variables
were factors in the eviction notice that Bill King had been served only days
before the murder.

The arrangement within the apartment wasn't exactly equitable. Bill King
had taken possession of the sole bedroom, although he allowed Louis Berry
to use one of the room's two closets for his belongings while he himself used
the other for his. Everyone else—Louis Berry, Shawn Berry, or Russell
Brewer—had to sleep in the living room, where the accommodations con-

sisted of a couch and a couple of mats on the floor. The dining room had been converted into a weight room, with a workout bench in the middle and weights distributed around it on the floor. The place had all of the homeyness that one might expect from the average bachelor pad. While it had originally been King and Greeney's apartment, the arrangement also allowed King to be in control, relegating others to satellite positions.

The Wall-Mart store sat up on a slight bluff overlooking the highway, and the deputies were parked on a grassy area at the edge of the parking lot, their truck perpendicular to the highway. Because the vehicle was facing the apartment head on, anyone peering at them from inside would have had no inkling that what looked like a run-of-the-mill pickup was actually a law enforcement vehicle with the words "Jasper County Sheriff's Department" painted on its doors. The apartment occupied by King, Brewer, and Berry was at the front of the complex, on the second floor. Thus, from their vantage point, the officers could look directly into the apartment anytime someone opened the door. In surveillance mode, the officers kept a constant watch on the apartment through binoculars. Their only other entertainment was listening to the exchanges with the county dispatcher coming in over the radio. A little way down the road on Highway 190 another team of officers, including Larry Pulliam, the man who had arrested Shawn Berry a few hours earlier, also lay in wait in an unmarked gold Crown Victoria.

The officers had been observing the apartment for less than an hour when a car pulled up in front of an adjacent unit where it could not be seen from the apartment. Several men got out, walked up a flight of stairs, and went into King's apartment. They departed only moments later. Soon the apartment door opened once again, and Chambers saw King and Brewer walk down the steps and head right for him and his partner. Chambers and Ledbetter had no specific instructions as to what to do other than remain "on surveillance," so they radioed the command center. "They're coming right at us," Chambers told the dispatcher. "What do we need to do?" In the short interval it took King and Brewer to walk across the highway, the officers received no response to their query.

As King approached the truck, he recognized Chambers. It was impossible for him to miss the lettering emblazoned on the truck's side as well. Chambers knew Shawn Berry from the local movie theater and he had seen King with Berry in Jasper's video game arcade. On occasion, King had been

one of a group of young men in Jasper who played paintball, an activity in
which some of the local law enforcement officers also occasionally participated. It was immediately obvious to Chambers that King had figured out
what Chambers was doing there, even though neither of the officers was
in uniform. "If they make it into the Wal-Mart, we'll probably never see
them again," Chambers said to Ledbetter. It was time for the officers to make
a move.

Chambers stepped out of the truck and walked up to King. "We need to
talk with you, Bill," he said. He indicated that there was a problem and they
wanted King and Brewer to ride over to the sheriff's department to sort it
out. By then, the second surveillance team had pulled up, and King and
Brewer were immediately separated, King staying with Chambers and Ledbetter. "King didn't ask what the problem was," Chambers later recalled. To
Chambers this was typical behavior, "like the guy with fifty pounds of marijuana consenting to have his car searched," he said. "He just tried to play
it off."

Chambers told King that he would need to be handcuffed for officer
safety, since their vehicle did not have a prisoner cage. King readily agreed,
and Chambers cuffed his hands tightly behind his back. On the eight-minute
ride over to the sheriff's office King and the officers exchanged small talk. It
was a strategy that Chambers liked to use to keep suspects at ease. "Once
things are sorted out, I'll give you guys a ride back to the apartment," Chambers told King. For his part, King was completely compliant. "No problem,"
he told the officers.

When Chambers and the others arrived with King and Brewer, the sheriff's office was brimming with law enforcement officers. The two men had
not yet been arrested, but they were kept separate, King brought into the
sheriff's office while Brewer sat waiting in a small office down the hall. King
and Brewer were allowed to take turns smoking outside, but they were monitored closely.

In the sheriff's office, King was the model of decorum. "Bill King was
nothing but a perfect gentleman the whole time," the sheriff recalled. "He
didn't even ask why he was there." When the sheriff asked King for permission to search his apartment, King readily signed the appropriate documents.
"I've got nothing to hide," he affirmed.

The sheriff immediately dispatched a team to search the Timbers Apartments. By now it was well past midnight on what had already been a long and intensely draining day. The apartment search yielded a cache of white supremacist literature, including a book on the history of the Ku Klux Klan, as well as drawings and other materials belonging to Bill King. The search team also found a pair of shoes that appeared to have bloodstains on them. The apartment was well stocked with cases of Bud Light and Coors Light, the same kind as the empty beer bottles that had been found at the crime scene. The brands were also consistent with those reported stolen from a local convenience store the day before. Of special interest to the officers, however, was the fact that the refrigerator at the apartment was filled with packages of gourmet meat. "These were things like mutton and salmon and things you don't normally find in some redneck guys' apartment in Jasper, Texas," is the way the district attorney, Guy James Gray, would later describe it. The packages were labeled "Patrick's Steakhouse"—a local enterprise that officers knew had been broken into just a few days earlier. At one-thirty in the morning, the law enforcement team roused the restaurant's owner out of bed and asked him to come over to identify the boxes of meat.

Patrick Lam, the owner of Patrick's Steakhouse, was a local eccentric. He was reputed to have been born in a Nazi concentration camp in Lyon, France, in 1944, the son of a Spanish general and a Belgian mother, both of whom were Jewish. Catholic nuns had rescued the infant, giving him the name Patrick to improve his chances of survival in case he was discovered by the occupying Germans. At the Timbers Apartments, the restaurateur confirmed that indeed the meats were from his establishment. King and Brewer were promptly booked on possession of stolen merchandise and placed in separate cells. Minor burglaries were the least of the sheriff's worries at the moment, but having a basis for arresting the two men gave officers more time to prepare a good "probable cause" document on the murder case.

WELL INTO THE EARLY HOURS of Monday morning, the sheriff's department was a hotbed of activity. The Jasper County jail can hold some fifty prisoners. To the right of the entrance to the cell area, there is a small room called the "multipurpose room"—in addition to interviews, religious services are conducted here by visiting ministers. The fifteen-foot-by-fifteen-foot room is less than inviting. Its cinder-block walls exude coldness. Three

of the four walls are painted an institutional cream color, like the jail's hallways, but otherwise they are unadorned. The fourth wall, painted navy blue,
has a one-way mirror that permits viewing into the multipurpose room from
the adjoining control room. It also has a mounted video camera. A stack of
plastic chairs and several folding tables are routinely stored in the room,
which is illuminated by two large panels of fluorescent lights. There is absolutely nothing in the room in which a prisoner might find reflected a sense
of the familiar or that might give solace.

By four in the morning Frame and Ford found themselves seated around
one of the tables in the multipurpose room interviewing Berry. They had
been there for hours, but the officers were getting nowhere with him. Frame
and Ford felt frustrated, knowing they had the goods on him, even though
Berry remained intransigent. Eventually, however, the suspect began to show
the effects of the prolonged interview. Frame could tell that Berry was extremely nervous. "He was sitting up, not relaxed, looking and listening to
everything we were saying. His eyes got big, he was licking his lips, picking
his fingernails, scratching, you know, fidgety." To Frame these were the telltale signs of a suspect who was beginning to break. It was dawning on Berry
that he had lost the game.

Frame had started the process of obtaining a "voluntary statement" from
the suspect (in current law enforcement parlance the term "interrogation"
is no longer used) by simply asking Berry about his pickup truck, where
he kept his keys, and his whereabouts on the previous evening. Berry was
also asked to identify some of the evidence found at the crime scene. He
identified a watch as Kylie Greeney's and the Zippo lighter as Bill King's. It
was Frame's way of warming the suspect up, a way of laying the groundwork,
setting the tone by alerting Berry to the fact that they had evidence, yet keeping him in suspense as to just how much they had. It was an approach intended to get Berry thinking about what the officers might know about what
had taken place out on Huff Creek Road the night before. Frame kept his
best cards for last, however, bringing in the torque wrench and the nut driver
with Berry's name on them, laying them on the table for Berry to examine,
letting the full implication of it all settle heavily into Berry's consciousness.

Frame and Ford were quite aware that they had to walk a very fine line.
At any moment, Berry could simply say, "I want to talk to an attorney,"
which would bring the discussions to an abrupt halt. At the same time, they

DETECTIVE CURTIS FRAME

needed to press Berry, whom they viewed as the weak link among the three men now in custody. Most of the evidence that they had pointed directly at him, and he was the only one of the three who had not served hard time. "Berry's the one to talk to," was the way the sheriff later put it. "These other two guys have been in prison. Obviously, from their tattoos, they're gang-bangers. We know these guys ain't the ones you want to interview. Berry's the one you want to concentrate on." So Frame and Ford hammered on him.

Berry's initial story was that King and Brewer had taken his truck that night, but Frame and Ford were not buying any of it. When more than one person was involved in a crime, it was a common gambit for a suspect to point the finger at others while minimizing his own role. Frame and Ford had been through this scenario countless times, enough to be skeptical of such a claim, even without all the evidence that seemed to implicate Berry. The officers' response was equally predictable: they jacked up the pressure on Berry. "You're probably going to end up alone on this deal," Frame told him. "If you want to take it, that's fine." However, Frame asked Berry to think about how he might feel sitting in prison while Bill King or Russell Brewer went free, maybe having sex with Berry's girlfriend. It was psychological war-fare that was aimed at making Berry contemplate what might be in store for him.

While the officers could see that the pressure tactics were having an ef-fect on Berry, he was clearly holding back. Frame and Ford were feeling frus-trated after hours in the cramped, hot room. At times their exasperation led to raised voices. "It really got loud," Sheriff Rowles later recalled, with what may have been understatement.

It had already been several hours since Sheriff Rowles had roused the Jasper district attorney with a late-night phone call, briefly outlining the crime and the nature of the evidence that they had gathered up to that point. When Guy James Gray arrived at the sheriff's office, the DA and Rowles con-ferred at length about the case before them. The evidence found at the apart-ment strongly suggested the possibility that Byrd's murder was a hate crime. As they talked, it occurred to Rowles that perhaps they should bring the FBI into the case, an idea that Gray agreed with.

They had already decided that they would follow this course of action when Rowles and Gray, aware that the interview with Berry was going no-where, decided to talk to him themselves. "Why don't we let them go smoke a cigarette, dip snuff, drink a cup of coffee, and you and I can take over for a while?" Rowles said to the DA. The two men entered the small room where Shawn Berry was sitting at the round foldout table looking drained and vulnerable. To Rowles, Berry appeared to be on the verge of imploding; he simply needed a little encouragement. Rowles and Gray played the classic good cop–bad cop routine. Rowles was the first to speak. "Shawn Berry," he said, "look at you. Look at yourself! You can't even breathe. You're having trouble taking a normal breath. Man, you're gonna suffocate on us here if you don't tell us what's happening. You're fixing to hyperventilate."

The DA's strategy, on the other hand, was to emphasize the gravity of the situation to Berry: "The sheriff and the DA aren't down here at three o'clock in the morning for nothing," he told Berry. "This is serious." As the man responsible for prosecuting the case, the DA was the only person in a position to offer Berry something in return for his cooperation. Gray looked Berry in the eye. "Usually the guy that talks first gets treated in a different fashion from the others," he told Berry. "You'd better be thinking about how you're going to handle yourself."

The sheriff then offered Berry a promise. "This is going to be a hate crime," Rowles told Berry. "I don't know what a hate crime is, but I know this man was killed because he was black. That's a civil rights violation, and this is gonna be an FBI deal, this is not going to be our deal."

The sheriff paused for a moment. He wanted Berry to hear clearly what was being proposed. As anxious as Berry felt, with his fear and exhaustion permeating the room, Rowles knew that the suspect's cognitive faculties were hazy at best. Berry was also no doubt trying to calculate what strategy might work best for him. "I don't have the authority to promise you much," the sheriff continued. "But there's one thing I can promise you. I know how the FBI people work. Somebody somewhere down the line gets a better deal than anybody else because they talk. And I'm telling you, they're gonna talk to all three of you, and somebody will get a little better deal than anybody else. And the only promise that I can make you is that you will be the first person that the FBI talks to. I'll make you that promise," Rowles said.

The sheriff's proposal may have been the first break in the clouds for Berry, who by then must have realized that he was completely cornered given that the officers had a mountain of evidence linking him to the murder. He was still nearly hyperventilating as Rowles and the DA talked to him, but the sheriff's words were finding a receptive ear. A few minutes after hearing the sheriff's proposal, Berry simply broke. He looked up at Rowles and Gray and in an emotional voice said, "They went to fuck with a nigger." The three men sat with the implication of that statement for a moment. It seemed to reverberate against the cold cinder-block walls of the room. Berry then said, "Give me a piece of paper and send the other guys back in here."

Sheriff Rowles and the DA emerged from the room and walked over to Frame and Ford, who were sipping coffee. "He's basically humble now," the sheriff told them. "He's willing to tell you about what he knows."

Berry's first statement was a significant breakthrough, notwithstanding its oblique quality and the fact that it did not enlarge on the idea that his friends had set out to deliberately "fuck with" a black person. He told the officers that the three suspects had driven out into the country late Saturday night in a failed attempt to find a party to which some girls had invited them. Frustrated, they headed back to town, where they encountered James Byrd walking down Martin Luther King Jr. Boulevard. Shawn Berry knew Byrd from around town and had given him rides before. According to Berry's account, King was opposed to picking Byrd up, but Berry did so anyway. On the way to the logging road they stopped, placing Byrd in the cab while King and Brewer got into the back of the pickup, a decision that Frame immediately saw as an attempt to control the unsuspecting victim. Once out on the logging road, King had been the first one to jump James Byrd, dragging him out of the cab of the truck. Berry claimed that he attempted to stop the assault, only to be threatened by King: "Nigger lovers can get the same thing." Berry reported that he then ran from the scene, while Brewer and King continued beating Byrd, and later King picked him up on the logging road. Berry claimed that he didn't know that Byrd was chained to the back of the truck or that he was being dragged behind them. After coming out onto Huff Creek Road, Berry remembered, Brewer turned and looked through the back window of the truck's cab and said, "Look at the motherfucker bounce!" That, according to Berry's statement, was when he first realized that Byrd was being dragged.

Although in Frame's view there were significant holes in the account, Berry's statement basically outlined the key elements of what had taken place, which was good. He'd put himself at the scene, and he'd put the other two suspects there as well. It was a useful statement from Frame's perspective.

It was nearly six in the morning by the time Curtis Frame handed Berry's signed statement to the sheriff. Rowles was sitting in his office, utterly exhausted. He had now been up for more than twenty-four hours, and they had been the most tension-filled hours of his life. The moment when he had first set his Calloway golf cap next to James Byrd's broken dentures out on Huff Creek Road already seemed like a long-ago memory. What was occupying the sheriff's mind now was his decision to go to the FBI. The nearest FBI offices were in Beaumont, more than an hour's drive away, and he wanted to be in Beaumont when the FBI offices opened.

SHERIFF ROWLES WAS FRESHLY SHOWERED and shaved but otherwise exhausted when he appeared, unannounced, at the FBI offices in Beaumont at eight o'clock sharp that Monday morning. He had hoped to meet with his friend Zack Shelton, an agent assigned to the Beaumont office, but Shelton had yet to arrive. The Jasper County sheriff was armed with a copy of Shawn Berry's statement, a document that was less than two hours old. A group of agents quickly convened to review the case, and an assistant made copies of Berry's statement for everyone in attendance. A copy was also faxed to the FBI office in Houston. At ten o'clock Rowles and one of the FBI agents headed off to the Jefferson County morgue in Beaumont to witness James Byrd's autopsy. The FBI was particularly interested in the elements of the murder that supported the possibility of a racially motivated hate crime. The fact that the victim had apparently been dragged to death behind a vehicle suggested a modern-day lynching. In addition, the white supremacist literature and Berry's intimation that it was a racial murder gave the case a possible civil rights dimension. It was this element that distinguished the case from a typical murder case, in which the FBI would usually have no role. It was obvious from the start that the sheriff had the FBI's attention.

Rowles had planned for a second "round table" discussion in the Emergency Corps Building at one o'clock on Monday afternoon, but he called to reschedule the meeting for three o'clock. His officers, as well as those from the Jasper Police Department, had been working on the Byrd case for well over twenty-four hours with no break. The sheriff instructed his personnel to go home for a short rest before the three o'clock meeting.

By the time Rowles reconvened his officers, some twenty FBI agents had arrived in Jasper, including the agent in charge from the FBI's Houston office, a man named Don Clark. It was clear to everyone that the Byrd mur- der had taken on a high-stakes profile, not only because of the raw brutality of the murder but also because of its racial overtones.

Tommy Robinson was assigned to escort the FBI agents out to Huff Creek Road and the logging road, where they immediately set about comb- ing the area for additional evidence. By the next day, Tuesday, there were close to a hundred FBI agents in Jasper, including the entire Evidence Re- covery Team from the Houston office. Specialists in soil samples and plant samples walked the entire three miles of the crime scene, from the site of the original scuffle down the logging road to the asphalt and up to the Huff Creek Church. The phalanx of trained eyes fanned out to search for evi- dence, scouring the entire area. Wherever there was evidence of blood, espe- cially along the paved road, they stopped and swabbed it for DNA. Their ap- proach was meticulous, and for Sheriff Rowles, the FBI's involvement was a godsend. The sheer size of the crime scene area dictated an immense expen- diture of personnel, which local law enforcement, even with the addition of the Jasper Police Department and the Department of Public Safety, simply could not manage.

The FBI's presence added considerable ballast to Jasper law enforcement's investigative efforts, but there was an additional motive for bringing in the federal agency. Guy James Gray put it succinctly: "The motive to go to the FBI was political protection," he said. "These types of cases had turned out badly in the past in East Texas. How did we know how it would be received in 1998? So the sheriff made the suggestion, and I agreed with it, that we go to the FBI and get them up here. At a minimum we've got some political protection. We're not hiding anything; we're inviting the federal people to come in and hear what we've got and help us get some more. And also, get- ting them in here before the media. That was a major cog in convincing, specifically the black community, that this wasn't 1920."

BY THE EARLY HOURS OF MONDAY morning, Bill King and Russell Brewer had been arrested on the suspected burglary charge, but law enforcement officers had yet to interview either of them. It was not until Tuesday that the officers were ready to interview Bill King, who was brought into the multi-

purpose room, the same small room where Berry had given his initial statement. Curtis Frame and Rich Ford, the officers who had interviewed Berry,
were present for the initial interview with Bill King. They were also joined
by three FBI agents, including Zack Shelton and his supervisor, a man named
Norm Townsend. Working in tandem, Ford and Shelton had already obtained several additional statements from Berry.

In the first meeting King had little to say but agreed to a second interview,
which took place later that same night. At this meeting he was placed at one
end of an oval folding table while the law enforcement officers asked him
questions. The presence of the FBI agents in the room constituted an unmistakable signal to King: law enforcement had brought in its top guns. According to Curtis Frame, Shelton was talking a good game with King. "He
was in a submissive mode," was Frame's recollection of King's demeanor.
"Bill King is sitting there with his hands on the table and he's looking and
he's listening to Zack." However, the interview took an abrupt downturn
when Agent Shelton told King, "We got some witnesses, we got some statements that saw you in the truck." The statement was, to be sure, a stretch
of the truth. Steven Scott had seen Byrd in a pickup truck with three individuals whom he described as white, but he had not been able to identify
any of them by name. It was the kind of truth-bending that is a staple of
such interrogations. Frame had no objections to the approach, but apparently such tried-and-true law enforcement tactics were not widely accepted
within the FBI, because Norm Townsend immediately grew uncomfortable. "We don't have this. You can't tell him that," Townsend is reported to
have said.

Frame still bristles at the recollection of the exchange. He viewed Townsend as perhaps a good agent in the typical coat-and-tie kind of crime that
the FBI is known for, but a rank amateur in the hardscrabble dirty realities
of dealing with convicted felons. Frame could see King processing the implications of this turn of events. "You can see the body language," he said.
"Bill King looks up, looks all the way around the table at everybody, leans
back, folds his arms and says, 'Y'all ain't got shit! I want my lawyer.' Well,
we're done then. We're through. Bill never talked."

The exchange revealed King for who he was—smart, nervy, and experienced. Unlike Shawn Berry, whose anxiety had been palpable, King's demeanor was more like that of a chess player in a complex game: he seemed to

recognize that the officers had run out of moves. It was as if he were taunt- *The*
ing them, knowing they were helpless to do anything about his recalcitrance. *Arrests*

The official FBI account of the interview is rather turgid:

> On June 8, 1998, at approximately 9:56 P.M., John William
> King, also known as Bill, was recontacted at the Jasper County
> Jail, Jasper, Texas. King was again advised of his Miranda Rights
> and was provided a waiver of those rights which he read, signed,
> and agreed to answer questions of Special Agents Townsend,
> Shelton and Brewer.
>
> King was asked about a watch, identified by his girlfriend, found
> at the crime scene. King stated that he had placed his girlfriend's
> watch in Shawn's truck on either Monday or Tuesday of this past
> week when they went to Wildwood to do the land clearing work.
> According to King they needed a watch and he got it and put it in
> the truck.
>
> *King acknowledged* that on Sunday afternoon he went with Shawn
> Berry to the Splish Splash Car Wash to wash Shawn's pickup truck.
>
> *King also* acknowledged that Saturday evening he and Brewer
> stopped by Tommy Faulk's house just to socialize.
>
> When the interview became accusatory, King requested an attor-
> ney at approximately 10:10 P.M., at which time the interview was
> concluded.
>
> During that interview King also acknowledged that he had accom-
> panied Berry to the car wash where they washed off the chain and
> the bed of the pickup.

Bill King's subsequent account of the two interviews differed from the accounts of Frame and the FBI. With respect to the first interview, he described
being instructed to go to the multipurpose room where there were three or
four FBI agents in addition to the Jasper law enforcement personnel from
the sheriff's department and the Jasper Police Department. The number of
people crowded into the room made it feel cramped, he said.

"I was told to sit down at a round folding table while everyone else stood
around me," King recalls. "It looked just like it does in the movies—intim-
idating—but there were no 'bright lights' being shined in my eyes." The FBI 51

agents took the lead in asking questions, asking King to identify such items
as his cigarette lighter, his girlfriend's watch, and other evidence. King readily acknowledged that the Zippo lighter with the name "Possum" marked on
it was his; however, he claimed to have lost it, along with a pack of cigarettes,
a week earlier. He thought he must have left them atop a pay phone at a local convenience store or else someone had stolen them, he said. He wasn't
sure. As for his girlfriend's watch, King said that he had kept it in Shawn
Berry's truck "to keep track of time while we worked out of town."

As the agents pressed forward with their questioning about the murder itself, King told them that he had nothing to do with it. "They asked me about
Byrd, and I denied all knowledge of anything," he said. He similarly refused
to answer questions about Shawn Berry or Russell Brewer. Instead, King said
that the trio had gone looking for a party that some girls had invited them to
that night and, failing to find it, had gone about creating some "mischief,"
such as running over mailbox posts out on the rural roads.

The FBI agents then produced Shawn Berry's sworn statements and asked
King to read them. "They were in Shawn's handwriting, and it was his signature all right," King said. King's response was to reprise what he had already told them of the night's activities, an account that contained no reference to the murder. King claims that the agents grew frustrated and drew the
interview to a close, asking him if they could talk with him again, to which
King agreed.

According to King, he was taken back into the multipurpose room some-
time later that night. He assumed it was after the FBI had again spoken with
Berry and Brewer. There were more agents in the room during this second
interview, as King recollects it, and there was a large trash sack on the table.
"I was told to have a seat and to look inside the bag. It was just like some bad
'B' movie. I started laughing, and asked them if they thought I was Willy
Foofoo or something. I refused to even touch the bag, so they got irritated
and opened it for me; then they had the audacity to tell me to pull the contents out and identify it. I was still smiling, rather sardonically, and told them
'No thanks! I *know* that my fingerprints are not on *anything.*' I wasn't about
to fall for some setup." King claims that the agents became upset with him,
opening the bag wider so that he could see that it contained a chain. He was
again asked to identify the bag's contents. "They asked what it was, and I said
something sarcastic, like, if they didn't know, it proves why they're called the

'Federal Bureau of Incompetence.'" King claims that at that juncture one of the federal agents became agitated. "No! It's the chain YOU used to drag Byrd to his death!" he remembers the agent shouting. The interview became very tense. King acknowledged washing Shawn Berry's truck the day after the murder. He was also asked about driving Shawn's truck to a friend's trailer home (the chain used in Byrd's murder had been hidden in a hole in the woods behind the trailer home). King also acknowledged having done that. The interview then came back to the events of the night of James Byrd's murder. King claims that the agent accused him of complicity in the murder. "I told 'em all to suck my dick and get me a lawyer," King claims. "One agent said to me, '. . . so you're refusing to cooperate?' . . . I ignored them, and asked again for a lawyer. All of a sudden, that hostile agent slams his fist into the table and screams at me, 'You're gonna fry for this, you little fucker! I'll see to it.' At that point, I told 'em to suck my dick again, and that the interview was over."

King was returned to his cell and never questioned again. Later, from death row, he reflected back on the interviews in the Jasper County jail. He seemed oddly bemused by it all. "I reckon ol' boy made some good on his threat, huh?" he said.

Bill King's stance had implications for the officers' efforts to obtain a statement from Brewer as well. "Brewer didn't want to talk," Frame recalled. "'Course, he'd heard through the jail communication that King had not talked, so obviously you know *he's* not going to. He wants to be as tough as King, right?"

JAMES BYRD'S FUNERAL was set for Saturday, June 13, 1998. In addition to elected officials, the event drew numerous prominent national figures such as Jesse Jackson and Al Sharpton. It also drew the Ku Klux Klan, mostly out of Cleveland, Texas, some seventy miles west of Jasper, as well as the Black Panthers of Dallas and a separatist Black Muslim group from Houston. The media, some from as far away as Australia and Europe, also descended on Jasper. James Byrd Jr., a man with a love of singing and dancing and a weakness for drink and drugs, a petty criminal who had been in and out of the local jail, was laid to rest in a funeral fit for royalty, at least by local standards. The cost of the burial, $30,000, was paid for by basketball star Dennis Rodman. In a

JAMES BYRD JR.'S GRAVE

gesture that captured the spirit of the community, following the funeral the
Jasper Ministerial Alliance, a coalition of white and black ministers, organized the tearing down of a fence that for generations had divided the white
and black sections of Jasper's public cemetery. Byrd's murder, the gesture
seemed to say, had not been entirely in vain.

Jasper now settled into an uneasy interlude. Weeks after the funeral, the
district attorney announced that Bill King would be the first of the three men
to be tried. He also indicated that it was his hope to secure the death penalty
for King. King's attorney filed for a change of venue, hoping that another
community might yield a more sympathetic jury, but his motion was denied.
The trial date was set for February 1999, seven months hence. Bill King, who
had lived in Jasper virtually all of his life, would be tried before a Jasper
County jury, but, in fact, the entire world would be watching.

The Unraveling

THE HOUSE ON LYNN STREET in Jasper, where the King family had lived for years, was a small, wood-frame affair with three bedrooms and a bath, situated directly across the street from the Louisiana-Pacific lumber company. Ronald King was employed as a millwright at the company, a kind of mechanical troubleshooter with a gift for repairing virtually any piece of machinery. The house had originally been on Louisiana-Pacific land, part of the company's subsidized housing for employees, but in the early 1980s, with the lumber industry in dire circumstances, the company had decided to divest itself of these houses as a cost-saving measure. Ronald was given the house outright; his only expense was the five hundred dollars he paid for a small tract of land across from the mill and the cost of moving the house to it.

Bill King was two years old when the Kings moved to Jasper, and seven when they moved to Lynn Street; Ronald and Jean's older children had long since moved out. Donald, the oldest, had joined the army while the family was still living in Picayune, Mississippi, before Bill was born. Donald eventually settled in Indiana and, in what was the first of several marriages, married a Korean woman who had given birth to the couple's twins. Carol, the next youngest of the King children, was married to a man working at a local plywood factory, and the couple was still living in Jasper along with their two children. Linda, younger than Carol by eighteen months, was also married and living in Jasper with her husband and their two children, although she would eventually end up divorced and living in Vidor, about an hour south of Jasper, a community infamous as the Ku Klux Klan capital of Texas. That left Ronald, Jean, and Jean's mother living in the house, in addition to Bill, although Carol and Linda were ever-present visitors.

Jean was especially close to one of her brothers, Johnny Knudsen, who still lived in Mississippi. Johnny visited the Kings in Jasper with some regularity and often brought along his two granddaughters, Samantha and Serena. Similarly, when the Kings made sojourns back to Picayune or New Orleans, where Jean's extended family lived, Bill frequently played with his two cousins, who were only slightly older. One particularly memorable visit occurred in 1984 when New Orleans hosted the World's Fair, to which Johnny Knudsen took Bill, then ten years old, along with the two girls. Bill had grown close to Samantha and Serena, although he'd never met the girls' parents.

When Bill was thirteen years old, Johnny Knudsen made one of his visits to Jasper and, as usual, he brought the two girls along with him. Ronald King had spent the morning watching Bill, Samantha, and Serena running through the house and playing in the backyard, and it was more than he could bear. It made him feel quite emotional to see Bill with them, especially Serena, with whom Bill shared a striking resemblance.

At one juncture, while the kids were playing outside, Bill ran into the house. Ronald felt the moment had come to reveal to Bill an important fact about his life:

"Son," Ronald said, "you realize that you're adopted, don't you?"

"No," Bill responded flatly. He did not appear to be particularly shaken by the revelation.

"Samantha and Serena are your sisters," Ronald continued, pressing the full implication of what he was saying.

Bill appeared to take it all in stride. "Well," he said, "I like my sisters better," meaning Carol and Linda. "Can I go out and play?"

That is all Ronald and Bill remember about the day Bill learned that he was adopted. There was an odd disjuncture in the moment—something so

potentially momentous received so matter-of-factly, as if it were rather trivial and mundane. Ronald might as well have announced that Jean was serving ham sandwiches for lunch.

Bill King was born on November 3, 1974. Johnny Knudsen's wife, Barbara,
had come into their marriage with a child, a daughter named Sylvia, whom
Knudsen adopted. Sylvia grew up and married a man named Sammy Rae,
with whom she had Samantha and Serena. Sylvia and Sammy could ill afford
another baby; their dire poverty was such that occasionally they and the girls
lived out of the family car. In addition to their financial problems, there were
severe strains in the marriage. In fact, Sammy had abandoned Sylvia while
she was in the hospital delivering Bill. Ronald and Jean agreed to take in the
newborn to help out, but they immediately fell in love with the child and
plotted to find a way to keep him.

Bill was only three months old when Ronald and Jean brought him to
their home in Picayune. Although this was a family adoption, neither Jean
nor Ronald was related to Bill by blood. Bill's legal name was Samuel Shane
Rae, which Ronald and Jean changed to John William King. They also had
Bill's birth certificate altered to indicate that Jean had given birth to Bill,
thereby erasing the traces of the adoption. Thus, while Bill had contact with
Sylvia's two daughters as he was growing up, he was not aware that Samantha and Serena were actually his biological sisters. He had also never met
Sylvia or Sammy, his biological parents.

Ronald claims that he made no conscious decision to keep the fact of his
adoption from Bill. Jean, on the other hand, lived in terror that Bill would
find out and was devastated to learn that Ronald had told him. "She was always afraid that he might think less of her if he thought he was adopted,"
Ronald explained. Her response to learning that the secret had been revealed
seemed to confirm her fear: "You didn't tell him! What's he going to think of
me?" she exclaimed when she learned that Bill now knew the truth.

While Ronald believed that Bill had received the news of his adoption
with equanimity, Bill's behavior suggested otherwise; not long thereafter Bill's
life started a slow but persistent downturn. It was as if the discovery had suddenly altered the trajectory of his life. The first signs were his faltering grades.
Bill King had been an excellent student in elementary school, consistently
making A's and B's, and he was not a problem in the classroom. On the contrary, the Kings had letters from teachers in which their boy was praised as

a model student and described as likeable, friendly, and polite. Now, as he entered adolescence full tilt, his grades were dropping precipitously.

Bill's friends changed as well. For example, Chris Thomas had been a good friend in the latter years of elementary school after the two boys had met at the school bus stop. Like Bill, Chris had a talent for things mechanical. He had built a transistor radio from a kit, for example, a project that intrigued Bill. The two boys frequently spent the night at one another's house and shared a passion for computer games, which they worked to solve for hours on end. The friendship had blossomed over the years, and Ronald remembers feeling pleased that Bill had such a friend, a child who was clearly smart, interested in school, and interested in technology. The fact that Chris Thomas was African American was not an issue in the King household.

What most impressed Ronald about Chris Thomas, however, was the child's relationship with his father. Ronald recalls going to pick the boys up at the Thomases' house and finding Chris's father sitting in a chair under the carport. The two men chatted for a while, as they sometimes did; Ronald was always struck by Chris's father's knowledge of the region. When the boys came out, Chris walked up to his father and placed his hand on his father's shoulder as he spoke to him, telling him that he was going to spend the night at Bill's house. That gesture, a spontaneous display of warmth between a son and father, surprised and impressed Ronald, and the image of it stayed with him. It seemed to strike a particularly emotional chord within the elder King, a man who was not particularly comfortable with such demonstrations of affection.

Bill King's relationship with Chris Thomas was one of the casualties of Bill's early adolescence. While the two boys continued to have some contact (a couple of years later Chris loaned the Kings a video camera to record the last weeks of Jean's life, for example), Bill's social interests increasingly gravitated toward less savory peers.

Bill developed an interest in tattoos in elementary school, when he would use pens to draw on himself and on friends. At the age of thirteen he attempted to tattoo a barbed wire pattern around his left wrist, but had found it difficult to complete the pattern on the underside. Ever since, King has had a fascination with tattoos. "I'm addicted to them," he would later say. "There's something about the needle. Some people are addicted to drugs or whatever; I've always been addicted to tattoos. Even watching someone get tattooed I have a strong reaction to that. It makes me want more tattoos for myself."

When King was in high school, many of the kids tended to gather at a tired old trailer home on McQueen Street, around the corner from the King house, where an older boy named Tommy Faulk lived. Shawn Berry's brother, Louis, who frequented Faulk's place, remembers that King was easy to get along with but that he had a penchant for being petulant and moody. "If he wasn't the center of attention, or if something wasn't working out, if the focus wasn't exactly on him, he'd leave." Often King would show up again later, after he'd cooled off, walking into Faulk's trailer as if nothing had happened. The other kids simply accepted the fact that King was this way. They liked "old Bill," as he was often called, notwithstanding his idiosyncrasies.

By then King had already established a reputation for having a way with girls. King would show up at Faulk's trailer with a girl's car and proudly declare, "I've got it for the night," or else he would talk girls into giving him money. King was quick to share such bounty with his buddies. But since the crowd at Faulk's tended to be a couple of years older than Bill, perhaps such largesse was fueled in part by the wish to be liked and accepted.

Tommy Faulk had a penchant for hanging around kids who ended up in trouble, although Faulk himself always seemed to evade being directly implicated. Ronald was sufficiently worried about this relationship that he instructed Jean not to allow Bill to go over to Tommy's, but on many occasions Ronald would return from work to discover that Bill was at Faulk's. "He don't have anyone else to play with," Jean would say in self-defense.

Ronald considered Faulk to be a bad influence. Tommy had no interest in school, and his parents appeared to place no restrictions on him. "His parents would pretty much let them do whatever they wanted to when they were over at their house," Ronald recalled. He also thought that Tommy Faulk's parents drank excessively. As far as Ronald was concerned, the Faulk home simply wasn't a good environment; yet Bill was there constantly. When Tommy Faulk began having serious academic problems, Bill was asked to tutor him, even though he was younger and behind Tommy in school. That only brought the two boys into greater contact and did little to remedy Tommy's academic difficulties. Tommy soon dropped out of school altogether, while Bill's own grades continued to plummet. Years later, when these

adolescent years had become little more than a longed-for nostalgia, Tommy *The*
Faulk would figure prominently in the days immediately before and after *Unraveling*
Byrd's murder.

"ALL MY LIFE, I'D FELT that I was different from everyone else," Bill King later recalled in describing what it was like to learn that he was adopted. It was a feeling he could not shake. He felt he did not fit in, that he was in the grip of something to which he could not put words. Learning that he was adopted at the age of thirteen seemed to be an answer to the question of why he felt so irrevocably dislocated. It wasn't that the thought had never occurred to him. As he grew old enough to notice, he began to realize that all his friends' parents were much younger than Ronald and Jean; in fact, they tended to be closer in age to Carol and Linda. This struck Bill as odd and it made him wonder, but not enough to ask. Questions bounced around in his mind, unspoken, much less answered. Ronald and Jean had been in their forties when they adopted Bill; by East Texas standards, they were already old enough to be grandparents. On the other hand, it wasn't altogether impossible, and Bill clung to this thread of possibility for an explanation of his existence once he was old enough to understand these things.

Then there was the conspiracy of silence. Jean and her mother, Eva, were committed to keeping the fiction in place that Jean was Bill's biological mother. It was a secret that Carol and Linda, both of whom had a great deal of contact with Bill, never betrayed. Ronald, aware of how important it was to Jean that Bill not know the truth, also said nothing.

The secret was necessary because of Jean's deep fear that if Bill learned that he was adopted, it would create a profound breach in their relationship. Her panic upon learning that Ronald had divulged the secret was the best indication of how tightly she had tried to sustain the myth that Bill was her child. Jean was deeply devoted to Bill. "She loved that boy with every bone in her body" is the way Ronald summed it up. From the very start, when they brought Bill home to help Sylvia out, Bill lit up their lives. Perhaps it was their middle-aged, empty-nest circumstance, for which the infant provided a reprieve, as if his new life meant a new life for them as well. The baby was pampered at every turn, the apple of everyone's eye. In addition to Jean, he had Jean's mother, Eva, as well as Carol and Linda to dote over him. "Bill grew up with four mothers and a father" is how Ronald summarized the situation. It was as if Bill had become the answer to an absence in their lives.

Bill King could be temperamental, and he had a low threshold for frustration and not having his way. If he didn't like something that was said, he could cut Jean or Ronald out of his life for weeks at a time. Ronald and Jean tried to avoid this at all costs. Keeping Bill happy became the hallmark of Ronald and Jean's parenting philosophy, and it meant that, more often than not, Bill got his way.

Bill King gradually came to feel a peculiar dual existence. On the one hand, he was spoiled and constantly fretted over; on the other, he felt a constant, profound dislocation within himself. The devotion from his "four mothers" could not overcome the feeling that he did not belong, that there was something wrong, or that there was something missing.

So treasured and yet so alone. That was the core truth of Bill King's life. His family was poor, yet they sacrificed to buy him the latest computer games and toys. Jean, in particular, could never find it within herself to deny the boy; the word "no" simply wasn't in her vocabulary when it came to Bill. He was her treasure, her comfort, her reason for being. "I was definitely a mama's boy" is the way Bill put it. Jean's mother was equally devoted to her grandson. Bill was like the family lap dog. Still, he felt incomplete, aware that something just wasn't right. All the pampering in the world did not seem to take the edge off of that feeling. Bill King knew that there was an empty place somewhere inside of him, a deep yearning for something, only he did not know what.

For all his manifest indifference to the discovery of his adoption, Bill was actually quite interested in it. He would occasionally ask Ronald, the only one willing to talk to him about the subject, about some of the details. He wondered about his biological mother and father and the circumstances that had led them to give him away. Bill also volunteered some observations of his own, such as the fact that when Bill's uncle, Johnny Knudsen, had taken him to the World's Fair in New Orleans, some people had actually asked Bill and Serena if they were siblings because they looked so much alike. "I remember the first time that Bill met Serena," Ronald later recalled. "She came over with Johnny one day, and Bill was standing in the door of the kitchen and I was in the living room. And Serena came in the front door and they stood there and just looked at each other for a few minutes, and then all of a sudden Bill just took off and came across the room and hugged her. I had to leave the room," Ronald recalled, becoming emotional again in the telling, "tears just came running down. He just took off and grabbed her and hugged her."

"I've always loved that boy intensely," Ronald said of their relationship. "I always let him know that I did love him, and had a lot of faith in him." However, Ronald was not a particularly demonstrative person. He was not the kind of father who hugged his children; especially with Donald, Carol, and Linda, he never showed emotions or physical closeness. He loved them but from afar. He was also extremely busy, working long hours at the mill where his job as a millwright meant that he could be called at any time, day or night, to come to the mill to repair whatever equipment or machinery was acting up. Ronald also had a work ethic that kept him attached to the mill; he was the consummate company man. Like his father, who had likewise been a millwright at a lumber mill, Ronald tended to hang around the mill even when his work was finished.

Ronald had been raised in strong southern Baptist churches, and although he no longer attended church, he was not a drinker or a carouser, and he was not inclined toward running off with his buddies and staying gone until all hours of the night. Instead, he tended to be either at the mill or at home in his shed, working with his CB equipment or talking on the CB radio to friends and truckers all over the country. He loved communicating through the airwaves and was constantly tinkering with his CB equipment in the small shed out behind the house. While Bill took care of his pet goats for his 4-H school projects, Ronald worked on his CB equipment. As he got older, though, Ronald also began to show Bill the ins and outs of the CB world. This is how Bill met Shawn Berry. Berry's CB radio was malfunctioning one day while Berry was sitting at a local truck stop when Bill came on the air and directed him to the Lynn Street house. Bill solved the problem, and it was the start of a long friendship that, in the end, proved the undoing of them both.

Bill's recollection of their relationship was less benign than his father's. "I never really felt that I could relate to him much. He just wasn't part of my life," Bill would later say. "At home he was the absolute authority. Authority but removed. There was no emotional engagement with him, he might as well have been a picture on the wall . . . I was scared of my dad when I was growing up, even though he never beat me or anything like that."

In addition to Ronald's reticence, perhaps one of the sources of this distance was the intensity of Jean's attachment to Bill. "Maybe Mother's closeness had something to do with that," Bill later hypothesized. Jean was overly involved with Bill. She tended to shield him from Ronald and keep him within her protective orbit. When Bill started running with kids who were getting into trouble with school authorities, Jean frequently lied to the truant officers who appeared at the door looking for him, telling them that he was in bed sick, when she knew him to be out with his friends. Similarly, when officers from the Juvenile Crime Division of the police department showed up at the house after Bill was caught shooting out the windows of the cars in a junkyard with a pellet gun, Jean did not report their visit to Ronald. Jean seemed incapable of taking Bill to task for his behavior, and Ronald didn't know much about what Bill was doing. As a result, Bill never suffered any consequences.

Jean also attempted to fill the gap left by Ronald's long work hours and emotional distance. "I'd say, 'Dad, let's go hunting.' And Dad would say, 'I'm too tired, I can't do it.' So Mom would take me or I'd go by myself," Bill reported. It was Jean who gave Bill his first shotgun, that rite of passage that marked every East Texas boy's coming of age, and it was Jean who took Bill hunting and fishing. "She was both a mother and a father to me" is the way Bill described their relationship. While Ronald felt usurped and preempted by Jean, excluded by her from a relationship with his son, Bill perceived her as someone filling a vacuum. "Dad was just never around," he said.

Not long before Bill's sixteenth birthday, Jean was diagnosed with kidney cancer. Although there had been no indications that she was getting ill—Jean seemed healthy and had not complained about any ailments—the disease was already inoperable. The petite, diminutive brunette with a high-pitched voice and soft, caring eyes quickly showed the ravages of the cancer, becoming weak and frail-looking almost overnight. In one of the last images of Jean during those final months, Ronald, using a video camera on loan from Chris Thomas's family, captured Jean walking slowly toward Carol's waiting car, wearing a bright red suit. Carol was taking her to lunch, and it would turn out to be Jean's last outing.

In other footage, Bill was captured riding his bike back and forth in front of the house, looking more a child than adolescent, as Carol's son, Michael, repeatedly pretended to crash his plastic three-wheeler in mock feats of roadside daring. In one image, the young Bill, now looking more adolescent in his sleeveless, black Metallica T-shirt and near shoulder-length hair with bangs falling across his face, helped Carol's husband sink fence posts along the property's boundary. In yet another, while Jean lay in her sickbed and Jean's mother sat knitting in a recliner as if at a wake, Bill looked in from the next room, again wearing his prized Metallica T-shirt, an electric guitar slung around his shoulder. As Ronald zooms in on him, Bill looks up from his strumming and says, while smiling impishly, "I live by this: Metallica forever!"

Two things stand out from this footage. One is the unmistakable impression of a family trying to absorb the impending loss. A palpable feeling of mourning held at bay pervades the images. Ronald had not been able to bring himself to tell Jean what the doctors had volunteered about her prognosis, so Jean did not know that her illness had no remedy and that she had very little time left. She was not aware, in other words, of the source of everyone else's singular preoccupation. Thus, while Ronald sits on the swing on the front porch, cradling the diminutive Jean like a newborn baby at his side, encouraging her to break through her shyness and say something for the benefit of the camera, one senses the negotiation of a complicated and distressing reality. Behind the jolly banter with the video camera, and the seeming ordinariness of children riding bikes in the yard and a teenage boy's rock star poses, there was the dreaded awareness of her impending death. It gave the video's veneer of normality a distinctly hollow feeling.

Carol was living in Beaumont at this time, and her apartment served as home base for the family in the final weeks of Jean's life, as they came in from Jasper to sit at Jean's side at Baptist Hospital where she lay dying. Jean's cancer was ravaging her body, and the ever thin, frail woman had taken a turn for the worse. She had also become terribly weak, her words carried on the thinnest of breaths. It was all anyone could do to get her to rise from her hospital bed and walk to the door. She was gaunt, with hollowed-out cheeks and colorless, pasty skin, lying there in a formless hospital shift, her white hair lost in the white of the bed sheets. She looked as if she were already dead and she spent a great deal of time in morphine-induced slumber, while Ronald stood an uneasy vigil, at times accompanied by Carol, or Linda, or Bill. No one acknowledged to Jean the reality that was absorbing them, namely, that there was no hope for her recovery and that her life would soon be over. The most glaring fact in the room went unspoken.

Bill was acutely aware of the feeling that his would-be guardian angel was slipping away from him. Donald, Bill's older brother by twenty years, had been summoned home from his army post in Germany to say goodbye to his dying mother. There had always been tension between Bill and Donald. Bill viewed him as an imperious, authoritarian bully. Though he was already gone from home for most of Bill's childhood, Donald's visits frequently involved tense and hostile interactions between Donald and Bill. As Bill grew older, he found Donald's visits more and more infuriating and intolerable. To Donald, on the other hand, Bill must have seemed like a pampered, spoiled baby whom he found insufferable. The devotion that Ronald and Jean shed on Bill, and their acquiescence to his every whim, was excessive. He was allowed no frustration, and no wish was considered too extravagant. This overindulgence, so absent in the poverty-induced austerity that had surrounded the Kings' natural children while they were growing up, simply did not sit well with Donald. (Years later, when Bill was on trial for the murder of James Byrd, Donald disowned Bill and refused to attend the proceedings, not even to offer support to his ill father.)

Learning that Donald was on his way home from Germany to be at her side had an immediate impact on Jean. She seemed to rally, as if her only biological son's visit were a momentary antidote to the cancer that was consuming her from within. She became alert. As Bill later described it, a peace and calm seemed to take possession of her.

Rather than feeling comforted by this development, Bill felt betrayed. To him, it was proof that Donald held the special place in her heart that Bill felt rightfully belonged to him. A strange fusion of emotions was at work within him—immense sorrow over the impending loss of his mother, mixed with immense anger at her for responding so definitively and dramatically to Donald's arrival at her bedside.

As the King clan gathered to await Jean's death, Bill gave every outward indication of being all but indifferent to what was going on around him. Donald's arrival, and the family's response to it, angered Bill. He was jealous of the fact that Jean, in particular, seemed to find such comfort in his presence. As he'd always done, Bill retreated inwardly, doing his best to seal over the dark rage boiling inside of him. He withdrew from everyone. On October 31 he announced that he was going to go trick-or-treating rather than accompany the rest of the family to the hospital to sit with Jean. Ronald was annoyed but wrote it off to Bill's usual petulance and self-centeredness. While Bill was out knocking on doors, competing with costumed preschoolers and elementary school-aged children to fill his bag with treats, Jean slipped away quietly, with Ronald at her side.

Bill King's seventeenth birthday was November 3, two days after Jean's death, and Ronald decided to postpone her funeral so that it would not coincide with Bill's birthday. In the interim, Ronald took Bill out to buy him a suit to wear for the funeral, in addition to making other arrangements. At the funeral Bill seemed detached, as if going through the motions by rote. He was quiet and withdrawn. Bill's birthday, too, was a somber event, and Bill spent the day in a silent rage, disengaged from everyone while the rest of the family mourned. To others, it seemed that Bill didn't care: "He didn't have much of a reaction as best I could tell," Ronald would later say. "He seemed ready to blame things on this, to anyone who would listen, but I didn't see him react that much," he said.

It was more than simple stoicism that everyone was seeing: "I didn't feel anything," Bill said. He felt as if something inside him had died. He was aware of a silent rage building within him, a feeling that felt larger than anything he could convey or explain, much less control. "I felt angry at everyone," Bill recalls. He was aware of feeling that he hated everything around him, although he had no sense as to why. Consciously, there was but a vague link in his mind between this seething rage and the loss of the woman who had been "both mother and father" to him. Bill attempted to repress these feelings, to bury them deep within, but he walked around constantly feeling that he was on the verge of exploding. "I felt like a hand grenade with the pin pulled out," he said of that time. It was the kind of reaction that might have alerted others to the fact that there was something awry in Bill; this was not a normal mourning process. However, no one seemed to notice, or, if they did, they took it to be just another manifestation of Bill's by now all too familiar petulance, failing to understand the deeper, darker implications of Bill's brooding, angry response.

Bill seemed unable to get a handle on himself or his life. He was closed off and disconnected from most people, yet he walked around with an edge and an attitude. No one seemed to be able to reach Bill—not Ronald, not his sisters. His friends experienced him as needy and vulnerable, yet taciturn and diffident. "Everyone felt sorry for him and wanted to help him" is the way Shawn Berry later remembered Bill. He had a way of letting friends know what he needed without coming right out and saying it. At the same time, Bill could be generous toward his friends. "He would do anything that he could to help you if it were possible," Berry said. The few friends he did have felt warmly toward Bill.

One of the traits that many recognized in Bill was his hardheadedness. When he made up his mind about something, there was no talking him out of it. He was uncompromising and rigid. Things often had to be his way or no way. Berry remembers, for example, that he couldn't simply tell Bill that there was a better way of doing something, such as fixing a carburetor on a car. King wouldn't listen, and he was adamant about doing things the way he was doing them. It was only if someone actually showed him that he was wrong, concretely, that he could tolerate a change in approach. It was as if Bill had to be in control of things for him to feel comfortable.

There seemed to be two sides to Bill King. On the one hand, there was a puppy-dog quality to him. He could look at his friends, especially his girlfriends, with needy big brown eyes and stir their maternal instincts. He had a knack for making people want to care for him. At the same time, he had an enormous need for control and felt anxious when out of his element. Bill was most comfortable when on his own turf where he could call the shots. He hated to leave Jasper, for example. Unlike many of his friends, who might go into Beaumont for a little excitement, Bill preferred familiar territory. He was not a person who was drawn to the bright lights of the big city.

IN THE ENSUING WEEKS and months after his mother's death, Bill grew increasingly uncooperative and disaffected. He tended to do what he felt like doing and not much else. Ronald had been temporarily transferred to the lumber mill in nearby Livingston and had moved there with Bill; but Ronald couldn't get him to go to school. Exasperated, Bill's father gave him an ultimatum: stay in school or move out. Bill moved out. He dropped out of school altogether and went to stay with Carol, her husband, and two daughters, who were living in the Jasper house on Lynn Street (Ronald had signed

the deed to the house over to Carol before he moved to Livingston). Bill took The
up residence in the shed next to the house, the same one in which Ronald Unraveling
would later live, but his stay was turbulent. He fought frequently with Carol
and her husband. Bill's willful and sulky disposition was tedious, but his antics, such as stealing Carol's car at night (which he wrecked on one occasion),
were also infuriating.

In late May of 1992, Bill and a friend named Frankie Self were sitting on
an old sofa in the shed, drinking beer, when Bill suggested that they try to
break into the building next door, a welding and machine shop owned by a
man named Don Elam. Bill was now seventeen years old and Frankie was
fourteen. They walked over to the shop, Bill in boots, Frankie barefoot, and
while Bill pulled back the building's tin siding, Frankie, being the smaller of
the two, wedged himself into the building, where he unlocked one of the
overhead doors for Bill. Inside, they found a variety of things that were of interest, including a 12-gauge shotgun with a folding stock, as well as a variety
of knives, tools, some bags containing Mexican money, a bracelet, and some
Corona beer. They also found a Mercedes-Benz parked in the building and
proceeded to break off its hood ornament. The two boys then carried their
loot back over to Bill's shed.

The following day, upon discovery of the break-in, the Jasper police found
a clear set of tracks leading directly from Elam's shop to the shed. Carol gave
the authorities permission to search the premises, where they discovered several of the stolen items. At some point on the day of the burglary, Bill and
Frankie had apparently discharged the shotgun by accident, resulting in a
gaping hole through the couch and out the back of the shed. A spent shell
casing was found on the floor. Bill King subsequently pled guilty to burglar-
izing the building.

Not long afterward, on a night in mid-September, Bill took Carol's Omni
without her knowledge and drove over to pick up Shawn Berry and another
boy named Bobby Perego. After stopping at Berry's grandmother's house for
a bag in which to carry their booty, the trio went to Neal's TV, a business on
North Fletcher Street, just a few blocks from the Jasper County Sheriff's Department. The establishment's name was misleading in that Neal's now specialized in such things as jukeboxes, pinball machines, video games, and cigarette machines. Perego's grandfather worked at Neal's, and Perego himself,
a part-time employee, had devised the scheme for breaking in after hours.

Bill dropped Berry and Perego off behind the building and parked in the dark while waiting for his co-conspirators to carry out the burglary.

Unbeknownst to the three boys, a nearby resident had observed what was taking place and called the police to report the suspicious activity, including a specific description of Carol's car. The police arrived while the two boys were still inside and arrested all three on burglary charges. It was Bill King's second burglary arrest in three and a half months.

In June of 1992, a month after his first arrest, Bill had been placed on deferred adjudication probation. Authorities had sought to have the probation revoked in October, following the second burglary, but a plea bargain resulted in Bill's being sent to boot camp instead. Boot camps were still fairly novel interventions at the time. They were intended to give young offenders a taste for penitentiary life, but, more important, to provide them with a highly structured experience that might increase their self-confidence and motivate them to get jobs or perhaps even to continue their education. Boot camp was an alternative to sending kids to prison and provided an experience that might encourage youthful offenders to turn away from a life of crime, the kind of life, in other words, that they showed every sign of leading prior to their sentencing.

Bill King went off to serve seventy-five days at boot camp, rising before dawn, learning to march in formation, taking instructions from a tough drill sergeant, and taking courses in how to feel good about himself and manage his life like a good citizen. Ronald and Carol attended his graduation ceremony in Beaumont, where a home video captured Bill marching in with his platoon, dressed in militarylike fatigues that were a size or two too large. At the awards ceremony, a dignitary called on the graduates to take home the lessons they had learned, to be contributors to society, to step up and play a constructive role in the world. Bill was especially proud of an intricate, Escher-esque mural that he and another attendee had painted during their stay. Ronald filmed the mural to document the accomplishment, although he was surprised to learn later from Bill that there were well-camouflaged derogatory messages about the boot camp's director that Bill and the other boy had embedded into the mural.

Bill returned to Jasper in mid-January 1993, having received ten years' probation. Ronald got Bill and Shawn Berry jobs at the lumber mill, hoping that it would be a new beginning for his son. Bill's assignment was to pick up and

deliver machinery parts that were needed throughout the mill. The man in
charge of the parts department was a gruff, unsociable character who treated
everyone who walked into his shop with a mixture of abruptness and disdain.
Bill received this same treatment until the man noticed Bill's identification
tag. "Oh, are you Ronald's boy?" he asked, his harsh edges abruptly evapo-
rating. Ronald was known throughout the mill and was well liked. "Yeah,"
Bill responded matter-of-factly. Bill claims to have been offended by the
man's newfound friendliness and used the exchange as a pretext for quitting
the job, a job that Ronald had arranged by calling in some favors. Bill rationalized his quitting, saying that getting special treatment from the parts
department man was an unfair privilege. It was an example of Bill's idiosyncratic superego, which allowed him to feel he was on higher moral ground
than everyone else even when he was being irresponsible. Ronald, for his
part, saw Bill's quitting as yet another example of his son's inability to get a
job and stick with it.

Unemployed again, Bill was just hanging out. Shawn Berry continued
working at the mill, but he also had a gift for mechanical things and bought
and restored used pickups as a sideline. One of his prized restorations was an
old El Camino, which he let Bill drive around while he was at work. Bill had
fallen in love with a rather attractive brunette he had met at a pinball gallery
named Keisha Atkins. Keisha, who five years later, on the night that James
Byrd was murdered, would spend most of the evening with Bill King, was at-
tending Jasper High School. Bill drove Shawn's El Camino up to the high
school and caused a commotion by hot-rodding around the school with tires
screeching so as to garner the most attention possible. School authorities
were not amused and called the police, who promptly arrested King for dis-
orderly conduct.

Although he could have had his probation revoked and been sent to
prison for the offense, Bill was fined instead. His probation officer, a friendly,
gentle man named William Sparks, whom everyone called "Sparky," repri-
manded Bill and tried to impress upon him the need to settle himself down.
Bill seemed responsive, promising Sparky, who also happened to be Shawn
Berry's probation officer, that it wouldn't happen again.

At home, however, things were not going well. Bill continued living in the
shed next to Carol's, but he and Carol were in constant fights about anything
and everything. He resented her attempts to set limits, shouting that she had

no right to try to "play mother" to him. He tended to become furious any-time she frustrated him. He demanded use of her car, and sometimes took it without her permission, sneaking her keys and driving off after everyone had gone to bed. Bill's demeanor at the house was insufferable. He was prone to temper tantrums during which he would hit walls, or punch holes in doors, or throw things. At one point he even threatened Carol, who along with her family felt terrorized by Bill. No amount of talking seemed to rein Bill in; he had to have things his way, and any obstacle to his wants was likely to spark an angry outburst.

By the spring of 1994, the King family had had enough. Carol and Ronald told Sparky that they were concerned about Bill and that he had threatened Carol. Bill was arrested for assault by threat. As he often did, Bill minimized the situation, acknowledging the conflict with his sister but protesting that it was merely an argument and that everyone was overreacting. While Bill's ac-tions would have been sufficient grounds for revoking Bill's probation and sending him to the penitentiary, Sparky opted to impose a "sanction" rather than revoke probation altogether. This meant that Bill would be sent to a restitution center in Beaumont rather than prison.

Restitution centers are like halfway houses where probationers work and perform community service while living in a dormlike setting. The main fo-cus of such centers is to help parolees look for employment. The Jefferson County Probation Department in Beaumont ran the Residential Services Unit to which Bill King was assigned. The setting was spartan, and the men's wages, such as they were, went primarily toward paying for their keep, resti-tution to their victims, and fines. Very little of their earnings ended up in their own pockets.

It apparently was not an arrangement that Bill King found congenial. Un-like the earlier boot camp experience, where Bill had done quite well and where he had complied with the harsh regime and the authoritarian structure imposed by the drill sergeants, at the restitution center Bill was insubordinate and hostile almost from the day he entered. His attitude was extremely neg-ative, with Bill refusing to perform assigned community service or chores at the center. He was also disrespectful toward the staff at the center, at times berating them. "He's immature and acts like a child when he doesn't get his way by throwing temper tantrums," read one restitution center report. "He has a feeling that he is too good for this place and should be allowed to do whatever he wants to do." It was a posture quite similar to that which Bill had adopted while living with Carol and her family.

One of Bill's complaints at the restitution center was that his room was too cold. When a staff member suggested he move to another room, Bill shouted an obscenity and threatened that if he got sick, they were going to be responsible for his hospital bill. When told that his language was unacceptable and that he would be written up if he continued to speak disrespectfully, Bill shouted back, "Fuck your writeups. While you're at it, write two or three," handing a pen to the supervisor on duty. When assigned to wash dishes the next day (such chores were part of the usual rotation of duties at the center), Bill refused, telling the staff member to go find a dishwasher.

Bill readily dismissed the staff's warnings that his behavior was going to create problems for him. "I don't give a damn," he answered. "You might as well send me back to my county because I'm sick of being here!" King simply refused to perform his community service assignments, staying in bed instead. At his wits end, the administrator at the restitution center called Sparky to recommend that Bill's probation be revoked and that he be sent to the penitentiary. Bill's response was to "abscond" from the center and return to Jasper.

Sparky liked Bill King and believed that he could be rehabilitated. King liked to recite quotes he came across in magazines and books, and Sparky enjoyed Bill's philosophical bent. The probation officer saw in Bill a glint of promise; he recognized talent and possibility in the slight, awkward adolescent with an impish smile. Bill also seemed to have something that a lot of the parolees that sat across from Sparky's desk lacked, namely, some semblance of a caring family. "His daddy loved him," Sparky would later recall. "The man tried to do everything he could for him."

Sparky could also see that Bill was a kid who seemed to be hurting. "I got a feeling from his friends and from his family that Bill had changed after his mother died," Sparky later told me. In his meetings with Bill, Sparky did his best to help Bill see the light. "Bill, you're going the wrong way, son. Let's make a change," Sparky would say.

It was this faith in the boy's promise that led Sparky to keep giving Bill chances, chances that Bill seemed hell-bent on subverting. Every new arrangement Sparky came up with, Bill undid. When Bill showed up in Jasper after running away from the Beaumont restitution center, Sparky made arrangements to get him sent to another restitution center in Liberty, Texas, rather than sending him to the penitentiary. Bill was no more responsive in that setting than in Beaumont. From there Bill was sent to another boot camp where he spent six months. Since he seemed to have responded well to the original boot camp experience, Sparky hoped that this might be the key to reaching Bill. But it was all to no avail. Bill seemed unable to settle down, to hear the message, or to contain himself. Everywhere he was sent, he seemed to bump up against the rules and against those in positions of authority. Bill was acting as if he were simply incorrigible.

In desperation, and largely because he had run out of other options, Sparky sent Bill back to the Jefferson County Residential Services Unit, the same place from which Bill had run away after a two-and-a-half-week stay over a year earlier. It was not an easy sell to the administrator of the unit, who remembered this parolee all too well. Bill knew that this was his last chance to avoid being sent to the penitentiary, but his second stint at the restitution center in Beaumont was a mirror image of the first. In the span of just a couple of weeks he refused work assignments, he was insubordinate, he lied about work assignments, and he pocketed money that was supposed to go to the restitution center. He also refused to take prescribed medications for what by now had been diagnosed as a bipolar disorder. The last straw was when Bill went off to work at a restaurant called Casa Olé and did not return for two days.

Bill King appeared indifferent to the fact that unless he changed his ways he was destined to spend time in the pen. He was like a moth drawn to a flame, as if the prospect of prison had allure. He was unable to control himself and unable to respond to any effort to help him redirect his life. He seemed compelled to bring about his own demise, almost willfully pursuing a course that would land him in a hard-time prison. Three and a half years later, during the punishment phase of King's capital murder trial, Sparky was asked if the State of Texas had done everything within its power to shepherd Bill King toward a different life. "Yes, sir, everything I had available," was the only thing the parole officer could say.

Sparky considered Bill King's demise a personal defeat. When I later interviewed him, he tried to summarize his impressions of Bill, the teenager in whom he had had such faith. "Bill was an enigma," he said. "I wish I could

have met him before his mother died," Sparky added wistfully, still harbor-
ing the belief that Bill King could have been saved.

Bill King had been sent to facilities in five different settings in efforts to
keep him out of prison. He was now twenty years old. His place terminated
at the restitution center and his probation finally revoked, the penitentiary
was now the only remaining option. On June 8, 1995, he was sentenced to
eight years in prison. With the exception of the fourteen-month interval following his first boot camp experience, Bill King had been in some form of
state custody almost continuously since the age of seventeen. He was now on
his way to the Beto I Unit, located near the community of Tennessee Colony
in Anderson County, a hard-core prison known for its racial tensions and
prison gang activity. It was not the kind of prison where smaller white men
tended to fare well.

Planet Beto

BILL KING ARRIVED at the George Beto I Unit in Tennessee Colony, Texas, in August of 1995. At the time, the twenty-year-old King was just another small-town hothead who had failed to get his life in order. In his prison-issue whites, his hair cut short and his brown eyes casting a weary glance out onto the medium-security cellblock to which he had been consigned, he felt nameless and indistinct. Only hours before, King had arrived at Beto (pronounced BEET-o) in a specially outfitted TDCJ bus—with barred windows and a locked steel-mesh screen separating the shackled prisoners from the driver and an armed guard. The new inmates were herded up to the infirmary's second floor on the prison's North Wing for processing. It was here that Beto authorities screened for medical conditions requiring special attention and where the Classification Committee determined an inmate's custody level, job assignment, and cell assignment. Bill King's medical records indicated that he suffered from bipolar I disorder and borderline personality disorder. He also told the intake team at Beto that over the last two years he had attempted suicide on four occasions: twice by overdosing on drugs, once by attempted hanging, and most recently, while in the county jail

after this last arrest, by cutting his wrists with a razor. King attributed those *Planet*
episodes to "family problems" as well as to the fact that he was unemployed, *Beto*
although he reported that since his incarceration he was no longer feeling sui-
cidal. Medical authorities placed King on the active psychiatric case load,
which meant that a psychiatric resident would periodically review his functioning, and he was placed on a daily dose of 75 milligrams of Trazodone, a
potent psychotropic medication.

Each of the arriving inmates carried his records from the TDCJ processing unit in Huntsville as well as a document called a "Travel Card," which
contained an inventory of tattoos and other identifying features such as scars
and birthmarks. The Travel Card was insurance against misidentifying an inmate or the possibility that an inmate might exchange his identity with that
of another inmate with less time remaining on his sentence. Bill King's Travel
Card indicated that he had a handful of tattoos, all of them typical and none
suggesting gang membership. King was assigned to J block in the North
Wing, and when all the prisoners had been processed, he was escorted to
his cell.

Leaving the infirmary with his belongings in a paper bag, Bill King and
his group walked out onto the prison's main hallway, an ample, thousand-
yard-long thoroughfare extending from one end of the Beto Unit to the
other. A thick, mustard-yellow line marked a path near each of the opposing
walls along which prisoners were to walk in silence and in single file. The
broad center swath of the hallway was reserved for the use of corrections
officers. The prison felt imposing. All along the main hallway was a series of
crash gates, staffed by teams of corrections officers, leading directly into various cellblocks, each of which was three stories high. Far in the distance, King
could see the crash gate that marked the end of the North Wing of the
prison. Beyond was the Searcher's Desk, the prison's nerve center, and, beyond the Searcher's Desk, the South Wing, which housed minimum-security
prisoners.

The crash gate into J block made a massive sound as it was opened and
closed behind the entering prisoners. The gate's thick round bars, extending
upward to the ceiling three floors above, were a creamy coffee color, like all
the metalwork at Beto. There were times during the day when work details
and educational programs were under way and the prison was relatively quiet.
But in the evenings, like this one, when King was walking through the cell-

77

block for the first time, the din of prison life escalated into a chaotic mix of shouts, music, crash gates opening and closing, and the metallic clanging of individual cell doors. The cement floors and cinder-block walls only served to amplify these sounds, their coherence fragmented as they ricocheted throughout the prison. The veneer of order that characterized many of the daylight hours at Beto quickly yielded to this cacophony, creating an atmosphere of palpable tension.

For Bill King, everything around him that first evening seemed contradictory and marked by a vague sense of foreboding. It was as if something horrendous were about to happen at any moment while, at the same time, things seemed inexplicably held in check. A feeling of incipient violence permeated the Beto Unit, a coarse, raw seething that was a product of this odd agglomeration of approximately 3,300 broken, angry, and depressed eighteen- to twenty-five-year-old men with plenty of fire in their hearts and a surplus of testosterone in their veins. Prisons such as these are termed "gladiator units," for good reason. As a corrections officer escorted King to his assigned cell, King felt that all eyes were staring at him. He could sense the taking stock, the appraisal of the initiate, as if to declare that yet another prison virgin had arrived on the unit. At the time, King was only five foot seven and did not appear likely to make much of a show of himself when the time came to "check his papers."

Like all the cells in the prison, King's was small and cramped. Each cell had two bunks, over and under, each with a 5-inch mattress sheaved in plastic for easy cleaning. The mattresses were covered with white sheets and matching white pillowcases, although in winter inmates were also issued olive-drab wool blankets. King's cellmate already occupied the lower bunk, so King took possession of the upper bunk. His cellmate happened to be white. Prison authorities say that cell assignments are not made on the basis of race but rather a prisoner's size because a larger inmate can easily victimize a smaller cellmate.

Above King's cell door were two metal shelves, each with a small lock box for prisoners' private possessions. King placed the contents of his paper bag into the available box, although he had not yet had the opportunity to purchase a lock at the commissary to secure them. With the exception of the bunks and the shelving, the only other appointment in the cell was a stainless steel fixture that was a combined wash basin (cold water only) and toilet;

one button activated the flow of water, another flushed the toilet. There was room to stand between this fixture and the cell door, but not much. On the wall at the rear of the cell was a large ventilation register that helped to circulate air; the George Beto Unit is not air-conditioned. Given the humid heat of an East Texas July, the prison's ventilation system was providing very little relief at the moment. Although King could look out through the bars of his cell door and see the cellblock's narrow hallway and, beyond it, the back side of the adjoining cellblock, the walls separating the cells were solid.

On the way to his cell, Bill King had noticed that there were very few white prisoners. The prison's demographics reflected the skewed relationship between crime, race, and poverty: half of Beto's inmates were African American, twenty-five percent were Latino, and the remaining twenty-five percent were white, not counting a handful of Asian Americans. Out of the din King had been surprised to hear the strains of a familiar Guns N' Roses song, "Welcome to the Jungle." King had the kind of mind that readily responded to such irony, and he felt a mixture of pleasure and anxiety as he listened to lyrics about living like an animal in the jungle, for they seemed to foretell what was in store for him at Beto.

Later that evening, while in the day room, King discovered just how much of a jungle he was in. He was alone, walking through a sea of faces of young men staring blankly, none making eye contact, and none accessible or welcoming. It was here, on his first night at Beto, with two television sets blaring from their respective corners of the room and with clusters of men gathered around the chess and checkers games, that King says five or six African American inmates assaulted him.

As blows and kicks rained down upon him, King says he fought back as best he could, the implication being that he had stood up for himself. Although he says he lost a tooth and suffered bruises, cuts, and scrapes, he was not otherwise seriously injured. While his attorney, Sonny Cribbs, later implied at King's trial that perhaps he had been sexually assaulted at Beto, King denies this. No witnesses to the assault intervened to break it up, and there is no official report of this incident. Bill King kept this assault, with its attendant anxieties and rage, to himself.

The common assumption that prisoners join gangs for protection is only partly true. A prisoner gets invited to join a gang only if he has demonstrated that he can "bow up" under such initiations. Prisoners who prove their mettle, who stand and fight, are the inmates that gangs are interested in recruiting. The weak inmates, the ones who crumble under this reign of terror, simply become chattel, bought and sold, or their services traded for other favors. At best, if they have a steady check coming from family or friends back home, an inmate might buy himself some protection, but this typically comes only after he has had a taste of the alternatives. A prisoner didn't simply step into the day room at Beto and declare that he was willing to pay for protection; some prisoners were so terrorized that they turned over their commissary funds and were still victims of the gangs around them. How a new inmate fared, how he accounted for himself in these "tests," made all the difference in the kind of life he would live while at Beto. Prison officials tend to downplay these accounts, suggesting that there is more than a thread of mythology in them. On the other hand, such accounts are persistent, and even the Beto Unit's warden acknowledged that some of this activity went on within his prison and that it is simply impossible to monitor every square foot of space within the large institution.

King would soon learn that terror was present in abundance within this milieu where day-to-day life was governed by fear: fear of assault, fear of rape, fear of humiliation. While gangs could be as predatory toward their own kind as they were to inmates of other races, much of the violence at Beto revolved around the politics of race, since that was the basis for gang affiliation. In some form or another the gangs held sway over every prisoner within Beto's walls, and every new inmate became a factor in the complex equations of gang power. In this jungle, brute force was the only force to be reckoned with; everything else yielded to it. Within Planet Beto, as prisoners often referred to the prison, an inmate's place within the social hierarchy was a function of a single, simple variable: the ability to withstand and impart brutality.

To be surrounded by a group of men in the day room, the recreation area, the showers, or in a lonely corner of the prison away from anyone who might care or be in a position to do anything about it, was to be subjected to a profoundly frightening experience. Being kicked and slammed against the cold cement floor, having hair torn from the scalp or eyes gouged, feeling teeth snap and spitting them to the ground from a lacerated mouth into a pool of blood—such experiences have an effect on a man's mind. They activate deep anxiety and helplessness. There is no place to turn and there is an acute awareness that one is completely alone. Prisoners know the reality of their circumstances: the last thing an inmate would think of doing is to report his assailants to the authorities. Reporting an assault would compound this terror, not lessen it. There were too many prisoners and too few guards. There were too many corridors, and cells, and awkward spaces out of view from the authorities, if only momentarily. It is clear that corrections officers are not entirely in control of these institutions, and it is the gangs, and the whims of angry men with a propensity for sadism and cruelty, that hold the cards. Some inmates who can't join a gang decide it is better to submit, to become a "ho," than to have the rest of their teeth kicked out or risk the possibility of having one's throat slashed with a razor-sharp blade fashioned from a piece of plastic or a pilfered metal strip.

No one walking Beto's halls has any doubt that the surrounding predators are capable of doing the unthinkable. The kingpins don't brook snitches or anyone who defies them for any reason, for to do so would threaten their grip on the reign of terror and subvert their control in a world where being in control is the only thing that counts. Empathy, sympathy—these sentiments are completely anathema here. Their presence, if detected, becomes the basis for more terror, not less. Like a beast that has picked up the scent of fear, feelings of vulnerability or compassion only activate a feeding frenzy in which the weak are consumed. For most, the only protection, in fact, is to become like them, to turn off emotions, to become hardened, cold, and ruthless as well. But no solution actually guarantees safety in this environment of competing gangs, and competing pimps, and competing kingpins. No prisoner is ever truly safe, whether he has paid for protection or has his gang "patch." He might easily find himself in the wrong place at the wrong time. Thus, for every prisoner, whether a gang member or a "ho," virtually every moment at Beto is a time for worrying about being victimized once again.

Down the hallways, where a faint odor of bleach was ever present, in the day room with its picnic tables and ever-droning televisions, and in the cells with their grimy bars, chipped paint, thin mattresses, and stainless steel fixtures, the prisoners on Planet Beto made their way through their daily routines. Work details were broken up by meals and educational courses (like Bill King, most prisoners were high school dropouts, although King had earned his GED before coming to prison). Some also got to take more advanced classes. King, for example, took a college-level course in computer drafting as well as a course in cabinetmaking. Then there were the head counts every four hours wherein prisoners were herded back into their cells to be tallied up, like so much inventory at a warehouse. Between these activities there was nothing but empty space, the silent ticking of the clock. The endless waiting was filled with daydreams about home, about life on the outside, about the "free world" and how different it was all going to be if they could just get out of this place.

Bill King had gone through several cycles of those thoughts, sometimes writing home about grand ideas. Early on, he even wrote to say that he'd found Jesus. He also wrote to say that he was finally figuring things out. He said he could see the error of his ways and regretted having treated his sister so badly, having been so selfish, and so on down a lengthy list of violations and trespasses and failures of civility. The empty moments in the day were filled with such reflections. They were a trace, perhaps, of the very notion of the penitent, the same notion that gave birth to the idea of the penitentiary—a place where those who had transgressed might engage in meaningful reflection about their lives and their relationships to God. Such reflection, it was hoped, might lead a sinner toward the light.

Today's concept of the penitentiary is all but drained of faith in the power of such reflection. Instead, penitentiaries are now first and foremost simply places where hardened criminals are locked up. So Beto was governed by, more than anything, a sense of hopelessness. Few within the Texas Department of Criminal Justice believed they could meaningfully affect the lives of significant numbers of these prisoners. Some prisoners found Jesus, some just matured, some found a trade, but many of them simply ended up here, or somewhere like it, again. The Texas prisons, like prisons all over America, were mostly bastions of futility, where no one could figure out what to do to turn prisoners' lives around, to get them to participate constructively in the social order. On the contrary, many prisoners ended up more disaffected and marginalized than they had been before. Many, in fact, became increasingly hardened by the realities of prison life.

The cynicism of the criminal justice culture permeated every detail of life within the prison. For the corrections officers, or COs, there was little idealism to hold on to, to shape their work and their relationships with their charges. So many prisoners were adept at the art of the scam and manipulation that COs of necessity adopted a skeptical stance toward them. Then there were the frequent assaults on officers that served to further distance them from the prisoners. The era of grand prison reform movements was long gone, an old shipwreck on the shore, broken down by the brutal realities of criminals who refused to change or often became worse, broken down by the sheer numbers of the prison population and the high recidivism rates that tended to erode hope and idealism.

The main hallway at Beto, with its strategically placed crash gates manned by clusters of corrections officers in their blue-gray TDCJ uniforms, gave an appearance of control and order. Files of prisoners wearing their prison-issue whites walked silently within their designated lanes, framed by towering walls and the ever-present cream-colored iron bars, a corrections officer at the head of the line and another at the end as each cluster of inmates was escorted to one destination or another. In truth, however, a dual reality was at work within the Beto Unit, one that dictated the day-to-day functioning of the prison, prescribing when prisoners might do what activities and monitoring them within their activities. The other was a reality over which authorities had substantially less control, the product of a strange culture bred of strange circumstances. In this reality prisoners had their own laws and their own conventions, a world within a world in which different terms defined what constituted a transgression and where consequences were determined by the peculiarities of prisoner logic. The two realities existed simultaneously, one overlaid upon the other. Paradoxically, the efforts to control and monitor prisoners' lives produced a culture that successfully subverted that very control.

Within the inmate world there were unspoken but unmistakable rules dictating a great deal of what went on within the Beto Unit. In the North Wing and South Wing day rooms, for example, prisoners grouped themselves, almost exclusively, along racial lines. Who got to sit on what benches in front of the two television sets that blared out the usual soap operas, sitcoms, and sporting events was also dictated by a clear but unspoken code. The official word was that prisoners voted, every hour, on what channel to watch, but such votes were manifestations of the struggle for power and control that lurked beneath the surface among the factionalized inmates. There were serious and often violent consequences for transgressing "the arrangements." Bill King claims that on one occasion, when a white inmate changed the channel on one of the televisions, a group of black inmates began pummeling him on the floor of the day room. A cadre of "woods" (white gang members) came to the white inmate's aid, and the result was a thirty-day lockdown in the North Wing during which inmates remained in their cells.

Evidence of this reality, the one created and controlled by the prisoners, was readily available. For example, despite the fact that tattoos are forbidden, the majority of inmates at Beto—white, black, or brown—got tattooed while in prison. Inks, needles, and electric motors all had to be obtained covertly and secreted away during the routine cell inspections and the frequent monitoring by corrections officers making their way up and down the cellblocks. Some prisoners had extensive tattoos, covering their entire bodies, including scalps, underarms, and genitals; others might have but a single tattoo, easily hidden under a T-shirt.

One of King's best friends at Beto was an inmate nicknamed "Dirtball," the prison's best tattoo artist. Dirtball's artistic talents were in high demand among the Beto inmates, regardless of their race. King himself had a fascination with tattoos. He would later tell me that the mere sight of a tattooing needle stirred strong feelings. Dirtball first agreed to complete the barbed wire tattoo that King had started on his wrist as a young adolescent. It was the beginning of a long association. Dirtball was a talented artist, and the images he rendered on King's body had subtlety, nuance, and considerable detail. The artistry was especially striking in light of the fact that Dirtball had only crude instruments, such as pilfered electric motors, and needles and inks that were subject to the vagaries of prison contraband and prisoner ingenuity.

One of King's tattoos took more than sixteen hours to render. It was done in four sittings because a head count occurred every four hours. Dirtball would disassemble and hide his "instruments" until the head count was completed, after which the equipment was reassembled and the work continued. This particular tattoo consisted of a warped portrayal of the Crucifixion: Satan being crucified by Christ and a bishop. The words "Jesus Loves" were written across Satan's body, as if to say that he was the victim of a perverse and cruel love. This image, like several others on King's body, played on shifting or inverted assumptions about good and evil.

According to King, the rest of his tattoos had been copied from or inspired by images that he and Dirtball had found in magazines and books. One arm was primarily devoted to tattoos from *Tattoo Magazine,* the other,

to cartoon figures from comic books. However, that claim was more than a
little disingenuous. Covering most of Bill King's right side was a large tattoo identifying him as a member of the Confederate Knights of America. This "patch" was a way of "marking" gang members. The tattoo contained a central emblem or coat of arms that was divided into three sections. In one was an image of a burning cross. Next to it was the three-legged Klan triangle symbol (the same one found on his Zippo lighter). Below them was a Rebel flag. Two Confederate Knights were crossing swords in the center. Along either side, from top to bottom, were thick lightning bolts that ran the length of the tattoo. Beneath the patch the words "Aryan Pride" were tattooed in bold block letters. King also had several additional pairs of lightning bolts tattooed on his body. The tattoos appeared to be testimony to the indelible character of King's beliefs.

In addition to the tattoos expressing racial views, King had many tattoos that invoked dark, satanic themes. He had numerous tattoos of baphomet symbols, and a large spiderweb design extended from his left armpit out toward his hand, which must have been a particularly painful tattoo to endure because of its location. There were goats' heads and other evil-looking creatures, including a large baphomet on King's scalp that depicted a monk worshiping Satan. King even had the name "Tinkerbell" tattooed on his penis.

Most inmates sought to memorialize their stay on Planet Beto with some ink, like a rite of passage through the dark waters of the correctional equator. Ironically, tattooing is forbidden by TDCJ, in part because of its obvious links to gang membership. In theory, the discovery of new tattoos could be the basis for disciplinary action, although corrections officers had too many people to watch in too large a space and through too many different activities to make tattoos a high priority. Notwithstanding daily showers, cell inspections, visits to the medical unit, and the occasional strip search, Bill King managed to get through Beto with no apparent awareness on the part of the authorities that his body had been so thoroughly tattooed. It was all part of the dual reality, the acknowledged and the unacknowledged reality, the TDCJ-defined world and the inmate-defined world.

BILL KING ARRIVED AT BETO with the same attitude and disposition that he had been dragging along for years. Some days he refused to go to work assignments, for example, and stayed in his cell as much as possible. Within the first few weeks of his incarceration he was written up twice for refusing to work, for which he was punished by having privileges withdrawn. King seemed to have a bad attitude toward everyone, especially the authorities.

As the days at Beto turned into weeks and months, King became even more of a hardhead, keeping to himself and doing his best to watch his back. It was an attitude that did not go unnoticed among the white gangbangers at Beto. They had watched him closely, beginning with the first "paper checking" in the day room on the night he arrived. The word was that King appeared to be peckerwood, or "wood" material. According to the perverse logic that ruled the prison's reality, every act that caused King to sink lower in the eyes of prison authorities simultaneously raised him in the eyes of fellow inmates. There were three white gangs at Beto. The Aryan Brotherhood and the Aryan Circle were the largest and best known, with chapters in prisons all over Texas and across the country. The third was a small group known as the Confederate Knights of America, whom few outside of Beto had ever heard of. At the time of King's arrival, Russell Brewer, whose cell was at the other end of the hall from King's, was the head of the Confederate Knights of America at Beto. The CKA was comprised of a small band of "woods" who for a variety of reasons had not joined one of the larger gangs. Some had simply not been invited; others did not like taking orders and found the role of mere foot soldier within the ranks of the highly regimented larger gangs unappealing. It is likely that King, who for years had not found it easy to take orders from anyone, simply didn't fit the larger gangs' mold of the ideal conscript.

Within six months of his arrival at Beto, King was invited to join the CKA. His gang member status was soon reflected in his correspondence to friends and family back home, many of whom noticed that King had taken to closing his letters with his newly conferred prison nickname, "Possum," instead of his usual "Bill." It was a nickname that King earned because of his penchant for staying up all night. King preferred to sleep during the day after completing his job assignment on one of the "hoe" squads working the prison's nearby fields where seasonal crops were raised. While most prisoners were hanging out in the day room or finding other forms of diversion, King slept in his cell. At night, however, he seemed to come to life, reading, writing letters, and working on his legal files.

Like every other white or black kid growing up in Jasper, Bill King had heard of the Ku Klux Klan. However, neither the Klan nor similar ideologies had been a meaningful part of his life during his formative years. He did not come from a racist family, and his parents had relationships with African Americans. As a child, he had spent the night in black children's homes and they had spent the night at his. Thus, white-black racial issues had not been particularly salient in King's life, though they were part of the culture within which his life unfolded. Life at Beto, and his newly minted membership in the Confederate Knights of America, soon changed that.

The CKA became a defining feature of Bill King's world. For one thing, gang membership provided a measure of protection and safety. Despite the fact that few of the members of the CKA were physically imposing, there was a degree of strength that came with numbers; to mess with them might easily create problems that everyone wanted to avoid. For example, a sufficiently raucous fight in the day room or the rec area might require prison authorities to intervene by locking down a cellblock or even an entire wing. Such lockdowns could extend for thirty days or more, during which prisoners were not permitted to leave their cells. Prison meals were delivered in sacks, and they were even less savory (lots of peanut butter sandwiches, for example) than the usual cafeteria fare. Most important, lockdowns represented an extended period during which the day-to-day transactions that were the staple of prison gang life could not be carried out. Lockdowns, in other words, were not good for "business." Thus, if members of a gang were willing to stand up, the threat of a lockdown gave a small gang like the CKA some leverage, even though they were hopelessly outnumbered and outgunned by the larger white and black gangs.

There was plenty of white supremacist propaganda floating around the Beto Unit among the white gang factions. Much of it was mailed to prisoners from hate groups who know that prisons are fertile recruiting grounds. From the various Aryan organizations to the Ku Klux Klan, there were countless permutations of groups with their own version of similar hate-infested ideology. The multitude of factions was a product of the petty squabbles and power plays so prevalent within the white supremacist movement and other extremist groups. The material circulating within the prison included hardcore anti-government views, such as those contained in *The Turner Diaries* and similar treatises espousing the overthrow of the government and the establishment of a white, "pure," Aryan nation. King became an avid reader of this literature. Hatred of blacks, Jews, and Mexicans was the staple of these screeds, views that King and his fellow white inmates discussed during the day or in their cells at night.

In an inversion of the societal power structure of the outside world, where whites typically called the shots, black and Latino inmates significantly outnumbered the "woods." At Beto whites felt oppressed, victimized, and at times under siege. In this atmosphere, inmates like King were receptive to the venomous white supremacist literature being passed around the cellblocks. It was a circumstance that added to the generalized sense of being embattled, and it fostered that peculiar solidarity that comes from shared tribulation. For the white inmates, Hitler and the Nazis provided a common source of ideology and symbolism. For example, King once wrote, in reference to his multiple tattoos of lightning bolts: "These 'SS' bolts represent those of us here in prison who fought unbelievable odds to earn a measure of respect. They're for all practible purposes, representative of the Shutzstaffeln who fought to the death during their last stand at Nuremberg. They were vastly outnumbered by the allies, and attacked six times before losing their first man. Every wood in Texas prison who wears these bolts knows about the 'last stand' at Nuremberg."

The immediate and ongoing tensions between white, Latino, and black inmates fed into this matrix of hatred and paranoia. The hard-core racism that permeated King's CKA world, filling it with diatribes in which Jews, African Americans, and Mexicans were viewed as the sources of all evil and the greatest threat to the "purity" of the white race, were born, to a significant extent, out of these prison circumstances. The constant and pervasive stress produced a warped consciousness; inmates developed views of both the prison world and the "free world" that were shaped by the forces that governed their daily lives and from which there was no possibility of insulation. These views were then projected and imposed onto the "free world." The members of the CKA and the other gangs came to believe that the strange reality they were living was in fact a meaningful reflection of life in society and that the lessons learned at Beto were applicable beyond the prison's walls.

Gradually, as his stay at Beto continued, disparate fragments of thought and feeling began to coalesce for King and take a definite form. Talk among white inmates, who secretly passed around their supremacist literature and huddled in furtive groups in the corners of the recreation area, was about the imperiled state of the white race. King, like many inmates, had come to Beto without racist beliefs or at least without any particular identification with such politicized racial ideologies. However, he began to find in them a kind of solace. These beliefs provided an explanation, or an ideological reading, that structured day-to-day encounters with the oppressive prison conditions and demographics that made white prisoners underdogs; they provided a conceptual device to help bind the anxiety of their circumstances. Through this mechanism they also fashioned rationalizations for the lives they had lived and the failures they had brought upon themselves. In other words, the ideologies helped sustain their denial regarding why they were there in the first place, allowing a sense of their own victimization to displace the more difficult questions about their lives and motives.

Regardless of race, almost all of the prisoners at Beto were young men who had grown up within society's dark underbelly. They tended to be uneducated high school dropouts who, like King, came from poor homes. Many also came from families that were broken and where abuse was commonplace. Though almost everyone at Beto shared some version of that past, somehow its edge was removed by the intense alliances of the race gangs, who provided a semblance of belonging, a semblance of family and allegiance, notions with which few of these inmates—white, black, or brown—were familiar. One might have viewed this as a triumph of the human spirit, keeping alive as it did a sense of hope and humanity, were it not for the fact that those sentiments formed around, and found representation in, the malignant ideologies of the race gangs. The very vessels that invoked or preserved these feelings also corrupted them and rendered them hardly recognizable. It was a sad paradox: through their shared hatred of others they found a sense of love among themselves. It was within the currents of racial hatred that many of these men found something that had eluded them for most if not all of their lives. They found, in other words, a sense of belonging, trust, and camaraderie. Individuals whose lives were comprised of shredded scraps of human experience, whose psyches were fractured by the harsh realities of life on the margins of the American Dream, found a measure of hope and coherence in the hate-filled diatribes of the race gangs, as if their ideologies created an emotional scaffolding, providing a home to the homeless, protection to the would-be victims, and a feeling of power to the powerless. However, if this shared crucible forged deep bonds, it also created within the prisoners an intrapsychic version of the predator, making many of the prisoners hybrid creatures, psychologically speaking: simultaneously victims and aggressors.

THE PRISON GANGS AT BETO were in constant tumult. For one thing, there were frequent fights with other gangs over turf, new recruits, and control of the amenities available at the prison. They were also prone to continual squabbles over larger and smaller points of ideology, pride, greed, and envy. Since prison gangs are outlawed, their membership and leadership were constantly changing as members were placed in the Administrative Segregation block to remove them from the general population, were transferred to other units, or were eventually released. There was also a consistent flow of new recruits. Thus, the gangs were always in a state of great flux.

Russell Brewer was the leader of the CKA at Beto, but in time King ascended to the leadership of the small group. For one thing, King was articulate and he could write well, qualities that soon thrust him into the role of spokesperson. King was also somewhat charismatic and had a knack for getting people to do what he wanted them to do. He became deeply committed to the group's ideology, which was really an amalgam of ideas and notions drawn from the white supremacist literature circulating within the prison. There were no new ideas in the CKA "platform"; it was simply another prison gang born out of the peculiar circumstances of prison life, where race seemed to be the natural font from which to draw.

The friendship that would eventually motivate Russell Brewer to volunteer to take the fall "for everything" in order to save King's life was not always a smooth one in the Beto days. There were tensions and differences related to "policy," and there was also competition between the two because of their respective ages: Brewer was six years older than King. At one point during King's stay it was discovered that Brewer had actually been married to a Mexican American woman and that he had sired a child in that union. King says that Brewer asked his wife not to visit him for fear that fellow gang members would discover this racial transgression. Though not necessarily related to Brewer's marital situation, around this time in a fit of anger King threatened to expel Brewer from the CKA and directed him to have his "patch" removed or face the consequences, a threat whose full implications were left to Brew-

er's imagination. In the end, Brewer accepted King's leadership of the CKA
and took his place as a committed follower and acolyte to the young man
from Jasper who had come to Beto with lots of attitude but no history of violent criminal behavior.

Feeling powerful and the zeal of a true believer, Bill King had found a home within the CKA and Beto's gang culture. He no longer felt alone. However, it would prove to be a high price for a temporary feeling of tranquility and groundedness. He once wrote me to ask about the story of Robert Johnson, the famous Mississippi blues player, who was said to have made a deal with the devil at a nearby crossroads, trading his soul in exchange for the promise of musical greatness. Over the course of his two years at Beto King, too, had made a significant, if unspoken, bargain of sorts. It was a gradual transformation, marked by a vow to the CKA to uphold its values and beliefs, but it extended beyond the specific parameters of the racial views espoused by the CKA. In his own way, King had signed on to the dark side. His tattoos reflected this, with their satanic imagery and violent implication. He had chosen evil rather than good, celebrating it, invoking it, allying himself with it as he attacked and subverted and disparaged all that society deemed right and wholesome. It was a society that he felt angry at, which he blamed for his troubles and misfortune. His newfound beliefs and ideology provided a means for venting the rage that he had been carrying all his life, siphoning it off like a release valve.

Over the course of his first year at Beto King's white supremacist beliefs gradually became increasingly important, although he tended to regard them like he did most everything else in his life: at some distance. Even after he joined the CKA, King's ideological commitments were situational and sporadic, not an organizing principle for his life. If there was a psychological utility to these notions, if they spoke to his circumstances at Beto, they remained only partly "him."

That changed in his second year when, months after he joined the CKA, everything seemed to come together for King; he experienced a moment of peculiar insight, like a religious conversion, in which he came to feel for the first time ever that his life made sense. A key catalyst for this moment was a man called Cajun Man, who was a somewhat mythic figure among white prisoners. Cajun Man had been in isolation in Administrative Segregation (reportedly, he had killed another prisoner, race unspecified) when

King first arrived on the North Wing. Word was that he had been one of only a handful of whites in the close custody unit and that despite his modest stature (he was only five foot six or so), he had accounted well for himself and ultimately been left alone by the rest of the prisoners, most of whom were black. Another reason for Cajun Man's lofty status was that he was a compendium of knowledge about the Ku Klux Klan, Hitler, Aryans, and anything having to do with history as it related to the white supremacist ideologies. Although his style was understated, Cajun Man was an effective communicator about white supremacist ideas, a preacher of sorts.

Cajun Man was eventually transferred to the minimum-security unit on the South Wing where King, too, spent the last ten months of his incarceration. Here the two prisoners became fast friends. King's membership in the CKA already implied a degree of immersion in white supremacist ideas, but in truth these were a hodgepodge of notions picked up here and there from different readings. Within the CKA, as with the other white gangs, white supremacist symbols were often appropriated without a real understanding of their meaning or origin. For example, King once told me that few white gang members had any awareness that the term "Aryan" was a reference to anything beyond Hitler and his teachings. After all, the vast majority of these prisoners were not particularly literate. Cajun Man, on the other hand, was viewed as something of a prison scholar when it came to these things, and he seemed to see in King a potential protégé, someone with the intellect and curiosity to be a worthy repository of Cajun Man's knowledge. When King announced that he was going to get lightning bolts and "Aryan Pride" tattooed down his shins, Cajun Man had urged him to wait: "Why don't you learn what this is all about before you do it," he told King. It was an invitation, in effect, to be mentored by Cajun Man, an invitation that King accepted. Cajun Man became King's closest friend and ally, an ever-present companion as the two of them worked out together everyday, jogging and using the weights in the recreation area. According to King, Cajun Man was not a member of any specific gang, though he was respected by all the white factions.

King once sent me a photograph of Cajun Man, taken after Cajun Man's release from Beto, in which he is standing between tall trees in a small clearing where large stones had been placed in a circular pattern, reminiscent of a pagan ceremonial space. Cajun Man is standing in the center of the circle, his full-sleeved arms—the product of Dirtball's handiwork—crossed before

him, looking bold. Cajun Man had had half sleeves until just before his release from Beto, when Dirtball had completed his tattoos. "You'll notice his
virgin patch," King remarked in the letter that accompanied the photograph,
"just like mine." Dirtball had a bad habit of leaving elbows for the last, claim-
ing they were the hardest area of the body to work. Filling out Cajun Man's
"sleeves" had required marathon tattooing sessions that had apparently been
quite debilitating: Cajun Man had suffered ink poisoning and had been sick
in his cell for a full week prior to his release. In the photograph he appears to
be of short stature, with blond hair and an intellectual look accented by his
wire-rimmed glasses.

King's ascendance to the leadership of the CKA had done little to alter his
moody, temperamental qualities. He continued walking around with an attitude. At one point Cajun Man had taken it upon himself to confront King
about how he was handling himself: "Why are you being such a hardhead?"
"What are you so angry about?" He encouraged King to lighten up and to
continue "educating" himself.

It proved to be a powerful intervention for King. Cajun Man seemed to
be the only one who could get through to "Possum," and King saw him as a
kind of benevolent paternal figure. One evening King found himself lying in
his bunk, pondering Cajun Man's questions and thinking about his life. Cajun Man had asked "Why?" and King found that his thoughts kept returning to his adoptive mother, Jean. He couldn't get her out of his mind, as
if some powerful magnetic force were at work on his emotions, pulling him
to her again and again. Their relationship still had a firm grip on him. Suddenly, King found himself sobbing into his pillow, terrified that someone
around him would notice. He became aware of missing her terribly. It was
the first time since Jean's death that he had acknowledged how much her loss
meant to him. "I realized I'd never mourned her," he would later recollect.

Ever since Jean's funeral, Bill King had felt dead inside. A whole universe
of feeling lay trapped there, as if beneath a hard, hermetically sealed enclosure. A cold rage festered within him, and while he allowed very few feelings
about Jean to come to the surface, the rage itself, like a disembodied specter,
had periodically broken through his defenses. Hence his outbursts when his
sister Carol "tried to play mother" and tell him what to do, outbursts that
could lead him to punch holes in walls and doors. He claimed to have no recollection of such outbursts afterward, but the splintered door and the gaping

hole in the drywall were proof enough. The link between these outbursts and Jean's death was not available to him, split off from the rest of his life as if something altogether foreign. Cajun Man's questioning had set in motion an emotional process that took King quite by surprise and momentarily subverted his persona as a hard-core white supremacist gang leader on top of the prison game.

Over the years King had developed a profound alienation, a feeling that he was different and simply did not fit in. As a child those feelings had permeated his life, but silently. No one around him seemed to be aware of the inner turmoil that was present in the boy who had a ready smile and an impish expression and who made good grades in school. By the time he arrived at Beto, that alienation was near complete. Learning that he was adopted years before seemed to have set him on a course. His sense of dislocation had somehow been given shape. Then there was Jean's death soon after. He'd felt safe with her, that he had an ally come what might. Ever understanding, Jean had been his tried and true, standing by him and always taking his side. She was the ultimate coddler, always giving him the benefit of the doubt and always forgiving. Jean had, as King himself had once put it, turned him into a "momma's boy"; he could do no wrong in her eyes, he was her baby.

And yet he was not. Ever since her death in that Beaumont hospital King had been haunted by a recurring thought—in the end, blood was thicker than water and that sense of betrayal was part of what fueled his anger at the world, his feeling of being the victim of a profound injustice. All of this— his discovery of the adoption, Jean's death and the turbulence that followed— haunted Bill King. It festered in him, an unacknowledged presence that seemed to seep into his thoughts in some derivative form, to surface unrecognized for what it was—a silent rage about his life and his chronic feeling of dislocation and abandonment. Why had his birth mother given him away? Why, despite all the years of thinking he was Jean's prized possession, had she betrayed him? When Donald had suddenly arrived and brought her such peace and calm, he had felt crushed, like a fool blindsided by his own naivete. These feelings churned in him. He felt the disquiet of his rage, but it was a rage with no name or clearly defined object. That night King realized not only that he had not mourned Jean, but also that he had not done so, in part, because of his feelings of betrayal. Cajun Man had unwittingly brought King to see something about himself that he had been unable to see on his own.

The white supremacist propaganda circulating within the prison provided *Planet* a channel for the pent-up and variously derived anger that so many of Planet *Beto* Beto's white prisoners carried within them. Bill King was bright, and the racial ideologies also drew his intellectual curiosity. In addition to reading the materials that were passed surreptitiously from inmate to inmate, King also started going to the prison library, where he read books that, though "approved," were germane to these interests, such as history books about the origins of cultures and languages. He became particularly interested in understanding the origins of the "Aryan people," and he became fascinated with genealogy, which became a major preoccupation.

For King questions about genealogy were, of course, overdetermined. He was adopted but had never met either of his biological parents, despite a relationship with his two biological sisters of many years. King's origins were unclear to him and the source of many questions. In fact, King's psychology rested in large part on two pillars: his adoption and his complex relationship with his adoptive mother, Jean, and, especially, Jean's death, which had required him to confront the fact of his adoption in unanticipated ways. It was not until he was at Beto that the full implication of this collection of feelings became clear to him, presenting itself in a torrent of emotion that night as he lay in his cell.

There was something organizing about the confluence of these feelings, Cajun Man's role as mentor, and the white supremacist ideology that served as the basis for their relationship. In some mysterious way, the released emotions appeared to function as a kind of adhesive for those beliefs, binding them together in a potent mix that was felt more than it was available for articulation. Something inside King had changed. Later, King would recall the moment with perplexity: "I'm not exactly sure what happened at Beto, but in the period of my 'conversion' I didn't have that rage or desire to self-destruction. I liked myself, as opposed to feeling that the entire world wants to see me fail [or be] destroyed. Had Cajun Man not shown me how destructive I was being . . . "

Such fusion of emotion and ideology is psychologically potent, the kind of process that once made Japanese Kamikaze pilots step into airplanes to conduct suicide missions, or that compels a young Palestinian to strap on an explosive-laden belt and walk into a crowded Israeli pizza parlor. It is the power of beliefs, and the way in which they tap, organize, and provide a structure for powerful feelings about our lives, that makes them become central to our psyches and our identities. Like Luther's disoriented response to the realization that his faith in the Catholic Church had eroded, once the link between ideology and emotion has been forged, anything that interferes with it is experienced as a profound psychic threat. Beliefs, even distorted and evil ones, hold us together. Once inserted into the fabric of our psychological makeup, they become indispensable to the maintenance of our sense of well-being.

King's experience in his bunk that night consolidated something; it brought his heretofore splintered and fragmentary ideological notions into an emotional matrix that was deeply wedded to the fundamental questions about his life and who he was. It made of King a true believer, giving him the kind of zeal encountered in religious conversions. It felt like a transcendent moment that yielded insight about the world, how it worked, and where he belonged within it. For the first time in his life, King felt he had a place. If for years he had felt dislocated and lost, like an untethered soul floating through a dark, cold universe, he emerged from this experience feeling anchored by an ideology.

He became even more immersed in issues of race, racial purity, and genealogy. The answer to lifelong questions about who he was became self-evident: he was an Aryan. He studied the origins of the "Aryan people" and, like other white supremacists, viewed himself as a guardian of "his race." He would soon write the following in the "yearbook" of a fellow inmate, just before the latter's release from prison:

> Despite the divisive ethnic slurs designed to separate us and belittle
> us, we are—each and everyone of us—Aryans.
>> A gifted race
>> A misunderstood race
>> A hunted and persecuted race
>> But Aryans nonetheless.

King's ideology of racial purity was a disguised or derivative answer to the question of who he was, where he fit in, and what his origins were. The disclosure of his adoption at the age of thirteen confirmed his sense of disloca-

tion but did not explain it. Who were his biological parents and why had
they given him up? And who or what did that make him? Bill King now had
an answer. He came to believe that he could trace his roots back to the Aryan
tribes, notwithstanding the fact that he knew almost nothing about his biological parents. He was white, and within the world of the white supremacist
movement, that pigmented fact could only mean one thing, that he was a de-
scendant of the great Aryan race. Bill King had now inserted himself as the
leader of a small group of inmates who viewed it as their mission to fight for
the salvation of that race and to subvert the U.S. government. The latter they
believed was orchestrating a plot to mongrelize the country. The CKA, like
other white supremacist groups, viewed anyone who developed meaningful
relationships with nonwhites, not to mention anyone who consorted with
them, as race traitors, pure and simple. In the unit bylaws of the Confederate Knights of America, King (who variously identified himself as the "Grand
Cyclops" or simply as "Captain"), included the following: "Aside from business and job oriented matters, members will not at any given time, engage in
in-depth personal socialization with individuals nor groups of minorities and
Jewish races." King's beliefs were an outgrowth of the milieu of prison life at
Beto and its amplified racial paranoia, but they were grafted onto his need to
have a clear identity where a "pure" racial genealogy served as a sort of personal authentication. They were, in other words, an attempt to consolidate
his ever-flagging inner equilibrium.

To the outside world, to the friends and girlfriends with whom King corresponded while at Beto, his transformation from lost, small-time criminal
to hard-core racist was easy to trace. The shift from "Bill" to "Possum" in his
letters to friends and family reflected, as if in shorthand, a personal transformation of enormous proportions. The letters also became laced with racist
rantings about white girls who dated black boys (in fact, he was obsessed with
interracial relationships) and boasts about the CKA and the other white
prison gangs.

After King deposed Brewer, who seemed to recognize King's leadership
skills and his greater intelligence, King wrote to friends back in Jasper about
his new role as the "Exalted Cyclops" of the Confederate Knights of America. In one letter to a "free world" friend, with whom he had spent time in
boot camp, King exhorted him to "Have the courage to be you!" and added:

"Bro, I am the Exalted Cyclops of the C.K.A. here in prison. A position which I've obtained through hard work and dedication to my beliefs and doctrines. An E.C. is the same as the Platoon guide was to us in bootcamp."

It was easy to see in much of this material that gang membership and racial ideology were partly in the service of repairing a variety of felt psychological deficits. For example, toward the end of the above letter King told his friend: "I know you possess in your inner self the will and drive to be a true Aryan Warrior." In one CKA document King wrote: "We do not choose to be common men," a statement he underscored by using multiple exclamation points for emphasis. Elsewhere in this same document he announced that CKA members "should strive to . . . be tolerant [and] control their temper and not take everything personally," an issue that gave King himself difficulty. Pop psychology had apparently made its way to the inner bowels of the Texas penal system and was now being put in the service of enhancing gang members' self-esteem.

Another document apparently written by King at this time, and later found by investigators in King's Jasper apartment, was seemingly a draft of a recruitment letter for prospective members of the Texas Rebel Soldiers division of the CKA. "Dear member," the letter said. "Welcome to the Texas Rebel Soldiers. This is the home, the training center, the very foundation of the Confederate Knights of America." The letter was a mini-treatise about the perceived plight of the Aryan race, a race, it argued, threatened with extinction. "For every Aryan kinsman who is accepted into this group, two are appointed to the U.S. Governments New World Order program, another makes the evening news with a campaign of terror designed to enslave humanity or as is often the case wipe the Aryan Race off the face of the earth." The CKA, the letter continued, was dedicated to a dream of a better world, one where the different Aryan peoples would be united. "Despite the divisive ethnic slurs designed to separate us and belittle us, we are—each and everyone of us—Aryans . . . A gifted race. A misunderstood race. A hunted and persecuted race. But Aryans none the less." The letter concluded: "Some would say this is a naive dream. Or even a fool's dream. Perhaps, but I say it is our only hope if we are all to survive. Apparently you believe it too. So welcome Aryan warriors both old and new. Welcome to the Confederate Knights of America. Welcome to the Dream." The letter was signed by King.

King also wrote up membership forms, bylaws, and a code of ethics for

the Confederate Knights of America. He became a tireless leader, promoter, *Planet*
and organizer. King now had a platform for his ideas and a newfound world- *Beto*
view within which everything seemed to fit and within which he was the
undisputed leader. Jasper's district attorney would later argue that King's vision for his fledgling CKA included taking it from Planet Beto and into the
"free world" to implement its racist ideology, to "prospect" for new members, and to hold "bashings" in an effort to further the cause.

An Uneasy Return

BILL KING WAS RELEASED from the Beto Unit on July 28, 1997, leaving behind his fellow CKA members (except Russell Brewer, who had been released
some months previous). King had arrived there two years earlier as a somewhat incorrigible twenty-year-old whose will the system had found no way
of bending and whose cooperation could not be enlisted. He was petulant,
oppositional, haughty, and full of himself. Neither the benevolent efforts of
his hometown probation officer, who was a friend of his father's, nor the
drill-sergeant types of the boot camp and the restitution centers had succeeded in getting Bill to change his ways. King had managed to thwart every
intention to help him alter the downward course of his life. The system had
run out of options and King had seemed indifferent to the possible consequences. Perhaps he was simply so accustomed to having his way that he
never imagined that anyone would really say "enough" or "no." If so, it was
a grave miscalculation. And, in a corollary miscalculation, TDCJ officials
had decided to send the incorrigible young Jasper boy to a renowned, hard-
time maximum-security prison as punishment for a parole violation.

King had arrived at the Beto Unit wet behind the ears in criminal justice

terms, having participated in a few minor-league break-ins. The Bill King
who left Beto two years later was a very changed person. He had bulked up
through a disciplined weight lifting and exercise program; in fact, he had become obsessed with being physically fit. He also left the prison with his racist and satanic "tats" and his CKA documents. Most important, he departed
Beto carrying the ideology that most of his fellow inmates left behind once
released. He was like a dark missionary leaving his church and going out into
the world. Most of all, he left feeling for the first time in his life that he had
an identity, that he belonged, that he was wanted and needed. He believed
he had resolved the persistent sense of dislocation and rejection that had
plagued him throughout his life, and his white supremacist ideology was pivotal to that sense of well-being.

King also left Beto more adept than ever at the cover-up. When he met
with the prison's Transitional Case Manager, the individual responsible for
planning King's release, King was amiable and cooperative. His Institutional
Parole Officer similarly described King as possessing "a very positive attitude"
and as "very cooperative in responding to the interviewer's questions [offer-
ing] avenues of improvement to increase his prospects of completing super-
vision successfully." King also talked about his realization that his "immature
actions" were responsible for his having been in prison and even suggested
ways in which he might "improve his attitude and behavior in society." King's
comportment had been exemplary during the latter half of his imprisonment, and it appeared that prison authorities were completely unaware of his
role in the CKA. "He denies any history of gang affiliation," the probation
officer noted in his report, adding that King's "institutional adjustment" had
been "satisfactory."

Bill King arrived back in Jasper at the end of July 1997 with no money and
not much to do. Unemployment was high in town, and Bill was not one who
found it easy to take orders from others. For a while he coasted on his ex-con
celebrity status. Some of the local teenagers were awed by the fact that he
had done hard time and, especially, by his tattoos, the likes of which few had
ever seen.

When he met the sixteen-year-old Kylie Greeney at the movie theater
two months after his release, she was impressed. "His tattoos were the things
that first attracted me," she later recalled. "I had heard that he showed his tattoos all around town. Like 'Tinkerbell' [the tattoo on King's penis], showing

everybody: guys, girls, he didn't care." Kylie was something of a misfit herself. She was not from Jasper, and many of the girls in the local scene were intimidated by the fact that Kylie was pretty and unconventional, dressing with a flair that distinguished her from her East Texas adolescent contemporaries.

Kylie Greeney was a forlorn child. Her father died of cancer when she was three years of age ("I have a picture, but no memories of him," she once told me), then her stepfather died. She and her mother had bounced around from place to place for most of her life—Nebraska, then Austin, Abilene, and finally Jasper. She was also something of a black sheep within her family. Her sister was the prized one, "married to a computer genius," as Kylie put it with more than a trace of envy in her voice. "She's the angel," Kylie said of her sister, "and I'm the bad one."

By the time she met Bill, she felt ready for something new. "I was tired of dating guys my own age who were immature. Someone older, someone rough is what I wanted." King fit the bill. For their first date Bill and Kylie went to the local VFW hall, and Kylie was taken by his dancing. When Bill thought that an older guy whom Kylie knew from work had fondled her, King squared off with him, though there was no fight. Kylie was impressed. The night was capped with a romantic Garth Brooks song, "The Dance," in which the country western crooner voices no regret for the pain and sorrow of his life because otherwise he would have missed the dance. It became the couple's song, and even later, when I wrote to King and suggested that there was something poignant and tragic about his life because it need not have turned out this way, he simply quoted the song's lyrics in response, as if to say that the pain of his circumstance was a small price to pay for the pleasures he'd had. He found it almost impossible to contemplate the possibility that his life might have been different. It was as if in King's view there was only one dance to be danced. To entertain the notion of alternate paths threatened to either wash away the few good and cherished things onto which he held tightly, or else open the floodgates to a well of sadness and remorse too enormous to absorb.

Kylie saw in Bill her knight in shining armor. She was his "featherwood," as white supremacists like to refer to their women; in fact, she almost had the word tattooed on her but was later relieved that she hadn't. Bill made her feel good and connected in ways she'd never felt before. She found his toughness and edge enormously attractive. It fostered the illusion of protection, not-

withstanding the fact that he frequently disappointed her. He was a powerful and compelling presence for the lost Kylie. "He had me like under a
spell," she would recall. "He had a power." King's verbal skills played an important role in his charm; she loved the way Bill spoke to her. "The way he
talks and uses words, [it] pulled me to him," she said. The allure was enormous, even though Kylie could also see another side of Bill. "He's a con artist," Kylie later said. "He's got that mystery about him. You want to believe
him. We'd go to his dad's and he'd ask his dad for money, then go to his sister and grandma, and tell them all the same story. His grandma would drop
everything to do for him."

Bill's relationship with Kylie was quite turbulent, although punctuated by
episodes of knee-buckling closeness and fever-pitch eroticism of the sort that
could momentarily make them each forget their accumulated mutual resent-
ments as well as the accumulated pain of their still young lives. Throughout
their courtship, Kylie was inclined toward angry outbursts and temper tantrums that seemed to completely take possession of her. She was also prone
to deep anxieties and extreme jealousy that led her to see every girl whose
path crossed Bill's as a rival. Kylie didn't even like it when Bill went to the
movies without her since the theater was the focal point of Jasper's adolescent
social scene. Kylie knew that there would be other girls there, and she didn't
want Bill around them. Aware of her vulnerabilities, Bill did little to allay
Kylie's many anxieties, inclined as he was to flirting with other girls and staying out all night.

On the other hand, Bill wasn't exactly confident of Kylie's fidelity, either.
On one occasion he claims to have found her in a compromising situation with a girlfriend and two guys at her friend's apartment. In February of
1998 Kylie became pregnant, and when she told Bill, he assumed the father
was someone else. He and Kylie had been having unprotected sex for seven
months and she hadn't gotten pregnant, he rationalized. He was also thinking about the scene he had walked into with Kylie and her "friends."

Bill King was twenty-three and Kylie Greeney was seventeen when they
moved in together at the Timbers Apartments, just a few months before the
murder of James Byrd Jr. Kylie and her mother had been at odds for years,
so if her mother objected to this arrangement, there was little she could
do to stop her infatuated, headstrong daughter from moving in with Bill.
Notwithstanding the glow of a flowering relationship, Kylie soon learned

that Bill was extremely moody. He was easily frustrated, and when things—
rarely specified—were not going well at a job, for example, he often took it
out on her. Bill had a very bad temper: "He'd cuss me, call me names," Kylie
recalled. One night she prepared a chicken dinner while he was working a
roofing job. When Bill returned, he announced that he had plans to go out.
"You're not going to eat?" she asked plaintively. In the ensuing altercation,
Bill threw a plate of food across the room. Not known for keeping a lid
on her own temper, Kylie also threw things at Bill as the argument escalated
out of control. "The neighbors called the cops on him," Kylie said, which
brought this particular incident to a close. However, such altercations were
common in the couple's turbulent relationship.

"At times he scared me," Kylie later admitted. Yet he could also be very
sweet and sensitive to her. Consistent with his bipolar disorder diagnosis, he
suffered from frequent mood swings, according to Kylie. "One minute he
was this way, the next he would turn." Kylie was also convinced that he was
cheating on her. "He stayed gone when I was pregnant. Made me feel used.
He denies it, but he wouldn't come home at night. I just wanted to be a family, for him to be there," Kylie said. Perhaps Bill and Kylie both harbored this
wish, but they were too broken and too burdened by a lifetime of troubled
emotions to make that possible.

Bill King was circumspect about his racial beliefs, not sharing them with
most people. Kylie, however, knew his views well. One night, while Bill was
at work, Kylie went to visit her ex-boyfriend at his apartment. There were
three other young men at the apartment, two of them black, another white,
whom she knew but described as "strictly friends." Bill tracked Kylie down
at her ex-boyfriend's and knocked on the door. Upon entering the apartment, he introduced himself, but it was an awkward situation and after a few
minutes he simply walked out, only to return fifteen minutes later, angrily
commanding Kylie, "Get your ass out here!" In the parking lot Bill berated
her for associating with blacks. "He said he was going to burn a cross in front
of the guy's yard," Kylie said. "He didn't care that my ex-boyfriend was there,
it was because there were blacks there."

When later interviewed by the FBI, Kylie Greeney downplayed what she
knew of Bill's racist views. "I had the FBI at me all the time," she recalled.
"Questions, questions, questions. Meet, meet, meet. I didn't tell them the to-
tally honest truth. Some things I didn't want to tell them. Like his racial stuff.

He had a KKK book. I knew he had that and other papers. He was racial, but everyone is," she concluded. At the same time, Bill was effective at masking these feelings. Kylie recalled one night when they were eating dinner at a little Jasper restaurant called the Cedar Tree. A black man whom Bill knew was also eating there. Bill shook the man's hand and they made small talk for a few minutes, but no trace of King's racial attitudes was evident in that exchange.

Despite the constant fights and conflicts, Bill and Kylie struggled to create the foundation of something that might resemble a family. For the first time in his life Bill opened a checking account. Somewhere in all of his personal turmoil, King harbored white-picket-fence fantasies. He told Shawn Berry that he planned to do a lot of playing around before the baby arrived to get it out of his system. That Easter, in April of 1998, Bill and Kylie, who was just beginning to show, drove to Mississippi to meet Sylvia, Bill's biological mother. Sylvia had last seen Bill when he was three months old, and Bill had no memory of the woman who'd given birth to him. It promised to be an emotional reunion.

Bill King arrived in Mississippi proud to show his mother the young, pretty seventeen-year-old girl who was carrying his child. He was surprised to learn, shortly after their arrival, that Sylvia's spiritual beliefs tended toward strict Christian fundamentalism. King had long since turned his back on Christianity, viewing it as an "imposed" religion that was "unnatural" and foisted upon the Aryan peoples by the ungodly Romans. Instead, he claimed to be a follower of Odinism, the true religion of the Aryan race, according to Cajun Man and the literature he had read in prison.

These differences produced significant tensions between Bill and Sylvia almost from the start of his visit. Her religious fervor made him uneasy, and it felt oppressive. Kylie, too, felt that the heavy religious atmosphere was "weird." On the last day of the visit these tensions broke into the open. Perhaps emboldened by his and Kylie's impending departure, Bill decided to take off his T-shirt to participate in the family softball game, thereby exposing his full-sleeve tattoos for all to see. The children and, especially, the adolescents, were immediately drawn by curiosity, and Bill was surrounded by a gaggle of intrigued kids asking him about his prized tattoos. Sylvia became irate and in the ensuing argument angrily told Bill that he was "a product of the devil."

The much-anticipated reunion with Sylvia had turned into a disaster. The visit, laced with hopes that it might heal a long-standing wound, had unraveled amid the Easter season's rich symbolism of rebirth. Devastated and humiliated, Bill headed back to Jasper, driving Kylie's late-model Eclipse, with Kylie at his side. They fought all the way home about trivial things, neither acknowledging what had happened or what it meant. For Bill, the old seething feelings were back. The sense of equanimity brought on by his conversion at Beto had evaporated. As he had done for years, Bill retreated back into himself, into that dark, quiet inner sanctuary that allowed him to mask it all, sealing up his rage within a malignant introversion.

BILL KING'S LIFE APPEARED TO BE unraveling in the weeks preceding the murder of James Byrd. Fed up with Bill and struggling with pregnancy-induced nausea much of the time, Kylie packed up her things and moved in with Christie Marcontell, Shawn Berry's girlfriend. Kylie felt betrayed by Bill. She had discovered that, following a chance encounter at the Jasper Wal-Mart, he was again seeing Keisha Atkins, his old high school girlfriend. His late-night antics with his friends also had her feeling exasperated—half of the time she had no idea where he was or what he was doing. He would borrow her car, ostensibly to pick up a paycheck or run some errand, and be gone for hours on end. Kylie might later learn that he had been at a party without her, but more often she simply had no idea where he was; there was no making Bill account for his time.

For Bill King, the period immediately preceding the murder had been difficult, although he was not one to recognize, much less acknowledge, the emotional causes of his behavior. He seemed to encounter rejection at every turn. Five weeks earlier he had left Jasper feeling proud as a peacock: the soon-to-be-a-father had opened his first bank account and moved into a nice apartment with his attractive girlfriend, who also happened to have a recent-model Eclipse. King was going to show Sylvia that he was good, that he was worthy, and the reunion with the woman who had given him up when he was three months old was going to dispel the old feeling of being damaged and broken. He had headed off to meet Sylvia full of hopes and dreams.

The ill-fated trip to Mississippi had had a profound impact on him, once again mobilizing the rage he had felt off and on for years. Then there was his suspicion that perhaps it was not his child that Kylie was carrying. These

CHRISTIE MARCONTELL, SHAWN BERRY'S GIRLFRIEND

were all feelings that were part of the backdrop of conflicts that eventually led her to move out of the apartment just weeks before the murder, although they continued to see each other.

Russell Brewer showed up in Jasper shortly after Kylie moved out. When she met Bill's scruffy ex-con friend, Kylie was less than impressed: "He was lying on the floor of the apartment and looked disgusting, nasty, gruff," Kylie would later recall.

Bill had given Kylie no warning that a former buddy from Planet Beto was coming to town, much less that he would be taking up residence with him. "He's come down to visit for a week" was Bill's explanation.

Russell Brewer made Kylie extremely uncomfortable. "I didn't like him," she said. "I felt weird around him." One week turned into two.

Many people have said that Brewer's arrival seemed to mobilize a dark force within King. "He just wasn't himself after Russell came to town," Kylie said. A day or two after Brewer's arrival, King, Brewer, and Louis Berry went off to Galveston for a weekend of partying. Irate about the trip (because she was convinced that the trip involved girls), Kylie scrawled "You're a liar" on Shawn Berry's truck for King to see when the trio returned. "She was psycho-jealous," Louis recalled.

There is no evidence that in the eleven months following his release from the Beto Unit King engaged in any illegal activities. On the contrary, there were indications that he was making efforts, if flawed ones, to pull his life together. However, Brewer later testified that after the Galveston trip, the two of them, along with Shawn Berry, embarked on a crime spree in Jasper. In the span of three days they burglarized a motel's pool-side party room—making off with fifty bags of potato chips—and broke into a liquor store a few miles out of town where they stole a dozen cases of beer. The following night the trio broke into Patrick's Steakhouse, stealing so much gourmet meat that the haul would not fit into the freezer at the apartment. They filled a couple of coolers with meat and organized a barbecue on Saturday, the day before the murder, to cook the rest of it. The barbecue only added to King's frustrations, for Louis Berry and King's lifelong friend Tommy Faulk had allowed the party to end up at an African American friend's house. Faulk and Louis Berry had obviously miscalculated the dynamics involved in the reactivation of the King-Brewer relationship, as would Shawn Berry a few hours hence, with tragic consequences.

For the socially anxious Russell Brewer, King's life in Jasper must have seemed idyllic. There were plenty of parties, lots of girls, lots of drinking, and lots of action all the time. And, as often as not, Bill King was at the center of it. In contrast to the life they had shared at Beto, Brewer found Jasper to be a town with no shortage of excitement, thanks to Bill. There was the Galveston trip, but Brewer had also gone off for a couple of days with a woman who lived in the apartment next door, ostensibly to help her move her belongings from Louisiana to Jasper. Then, in town, there had been party after party, with barbecues, horseshoe and volleyball games at the river, all-terrain-vehicle rides, and paintball games in the pine forest.

Almost everyone thought Brewer strange. "We'd party at the apartment, have girls over and play drinking games at the counter in the kitchen," Louis Berry recalls, "but Russell wouldn't drink. He'd mostly sit on the couch watching. If someone said something that was funny, he'd laugh for a second, but then go back to just sitting there." Brewer seemed lost and disconnected. King was the only person Brewer would actually talk to. The two ex-cons seemed to be in a world of their own, and being together again appeared to stir a strange nostalgia. King and Brewer would slip into prison lingo in front of everyone: "Hey, Russell, you got so-and-so in your 'house' with you last night taking it in the ass, he's raping you every night and you know you like it," King is reported to have said to Brewer. They boasted about their Planet Beto days. One incident that Louis Berry thought was particularly strange was coming home to find King and Brewer preparing a concoction they called "jack smack." King had opened a can of mackerel and combined the contents with some Ramen noodles—food items they had been able to purchase at the prison commissary—to make a "spread." As King and Brewer sat on the kitchen floor eating the concoction and talking in prison lingo, they seemed to be completely absorbed in what was essentially a recreation of their prison experience. When offered some of the "jack smack," Berry refused. "It was nasty," he said.

Ever since his return to Jasper, King had been trying to find his place, to relocate himself in a world where he had never felt at home to begin with. He had tried desperately to find a way of reengaging that world, but nothing was quite right. King's friends observed that his clothes were dated, and his music collection was, too. He spent hours copying Tommy Faulk's more recent tapes and CDs, and he tried to pry money from his grandmother to buy a new wardrobe, although he often used the money to buy alcohol instead. Notwithstanding the partying, and the womanizing, and his drifting along doing pretty much whatever he felt like doing, there was a part of him that wanted to find a place in Jasper. He wanted to feel normal, perhaps marry Kylie and be a father to their child. There was a war raging within him between these conflicting aims and wishes.

Russell Brewer's arrival, however, was a turning point in King's life, throwing King into an altered state. It was as if their shared Beto experience, which had given King a sense of identity and belonging, was being relived. King and Brewer reinforced within one another a peculiar mind-set, one perhaps also flush with unacknowledged homoerotic feelings, the kind of feelings that led them to banter about getting "fucked in the ass and liking it" or to pepper their speech with "Love ya bro" and "daddy loves you" pronouncements. These feelings had derived, in part, from the white supremacist movement's ideology of racial identity and from its fusion of genetic theories and longings to return to a mythic home. Within these notions King had not only felt he belonged, he'd also felt like a powerful, righteous warrior. As fate would have it, Russell Brewer arrived in Jasper at the very moment when King was once again experiencing feelings of hopelessness and fragmentation. As if by some malevolent design, the structures that held King's life together were falling apart all around him—he had been rejected by Sylvia, Kylie was moving out, he had no car, no job, and he was being evicted. The timing of Brewer's arrival could not have been less fortuitous, coming as it did at the very nadir of King's post-Beto life.

Perhaps King recognized that he was at the end of the road, that things were about to unravel under the weight of an enormous centrifugal force that he was helpless to contain. The feelings of equanimity and power that he had found in his Beto conversion had by now almost entirely dissipated, no longer providing needed ballast. Instead, King felt himself battered by all that was taking place around him, most of it a product of his own doing, of his own limitations. For a brief moment, Brewer and the whirlwind of social activities that were largely occasioned by his visit seemed to ward off King's sense of fragmentation. With Brewer, King launched into a crusade of avoidance. In the days preceding June 6, the two men lost themselves in an orgy of crime and merriment, Brewer, the acolyte, enthralled by the world that King was showing him, and King unconsciously fleeing the implications of his crumbling world. Bill King had reverted to being "Possum." The dark forces in which he sought refuge, where he looked for a font of sustaining power, were instead about to destroy the lives of four flawed individuals whose destinies had brought them together.

A mere five weeks after Bill King's ill-fated reunion with Sylvia, he and Russell Brewer and Shawn Berry would find themselves driving around town on a Saturday night, upset that they'd found no girls and no party, tearing up rural mailboxes to vent their frustration. They pulled one from its post with a logging chain that lay in the back of Berry's pickup truck. On their way back into town they encountered James Byrd, making his way home from a late-night party. Byrd slid himself onto the bed of the primer-gray pickup truck. He was feeling momentarily relieved that he'd gotten a ride, and he accepted the invitation, offered through the small, sliding window that was open at the back of the truck's cab, to help himself to one of the beers in the cooler next to him. The foursome wove their way through Jasper's darkened back streets in the old, battered truck as the unsuspecting James Byrd sipped his beer. Byrd must have thought that the night was still young, that there was more partying in store with the three white boys riding quietly in the cab of the old truck, whose shock absorbers were spent and whose springs and joints creaked at every turn.

Not the 1920s

BUILT IN 1889, the Jasper County courthouse is a majestic, toffee-colored, three-story structure occupying the back half of an attractive square dotted with ancient pecan trees and crepe myrtles. A handsome gazebo, surrounded by azaleas, sits off to the side. A few benches and picnic tables on the grounds lend a casual air to what was once the commercial center of town, although most of Jasper's businesses are now spread along the two highways that intersect on the southeast end of town.

Guy James Gray typically worked late into the night. His office was one of a suite of offices allocated to the Jasper County district attorney on the ground floor of the west wing of the courthouse. A secretary, along with the DA's two investigators, a copier, and a coffee machine that was in high demand occupied the first office in the suite, whose door opened to the main hallway. In the adjoining office was Gray's personal secretary, and beyond that was Guy James Gray's office, which was rather spacious. That impression was enhanced by its ample windows, the kind often found in nineteenth-century buildings. On his wide mahogany desk were neat stacks of mail and documents, as well as a computer and a black telephone with multiple lines.

Along the walls surrounding the desk was a chocolate-brown vinyl wrap-around countertop on which various family photographs were arrayed and beneath which were sets of shelves and filing cabinets. On the wall facing his desk, beyond two leather upholstered chairs, were bookshelves containing various lawbooks and the Texas Penal Code. It would be some time before Gray's office walls were decorated with mementos from the defining moments of Gray's career as a prosecutor: courtroom artists' renderings of the King, Brewer, and Berry trials, photographs of the DA with Attorney General Janet Reno, or Gray and Sheriff Billy Rowles standing proudly in front of the courthouse.

Guy James (everyone who knew Gray called him by both names) sat at the leather upholstered desk chair that matched the two on the other side of his desk. The DA had steady blue eyes and he was balding, a fact about which he was a bit self-conscious. By East Texas standards he was of moderate stature, and he had rather short arms and small, almost delicate fingers. However, Gray's demeanor projected a larger, more commanding presence than his physical attributes might suggest. Gray had been the Jasper County district attorney since 1979. His East Texas drawl and his laid-back style might have made him easy to miscast as a hardscrabble, ill-educated country boy, but the facts were otherwise. Gray was as close to blue blood as people get in East Texas. His grandmother had been a cousin to Robert E. Lee, for example, and his family had been living in and around Jasper County for five generations. Gray was a graduate of the University of Texas School of Law, the best in the state. He may not have been at the top of his class, but he was a sharp legal tactician and an able prosecutor. Behind the simple country lawyer demeanor was a tenacious, incisive mind.

Guy James Gray was the ambivalent point man and chief architect of the state's prosecution of Bill King and the two other men charged with the murder of James Byrd Jr. Given the nature of the crime and the charged atmosphere that immediately enveloped it, the DA did not relish his role. He had first been under the impression that the U.S. Department of Justice was going to take over the case. Beginning with the visit of Sheriff Rowles to the FBI office in Beaumont the Monday morning following the murder, the feds had taken a keen interest in the investigation. There had been specific discussions suggesting that federal authorities might prosecute the case under federal hate crime statutes. Such a development would have placed both

Gray and Rowles in consultative roles, with the sheriff appearing as a key witness. That would have been a very congenial arrangement as far as the Jasper
DA was concerned.

Not long after the murder, however, Mike Bradford, the U.S. attorney in
charge of the East Texas region, had called to notify Gray that after considerable research his office had concluded that it was unlikely that they could
prosecute the Byrd case under the federal hate crimes statutes. "Lord have
mercy" was all Gray could bring himself to say in response. Things would
have been much simpler for the DA and his team had the feds taken the reins.
The trial of three white men charged with one of the most heinous murders
in recent history was now squarely on Gray's shoulders. He was acutely aware
of the challenge he faced. "This was a dangerous, dangerous case. Whoever
took this case to trial, if they messed it up, it would have history book consequences," the DA noted gravely. Gray was convinced that failure to get a
conviction in this case would mean the end of his professional career. "I
might as well resign, get a hair transplant and a face lift, and go somewhere
else to live," Gray said.

The Jasper DA took a cynical view of the federal attorney's explanation for
not taking the case. The official reason was that the feds were unsure that the
case fell under federal jurisdiction. The federal hate crime statute requires
that a defendant be in the process of violating specific civil rights, which the
feds were not sure they could prove in the Byrd murder. However, Gray was
convinced that political considerations played a part in this decision as well.
"This was a tough case," he would later volunteer. "They'd rather me handle
it. They could come in and help me, but if something went sour, they weren't
directly responsible for it," Gray noted. "I don't think they were willing to
take the all-or-nothing gamble," he said. "We took a shot at all the marbles
[going for the death penalty], but it was very risky." This decision may have
been an act of prosecutorial courage, but it was also the product of the simple
fact that Gray, Rowles, and the community of Jasper had their backs against
the wall. There was no one else to pass the case on to. Gray and his team were
going to have to take on this challenge and hope for the best.

Although the Jasper district attorney's office was handling the case, the
U.S. Department of Justice offered immediate assistance, and getting federal
agents in early had already paid big dividends. Within twenty-four hours
of the murder, FBI agents were combing the crime scene for additional evi-

dence. The FBI's presence had also provided political cover, given that his-
torically in East Texas it was rare for whites to be brought to justice for mur-
dering blacks. The FBI's involvement communicated a clear signal that local
authorities were not trying to sweep things under the rug. Quite the contrary.
The DA's office was actively prosecuting the case. Eventually, the FBI would
set up a command post in Jasper, and, nationwide, close to two hundred officers would not only gather and analyze physical evidence but also interview
Bill King's current and former friends and his fellow inmates at Beto.

The FBI represented an enormous infusion of investigative resources, ex-
ceeding by a significant margin anything that Jasper County could have mustered. For example, when it had become evident early that DNA would play
a pivotal role in the case, the FBI arranged for the expedited analysis of this
evidence. Blood and hair samples from the victim and from King, Brewer,
and Berry, along with samples taken from cigarette butts, beer bottles, and
blood and tissue specimens found on the truck and at the crime scene, were
packaged and transported to the Houston airport by a caravan of federal
officers. There the evidence was placed aboard a commercial airliner and
flown to Washington, D.C., under escort. Upon arrival in Washington, the
plane's passengers were required to wait until the escorting officer had de-
planed and transferred the evidence to a van from the FBI lab in Quantico,
Virginia. The FBI also put its best DNA analyst to work on the samples, and
preliminary results were obtained in record time.

Gray had never prosecuted a case with such resources at his disposal. But
it was also true that he had never prosecuted a case in which the stakes were
so high. Within forty-eight hours of the discovery of James Byrd's body, the
national and international media had descended upon Jasper, their remote
broadcasting trucks lining the courthouse, their anchors, producers, and
camera crews taking up virtually every motel and bed and breakfast in town.
Some were commuting daily from Beaumont, over an hour away. "We were
under siege," is the way one local would later describe the media's presence.

On the afternoon of Tuesday, June 9, Jasper law enforcement officers held
their first press conference, an event that quickly turned into a public relations disaster. The plan had been for Guy James Gray to meet Sheriff Rowles
at the county jail, where the three suspects were being held. The media, lying in wait at the jail's entrance, swarmed the DA as he exited his car. Gray
managed to make his way into the building through the camera crews and

the microphone booms as anchors shouted questions at him. The strange and unanticipated gauntlet left the DA feeling rather disoriented. Inside the building, Gray went straight to the sheriff's office, where a media consultant from the Justice Department was waiting to help Gray and Rowles pound out an official statement to be read by the sheriff to the waiting press corps.

The press conference was not a pretty sight. Sheriff Rowles emerged from the jail to stand before a bank of microphones and cameras, where he awkwardly read the prepared statement with Gray standing at his side. Looking down at the sheet of paper, the sheriff stumbled through, making little or no eye contact with the reporters. It was evident that he was anxious and uncomfortable, and it made the sheriff look as if he and his community had something to hide, which may have been precisely what many in the media assumed. Things only got worse at the conclusion of these prepared remarks, when the reporters started peppering the sheriff with questions. "Were these guys members of the Klan?" "How many Klan in Jasper?" "How many people have been prosecuted in Jasper for race-related crimes?" "How many African Americans are employed in local banks?" All too many of these questions received the same answers: "No comment" or "Case under investigation."

It was readily apparent to Gray and Rowles that the press conference had gone poorly. The two men retreated back to the sheriff's office. There they immediately agreed to revamp their approach to the press, namely, forgoing the services of the media consultant and dispensing with written press releases and similarly prepared statements. "We decided to go out there and look them in the eye and just answer questions as best we could, and as honestly as we could," the DA would later recollect. Feeling more in their element, the character of their interactions with the media started to change. The tone of the daily press conferences that followed grew less testy and more candid. However, the experience left Gray with a bad feeling: "Nine out of ten of them came down here to crucify a pot-bellied sheriff and a country lawyer DA for being backwoods and country," he would later say with more than a trace of indignation. "They were expecting a redneck law enforcement and a redneck prosecutor. Simpletons," Gray said angrily.

However painful that first press conference was, the experience brought home an important lesson to the Jasper DA, namely, that the whole world was looking over his shoulder. Every step he took in this case was under close scrutiny. Gray was carrying an enormous burden. He wasn't merely prosecuting a brutal murder, he was, in effect, representing Jasper, the region, and the nation's legal process before the court of national and international public opinion. Gray had enough on his mind without being distracted by such considerations.

In addition to the external pressures brought to bear by the media, there were also substantial local pressures. Beginning on June 7, from the moment on that Sunday afternoon when James Byrd Jr.'s remains had been positively identified, rumors began to spread throughout Jasper regarding what had transpired and why. Within Jasper's African American community there were concerns that Byrd's murder was part of a broader Klan conspiracy and that anyone caught walking in the street might be the next victim. An atmosphere of rage, fear, and anxiety permeated Jasper's black community. For whites in town fears were mounting that the gruesome murder might incite reprisals. Jasper was experiencing waves of tension, and there were rumors that many in town, white and black, were arming themselves. Gray and Rowles were deeply concerned about the unbridled rumors, fearful that a misstep might ignite a conflagration.

Before the Tuesday press conference, Sheriff Rowles had called the president of the Jasper Ministerial Alliance, an African American preacher named Bobby Lee Hudson, and asked whether he and Harlan Alexander, the chief of police, might speak at the alliance's monthly meeting which, fortuitously, was scheduled at noon that day. The Ministerial Alliance was comprised of the majority of the community's white and black ministers. The ministers had been meeting together for years. They trusted each other, and for years the group had been organizing events such as Sing with One Voice, where the choirs of most of Jasper's churches sang together. The event culminated with the ministers themselves taking the stage and singing a hymn. Some of the ministers also took turns giving sermons at each other's churches, and they had developed an unusual degree of collegiality and mutual respect notwithstanding their theological differences.

The decision to come to the Ministerial Alliance meeting reflected the degree of concern and anxiety that law enforcement officials felt regarding the tensions in town. Rowles, Alexander, and several FBI agents were present at the Tuesday meeting and shared with the ministers key elements of what they knew and what actions they had taken. For example, they discussed the Probable Cause document that they had presented to the Jasper Grand Jury as the basis for the charges being brought against King, Brewer, and Berry. It was an unusual step for law enforcement to have such a meeting with a community group, and it reflected their level of concern.

"It was a calculated risk," Gray would later recall in reference to this meeting and a similar meeting with the Byrd family. "But we had to satisfy them that this was not 1920." Gray was referring to two lynchings that had taken place years ago in neighboring counties, including one in which, like James Byrd, a black man had been dragged to his death behind a pickup truck. The perpetrators of those lynchings had never even been accused, much less tried in a court of law, but the incidents had not been forgotten. On the contrary, accounts of the lynchings had been handed down from generation to generation within Jasper County's white and black families, woven into the lore about the region's dark history of racial animus. While there was a public silence about these and other incidents laced with greater and lesser injustices, they formed part of an uneasily shared past, living on as part of a collective, if unofficial, legacy. Gray knew that it was essential to convey to Jasper's residents, especially its African American community, that in 1998 things would be handled differently. This time, local law enforcement had arrested and charged three men with the murder, they believed they had sufficient evidence to prosecute them successfully, and they were going to prosecute them to the full extent of the law. In other words, Gray was pursuing this as a capital murder case punishable with the death penalty.

It helped that Jasper, while no interracial utopia, was not the racist, redneck vestige of a "good old boy"–run town that most of the world assumed it to be. For example, Guy James Gray had a history of working with the black community and was open to input from community leaders. Within the parameters of what was possible and permissible, Gray had been responsive to such counsel, and his stance gave the DA credibility now that Jasper was facing a crisis. He was known as a straight shooter and a man who kept his word.

Even more important, the power structure of Jasper was not what it had been in the twenties and thirties. Jasper's mayor, R. C. Horn, and mayor pro-tem, Clyde Williams, were African Americans. The presidents of the school board and of the Chamber of Commerce were black, as were 20 percent of the district's schoolteachers. The CEO of Jasper Memorial Hospital, one of the community's largest employers, was black, as was the director of the Deep

East Texas Council of Governments, Walter Diggles, whose agency was responsible for funneling millions of state and federal dollars into fifteen East
Texas counties. On the Sunday morning when James Byrd's remains had
been found, it was a black Highway Patrol officer named Rodney Pearson
who had walked side by side with Sheriff Rowles down Huff Creek Road,
trying to put together the pieces of the nightmarish scene and to fathom what
had occurred. The image of those two law enforcement officers, one black,
the other white, working this case together as colleagues, would not have
been imaginable until the last decade or two. Such facts reflected significant
changes in the social realities of Jasper, changes that few would have thought
possible during the dark days of Jim Crow. Jasper may have been a poor community with high unemployment and many of its residents living in squalor,
but Jasper was a far cry from the racist town that the media crews had expected to find when they descended on East Texas in the summer of 1998.

To be sure, Jasper was no model of racial harmony. Gray knew Jasper well
enough to know that there was plenty of racism to go around and pockets
in Jasper and in Jasper County where "racial attitudes" ran deep. However,
it was also true that a core of whites and blacks shared a stake in the community's well-being. They formed a critical mass, an unspoken coalition, although Gray feared that perhaps this was a tenuous alliance on both sides.
Certainly it had never been put to the test by a circumstance such as this
murder, infused as it was with powerful, racially polarizing feelings. At James
Byrd's funeral, state and national dignitaries had attended en masse, including the Reverend Jesse Jackson and the Reverend Al Sharpton. Their presence was intended to show solidarity and support, but many locals were convinced that the media coverage simply provided a convenient stage, an
opportunity for implementing political agendas. Then there were the more
radical perspectives represented by the Ku Klux Klan from nearby Cleveland,
the Black Panthers of Dallas, and a black Muslim separatist group from
Houston, all of whom marched in Jasper in the weeks following James Byrd's
funeral.

Jasper's fragile white-black alliance might easily have unraveled had one of
the community's African American leaders stood by someone like Al Sharpton, or the Black Panthers, and endorsed a more radical posture. Similarly,
had the sheriff or the district attorney or some other white leader made a
statement or taken an action to suggest the presence of bias or support for the

Klan, that alliance might have easily fallen apart. Relationships that had taken years to forge might have quickly deteriorated, making it difficult, if not impossible, to prosecute the case in Jasper. The repercussions of such an unraveling would have persisted within the community for years. Gray knew this instinctively. At the time, there was plenty of uncertainty as to how Jasper's residents on either side of the color divide would respond to the crisis. In the face of these enormous strains, Jasper held on to a brittle peace.

All of these considerations were prominent in Guy James Gray's thinking as he sat at his desk at the courthouse, night after night, planning his strategy, studying the evidence, and trying to imagine how the pieces of this puzzle were going to come together.

The district attorney became completely immersed in his work. He thought about the case every waking hour. It intruded into his sleep nightly, frequently waking him up with a startle. He was a man possessed. "My nerves were so tight my eyes would just pop open at three o'clock in the morning," Gray recalled. He tried to examine the case from every possible perspective. What to do if a defense lawyer made this move as opposed to that one? He was constantly calculating, using every moment to speculate about his strategy, analyzing it, setting up traps for defense lawyers, pondering what kind of a jury he wanted. In fact, there were countless things to consider and only so many hours in a day to consider them. "I neglected my wife. I neglected my family. I neglected everything," he said. The trial of his career was consuming him. Uncharacteristically, Gray took to having several drinks at night when he arrived home, hoping to take the edge off and relax enough so that he might, for once, get a full night's sleep.

Gray had three significant decisions to make. The first was whether to try to strike a plea bargain with Shawn Berry. The second was to decide the sequence of the trials. The third involved developing an image of the kind of juror who might deliver a guilty verdict; such a verdict had never been rendered in a Texas capital murder case when it involved a white perpetrator and a black victim.

WHILE MOST PUNDITS ASSUMED that the cases against Bill King, Russell Brewer, and Shawn Berry were a slam dunk, the truth was otherwise. Shawn Berry's confession was problematic because it was far from consistent. His

DISTRICT ATTORNEY GUY JAMES GRAY

story had gone through several contradictory iterations with significant holes and gaps. As a result, the credibility of Berry's statements would become an easy target for any defense attorney worth his salt. In any event, the only way that Gray could use it was to put Berry on the witness stand, which meant offering him a plea bargain; otherwise the laws against self-incrimination would preclude Berry's testimony.

In other words, Gray's assessment of the case was not nearly as sanguine as that of the legal experts appearing on the nation's talk shows. Many of these experts had concluded that the outcome of the case was less a question of evidence and more a question of the will of the East Texas prosecutors and their ability to select a jury that would convict whites for the murder of an African American. However, without Berry's testimony, Gray and his team had very little on Bill King. A witness named Keisha Atkins had given a statement indicating that she had seen King, Brewer, and Berry get into Berry's truck in the early hours of June 7. In addition, Steven Scott could testify that as he was returning home from a Beaumont nightclub, he had seen Byrd pass by on Martin Luther King Boulevard at approximately 2:30 a.m. Byrd was sitting in the back of a pickup truck whose description matched one owned by Berry. However, Scott had been unable to identify any of the occupants; he could say only that they were three whites. A reasonably adept defense attorney could create an element of doubt about the fact that Bill King's lighter had been found at the crime scene, if not argue it away altogether, as it was an established fact that King had spent considerable time in Berry's truck in the days preceding the murder. The presence of the lighter did not prove King's presence at the crime scene that night, much less prove that he was an active participant in the murder. Mere presence at the scene of a crime, after all, does not prove involvement. From the vantage of the man responsible for prosecuting this case, these were not overwhelming facts to muster in a capital murder trial.

Gray had even less evidence linking Brewer to the murder. "We were completely naked on him" is the way Gray put it. The statement of Keisha Atkins that she saw Brewer in Berry's truck an hour or so before Scott saw Byrd getting a lift was about it. At the time of his arrest, Brewer also had a severely swollen and bruised right toe. In his statement to authorities after his arrest, Berry said that Brewer had kicked Byrd in the head during the initial assault at the clearing on the logging road. However, while the condition of Brewer's toe suggested a plausible circumstantial link to the murder, it, too, could be explained away easily by a moderately competent defense attorney.

Without Berry's testimony and without good DNA evidence (the results of which were not yet available), Gray's capital murder case against Bill King quickly started looking quite thin. It was this worry that intruded into the district attorney's sleep nightly, and he frequently awoke racked by an anxiety that somehow this case could slip away, a circumstance that he knew would be nothing short of disastrous. Such an outcome would also have far-reaching reverberations. Jasper's law enforcement officers and Jasper itself would be blamed, the former for somehow botching the investigation, the latter for somehow having incubated the very motives and feelings that created the crime. Gray was acutely aware of these possibilities. He could sense them in the questions he was being asked day after day by the media representatives, whose working assumption seemed to be that Gray and Jasper's white community were, at best, just a few degrees removed from the kind of virulent racist beliefs that were responsible for the Huff Creek Road horror.

The case against Shawn Berry was obviously the strongest. Berry's truck was clearly implicated, and Gray was certain that the blood found underneath the vehicle would turn out to be James Byrd's. Finding two of Berry's tools at the crime scene, with his name inscribed on them, only made the case against him stronger. However, Berry's girlfriend, Christie Marcontell, and her grandfather had hired an aggressive attorney named Joseph Hawthorn to represent him and the attorney's posture was complicating negotiations regarding Berry's possible testimony. Early on, Hawthorn, who went by the nickname "Lum," sent Gray a letter offering Berry as a witness in exchange for serving out the ten years' probation that remained on a prior burglary charge (when, at the age of seventeen, Berry and Bill King had broken into a local business). "I didn't even bother to respond to that letter," Gray says, indicating that Hawthorn's offer was so far off the mark as to not warrant an answer. Hawthorn's next offer was not much better.

"He [Berry's attorney] thought he had us by the short hairs," Gray later recalled. But the brutality of this murder and its raw, racial currents made it impossible for the DA to accept such a deal, which would have brought the opprobrium of the world down on Guy James Gray. It was simply unthinkable, a kind of legal low-balling that bordered on an insult as far as Gray was concerned. If nothing else, the proposal all but ignored the political context of this crime. It was so out of line as to be laughable were it not for the fact that this impasse created enormous problems for the prosecution. Without Berry's testimony, Gray and his team were entirely at the mercy of the DNA evidence, which was still being analyzed.

What Gray did eventually offer Berry and his attorney was an arrangement by which Berry would plead guilty to capital murder in exchange for his testimony. Gray had convinced federal authorities to take Berry into the federal penitentiary system, which would make Berry eligible for parole after twenty years. Berry would be in an air-conditioned prison (Texas prisons lack such amenities), and he would be given a false identity, making it possible for him to be out among the general prison population. If he turned the offer down, what awaited Berry in Texas was a very different scenario. If he managed to dodge the death penalty (not a foregone conclusion), he would likely be placed in Administrative Segregation where he would be allowed out of his cell for only one hour a day to exercise alone. Given the nature of this crime, Berry would remain isolated from other prisoners for his own protection. Twenty, thirty, or forty years of such isolation usually broke most men.

Committed to playing hardball, Berry and his attorney declined the DA's offer. Without Berry as a witness, Gray knew he was going to have to rely heavily on DNA evidence. But if a defense lawyer could raise the specter of contamination of the DNA evidence, the prosecution's case could quickly evaporate. Echoes of the O. J. Simpson trial, in which the famed athlete had escaped conviction because of a defense team's effective management of DNA issues, haunted these reflections. Gray was keenly aware that he had a lot less potential DNA evidence on King than the Los Angeles prosecuting team had had against Simpson.

The prospect of offering Bill King a deal was out of the question. For one thing, King was belligerent and absolutely uncooperative. During the interviews with Curtis Frame, the FBI, and the other officers, King had been mocking and derisive. More to the point, however, Gray was convinced that King was the key player, the leader of the three men. He was an avowed racist, and the materials found at King's apartment underscored how deeply immersed he was in such ideology. Even in the unlikely event that King had been open to it, the prosecution would not consider offering him a plea bargain in exchange for testimony.

Brewer posed similar problems in that, like King, he was uncooperative.

In addition, Brewer was almost useless as a witness because it would have been impossible to make him credible. Brewer's mind, as Gray put it, had been "burned out on dope." He was quite dull and inarticulate. He was also a habitual criminal who had spent a great deal of time in Texas prisons for offenses ranging from burglary to drugs. The prosecution simply could not put Brewer on the stand and expect a jury to believe what he had to say about this case or anything else. Thus, offering a plea bargain to Brewer in exchange for his testimony was never seriously considered.

This left Shawn Berry as the only potential witness for the prosecution. As they waited for the FBI to conduct DNA analyses on the evidence that had been shipped to Quantico, Gray decided to play chicken with Berry and his attorney. He gave them an ultimatum: they had a week to decide if there was any room to negotiate. Otherwise, he said, the prosecution would go for broke. When the DNA evidence came in, if it linked Berry to the murder, there would be no compromises and no deals offered to the defense. Berry and Hawthorn would have to decide now if they were willing to cooperate. Of course, there was no way that Gray was going to give Berry the kind of sweet deal that he and his attorney were proposing. The federal capital murder offer was the only offer on the table. The prosecution's posture contained, to be sure, more than an element of bluster. Both sides knew that, if King's trial started to unravel, the prosecution might feel compelled to come back to Berry for a deal.

Unfortunately for the prosecution team (and, as it would turn out, for Berry), Berry and his attorney demurred. Had Berry struck a plea bargain, King and Brewer could have been tried together in a single trial, which would have been Gray's dream scenario, assuming Berry's testimony could be corroborated. Despite the weaknesses in Berry's account, Berry's personal qualities made him the best prosecution witness of the three defendants by a long shot. He was not a known racist, he was not a member of a prison gang, and he had been steadily employed. Most important, he had an engaging personality, so his demeanor on the stand would likely have made him credible to a jury. Instead, the prosecution team would now have to think in terms of three separate trials, a daunting prospect. For one thing, it was already obvious that each trial would be a media spectacle. For another, the sheer expenditure of time and effort by the prosecution team would surpass by a significant margin any trial Jasper had ever seen, multiplied by three. Then

Not
the
1920s

125

there was the expense to Jasper County to consider, a poor county with an all but nonexistent tax base whose coffers would be completely drained by such proceedings. Jasper could ill afford to underwrite the cost of even one such trial.

WITHIN A FEW WEEKS THE PROSECUTION team received some welcome news from the FBI lab in Quantico. Preliminary DNA results indicated that all three suspects had James Byrd's blood on their shoes. Of the three defendants, Berry's clothing was found to have the most blood, thereby strengthening what was already a strong case against him.

The FBI's DNA analyses were a significant help, but Gray did not feel out of the woods yet. The amount of blood in question was quite small, especially when it came to King and Brewer. What they had was a single drop of blood on a pair of sandals assumed to belong to Bill King and a few more specks of blood on a pair of tennis shoes assumed to belong to Russell Brewer. Gray noted the possible limitations in this evidence: "They [the investigating officers] had gone through the apartment and gathered these things up," Gray recalled. "They didn't take them off of Bill King's feet and they didn't take them off of Brewer's feet. We had to prove that these sandals belonged to King and that he was wearing them that night. We had to prove that the tennis shoes belonged to Brewer and he was wearing them that night. . . . We've got blood on two pairs of shoes. That sounds awesome but you see how really weak it is? A good defense lawyer says 'Well, then, who spent the night at the apartment? What about any of the half a dozen of their friends? How do you know who's wearing this pair of sandals? These tennis shoes?'" Gray let the questions float in the air as if to conjure a nightmarish scenario in which a defense attorney systematically revealed fatal flaws in his case. It was well known, for example, that the apartment had become something of a hangout, with numerous people drifting in and out all the time. None of the defendants had been arrested at the apartment nor had any of them been wearing the clothes in question at the time of their arrests. Investigators had canvassed every potential witness who lived at the Timbers Apartments but could find no one who could place King, Brewer, or Berry at the apartment later that night, after Keisha Atkins had seen them leave together, much less identify what they were wearing.

Notwithstanding these potential problems, the DNA evidence strength-
ened the prosecution team's case significantly. The case was further buttressed
a few weeks later, when the FBI lab determined that cigarette butts and beer
bottles retrieved from the crime scene contained all three suspects' DNA.
This still wasn't incontrovertible evidence. It could be argued, for example,
that those items had already been in the truck and had merely been knocked
out during a scuffle at the crime scene. While the evidence was still circumstantial, the prosecution could more plausibly place King and Brewer at
the crime scene without Berry's testimony. The prosecution team's gamble
with Berry appeared to be paying off, revealing a significant miscalculation
on the part of Shawn Berry and his attorney. While Gray's hand was shored
up, it did not translate into fewer sleepless nights for the District Attorney.
"O. J. [Simpson]'s case was ten times stronger than that," Gray would later
recall. "[We had] reasonably good evidence, but it was not overwhelming evidence of guilt. There were gaps and loopholes in our proof."

BILL KING'S COURT-APPOINTED ATTORNEY was a middle-aged veteran
of East Texas courts named Haden Cribbs, who went by the nickname
"Sonny." Another attorney, Brack Jones, assisted Cribbs. Cribbs was from
Beaumont, and although he had experience with capital murder cases, he was
better known as a slash-and-burn divorce lawyer. For months, things had not
been running smoothly between Cribbs and Bill King. According to King,
the lawyer's strategy, from their very first meeting, had centered not on the
question of King's guilt or innocence but rather on how to help King dodge
the death penalty. Such a strategy did not sit well with King, who hoped that
aggressive representation might actually free him. King had consistently
maintained that he was not present when James Byrd was murdered. Shawn
Berry, he argued, had dropped him and Brewer off at the Timbers Apartments after the trio had picked up James Byrd on Martin Luther King Boulevard. King maintained, in other words, that Berry had then gone off to murder Byrd on his own.

In a statement titled "Logical Reasoning," sent (against his attorney's ad-
vice) to the *Dallas Morning News* in November 1998, King argued, as he
awaited trial, that "emotion and subjectivity ruin facts." He assailed the media for its role in both inciting and reacting to the potent emotions sur-

rounding his case. He also accused the media of circulating unsubstantiated facts without critical examination. Such "facts," he maintained, could be easily disproved if subjected to closer scrutiny. King viewed the entire process—the accusations against him and the extensive media coverage—as little more than a misguided attempt "to solve the many personal and societal problems of our complex civilization." The manifesto appeared to be a roundabout way of saying that the nation, like Jasper, was seeking to find a sacrificial lamb, someone to blame for the racial hatreds that fester in society. Bill King likened the whole affair to the once highly publicized controversy over "cold fusion." King argued that the case against him—like the pseudo facts that led two University of Utah chemists to report the astonishing discovery of "cold fusion" in 1989, which was quickly discredited when other scientists were unable to replicate the findings—was based largely on emotion, innuendo, and faulty reasoning. He also took on some of the published facts, including the interpretation of evidence found at the crime scene, the meaning of witnesses' statements, and the relevance of the Jasper district attorney's statements.

"Logical Reasoning" was a rambling discourse, at times reflecting Bill King's intelligence ("New facts attained as conclusions by means of a kind of logical reasoning known as the deductive method are drawn from given facts, or premises. Such facts are often 'fuzzy' because the premises, i.e. the facts, on which they are based, may be faulty"). The statement was also punctuated with perhaps telling quotations, attributed to Garrison Keillor ("Sometimes you have to look reality in the eye and deny it") and Mark Twain ("Get your facts first, and then you can distort them as much as you please"). However, "Logical Reasoning," laced as it was with occasional malapropisms, faulty grammar, and spelling errors, also revealed the fact that King was a high school dropout who had fashioned an education largely without the benefit of mentors or teachers.

The document was also a defense attorney's worst nightmare. In the essay King outlined what he believed his defense strategy should be, thereby preempting Cribbs and Jones. He also included a detailed account of what he claimed had really transpired on the night of June 6 and the early-morning hours of June 7, 1998, when James Byrd was murdered. This meant that the prosecution had a document authored by the accused that could be scrutinized for inconsistencies, gaps, and falsehoods. "Logical Reasoning," from a defense standpoint, was anything but logical. It also didn't help that King concluded the document with the following: "I, John W. King, remain White and Proud." If racial views were going to be a significant factor in the murder trial (a foregone conclusion), then such statements only served to fuel the very fires that the defense team was hoping to quench. The essay's closing, as well as the impulse to send it off to the newspaper in the first place, also betrayed the hubris and grandiosity that had subverted King time and again throughout his short life.

THE PROSECUTION'S CASE against Bill King and the others was beginning to jell. Two key considerations remained. First, Gray and his team had to decide whether to try the defendants on a straight murder case or whether to go for capital murder, which would open the door for the death penalty. Under Texas statutes, only the murder of a law enforcement officer and murders committed in the course of a felony crime are punishable by death. In order to prove capital murder, the prosecution would have to establish that James Byrd had been kidnapped as well as murdered. The problems with establishing kidnapping were readily apparent. Steven Scott had seen Byrd riding in the back of Shawn Berry's pickup truck showing no signs of distress or coercion. Presumably, Byrd could have jumped out of the truck at any time had he wanted to.

In his statement to investigators following his arrest, Shawn Berry noted that after Russell Brewer kicked Byrd in the head, the victim had fallen to the ground and not moved again. This account also undercut the kidnapping charge. If Byrd was unconscious or dead when he was chained to the back of the pickup truck, then the case for the death penalty was significantly undermined. James Byrd's autopsy, however, lent itself to a different story. The character of Byrd's wounds suggested the possibility that Byrd was alive and conscious for much of the time that he was being dragged. The fact that his elbows had been completely shredded, for example, might indicate that he had tried to prop himself up on them to protect himself as best he could from the logging road and the asphalt. The top of the victim's buttocks had been ripped out, similarly indicating that he had made an effort to hold himself up off the ground. Finally, the back of his head had notably fewer contusions and scrapes, perhaps because he was trying to hold his head up off of the ground. Had Byrd been unconscious, so the prosecution's argument went, the pattern of damage to his body would have been quite different.

This interpretation was precisely what Gray needed to argue in order to pursue the death penalty. It supported the view that Byrd was alive and conscious during his ordeal and that he had struggled against what was happening to him. Hence, it reinforced the kidnapping argument. In fact, according to the autopsy evidence, it was not until toward the end of the three-mile dragging that Byrd had actually been killed. At that juncture, when the truck rounded a left curve in the road, Byrd's body had swung to the right, sending it careening against a roadside culvert where it was severed into two parts. Byrd's head and right shoulder were left in a ditch by the culvert, while the rest of his torso was dragged on to the Huff Creek Church.

With the autopsy evidence, all of the essential elements of the prosecution's case were in place. The next issue was which of the three defendants to try first. Each option had its advantages and disadvantages. The evidence against Berry was the strongest; that was obvious. However, Berry posed the greatest challenge to going after the death penalty. Despite the evidence against him, Berry was a sympathetic character and was well liked within the community. In fact, many in town viewed Berry himself as a victim and wondered if perhaps there was truth to his account of having been swept along for fear of being attacked by King and Brewer. Berry had a history of good relationships with African Americans in Jasper, many of whom were as surprised as Jasper's whites that Berry had been implicated in this case. As the manager of the Twin Cinema, Jasper's only movie theater, Berry was a familiar face to almost everyone in town. He simply did not fit the profile of a racist killer, a fact that might convince a jury to be a bit more lenient. Berry, the prosecution team concluded, would be a tough death penalty sell. In Gray's experience, when a case involved multiple trials, if the first defendant received a lesser sentence, it invariably became much more difficult to obtain harsher judgments against the subsequent defendants.

Bill King, on the other hand, was the obvious choice. He was a member of the Confederate Knights of America, a white supremacist prison gang. Investigators had found documents in his apartment expressing "racial attitudes," books about the Ku Klux Klan, and membership forms, in King's handwriting, for potential CKA conscripts. King was also covered with prison tattoos, which, if Gray could find a way of entering them into evidence, formed an unsettling portrait due to their satanic, Klan, and Aryan content. It would not be difficult to depict Bill King (or Russell Brewer, for that matter) as a frightening monster, someone that jurors might readily want off the streets—permanently. "We wanted the death penalty," Gray would later reflect in reference to the prosecution's strategy. "So we made a conscious decision to gamble with our weakest physical evidence case but our best death penalty case. We just loaded up and took the shot."

ONE OF THE MOST DIFFICULT CHALLENGES facing the prosecution team now lay in selecting a jury in Jasper County. Gray's intuition told him that the jury he wanted for this case should be a departure from the typical capital murder case. In the latter, a prosecutor tended to dismiss schoolteachers, preachers, and more-educated individuals from the pool of potential jurors. People with these profiles tended to be bleeding hearts or inclined toward forgiving the trespasses of the accused. In either case, such views readily translated into a reluctance to vote for the ultimate penalty. However, given the overriding racial themes in this murder, Gray believed that such individuals might actually be more receptive to the death penalty.

Like a trained sociologist, Gray described the profile of the ideal juror who might be open to the prosecution's case against Bill King. "You're looking for jurors that our system of government and our system of justice have worked for. That's your best juror. Someone with an education, married, stable family, someone with a job who's been employed a long time, who has a house, a future, and who's pleased with our system." On the other hand, the county was full of people who might bring a very different set of attitudes to the jury box. "We have such high unemployment, no manufacturing jobs, there are economically disadvantaged parts of the county, they have more racism, they live in trailer houses, have cars on blocks in their front yards, high levels of unemployment. It's much tougher to handle a case like this [with this kind of a juror]. They feel more animosity toward minorities. It's a classic pattern."

A significant concern for Gray and his team was the possibility of impaneling a jury member who might be a Klan sympathizer. It would only take one such person to potentially tie a jury up in knots, resulting in a hung jury or worse. Ferreting out such individuals was no easy task. Gray brought on a man named Aubrey Cole, a retired Jasper County sheriff, to serve as his jury consultant. Although Cole was up in his years, he was still a formidable presence. He was a big man who had worked most of his life welding and farming, work that accounted for his strong hands and powerful shoulders. Some suggested he resembled a scarecrow. "Not pretty," was the way Gray summed up Cole's appearance, "but he's the smartest uneducated man I've ever met in my life." The respect that many in the community had for Cole was reflected in the fact that the Jasper County jail was named after him.

Gray had worked with Aubrey Cole for eighteen years before Cole's retirement, when Billy Rowles had taken over the reins at the sheriff's office. Apart from Cole's experience, in one way or another his years as sheriff had brought him into contact with nearly every person in the county. He also had excellent people instincts. With Cole at his side, Gray felt much more comfortable as he started reviewing the lists of potential jurors for Bill King's trial.

Jasper County had originally been populated by Civil War renegades and other individuals who preferred or needed the anonymity afforded by the region's inaccessibility. It was also an area where cotton plantations and the legacy of slavery had played a significant role in the region's economy and social relations. This history, coupled with the notable poverty that gripped most of the county, was fertile ground for racist attitudes. Throughout the county there were small communities where whites' racial attitudes toward blacks ranged from the enlightened to the regressive. Communities with names like Evadale, Buna, Kirbyville, and Roganville had established reputations on one end of the spectrum of racial tolerance or the other. In addition, there were countless smaller, nameless clusters where families had lived in little enclaves for generations. The pool of potential jurors for Bill King's trial would be drawn from this universe of possibilities. While the town of Jasper was not nearly as racist as many outsiders assumed, anything was possible when drawing randomly from Jasper County at large. Gray and Cole had their work cut out for them. The fact that each had grown up in Jasper County and their families had been in the area for generations was a distinct advantage.

Gray realized what was at stake in the jury selection process. "There are pockets of racism in East Texas that go back for generations," Gray told me. "Aubrey and I knew the old families and those pockets. Probably the single most important thing that we did in these trials was the jury selection—trying to see a juror's family, their background, what part of the county they

lived in, trying to see if they came from one of those old families that hadn't
grown out of the 1920s brand of racism. That was critical, absolutely critical
to being able to get a jury verdict." Putting together the facts of the case,
presenting the evidence, and trying the case would be fairly routine for an
experienced prosecutor. What was not routine—and what was essential—
was to avoid getting a ringer on the jury. "You really don't think you'd have
to duck and dodge that in the year 1999, when we tried these cases," Gray
would later reflect, "but you do. It's a lot better than it used to be. In 1930
you couldn't have picked a jury."

Gray and Cole worked the jury pool hard. "Over and over in the jury selection process we ran into people who had some racial feelings, and we had
to root them out," Gray said. "That was critical. It was also nerve-racking."
Operating largely on gut feeling and the kind of finely honed instinct that
comes from intimate familiarity, Gray and Cole surmised who was likely to
have racist feelings and who was likely to have less tolerant views for what had
happened that night out on Huff Creek Road. The most difficult challenges
were prospective female jurors. If they were married and had adopted their
husband's surnames, it was difficult to discover their links to those families
with attitudes that might well produce an obstructionist juror. In addition,
the media was monitoring the jury selection process very closely, many assuming that an all-white Jasper jury would never convict King and the others. In the end, the jury impaneled for King's trial had a single African American member, far fewer than most outside observers would have liked.

THE TRIALS OF BILL KING, Russell Brewer, and Shawn Berry became
something of an obsession for Gray, and he was driven by more than the wish
to seek justice. Horrendous as Byrd's murder was, the prosecution of these
three men represented an opportunity to redress a sense of guilt and silent
complicity that many whites in East Texas felt about the history of race relations in their region. Gray liked to repeat a story that he had heard his father
tell countless times about a lynching in neighboring Newton County that
had taken place in 1933. At the time, East Texas was dotted with illegal barrel-
houses, where men came to drink and gamble. Occasionally there were also
prostitutes at these establishments. At this particular Newton County barrel-
house, a white prostitute was reportedly found passed out on a bed next to a

black man. "There were no indications that they'd had sex, and both of them had their clothes on," Gray noted. However, the mere possibility was enough to incite the white men who discovered them. The black man was attacked, tied behind a truck, and then dragged around the Newton County courthouse square.

"My daddy told me that story a hundred times," Gray would later remark. Gray's father was superintendent of schools in Newton at the time. "Everyone knew who had done it," Gray said. The culprits' truck was recognized by countless witnesses, but none came forward and local law enforcement officials were obviously not inclined to investigate the lynching. According to Gray, it embarrassed his father deeply that people in his county, people who were his friends, had done this. "And they weren't necessarily white trash," Gray said. "They were 'decent people.'" Gray believed that his father was haunted by the incident for the rest of his life.

A decade later, in 1943, Billy Rowles's father was working at the Beaumont shipyards. The war effort had brought an infusion of African Americans into the ranks of shipyard workers, resulting in a decidedly uneasy coexistence among the white and black men who were working side by side for the first time. A rumor circulated that a black man had raped a white woman in town and the bosses reportedly shut down the shipyard, sending the white workers out to retaliate. Numerous African Americans were hanged during the ensuing riots. "Billy's daddy didn't leave the shipyard, he stayed there," Gray recounted. "In that day, the guy who didn't go with the mob ran the risk of being ostracized. Billy's daddy and his mama told him this story a hundred times, and they had that same feeling of embarrassment, that people he worked with and people he knew had gone out and killed blacks."

Aubrey Cole, the retired Jasper County sheriff, told a similar story. Cole's father was once driving a mule team through the town of Bronzon in nearby Sabine County, just north of Jasper, when he encountered a mob that had apprehended several black men and was in the process of hanging them. Like Gray's and Rowles's fathers, Cole's father had recounted the story to his son countless times. Gray remarked, "That story haunted Aubrey's daddy all his life, the sight of these black guys being hung. And he had not interfered. He had not participated at all, but he had not interfered; he had not stopped them."

Gray kept a copy of an old postcard in his desk with a photograph of a lynching that had taken place in East Texas in 1908. On the back of the post-card was a racist poem by T. DeBenning titled "The Dogwood Tree," which read, in part, "This is only the branch of a Dogwood tree; An emblem of White Supremacy." The postcard had circulated throughout East Texas at the time.

"Those were vicious, violent days," Gray recalled. "The use of force and intimidation was almost unbelievable to those of us living today." Gray knew of a few other lynchings that he had heard about firsthand over the years. "Horrible cases," he said. There were many unconfirmed stories and rumors about people and incidents in Jasper County and neighboring counties, es-pecially in the first half of the twentieth century. Within the black commu-nity there were also numerous stories of people who had simply gone miss-ing. Everyone suspected that these individuals had been killed, but their bodies had never been found. It was the kind of thing that never appeared in the newspapers, and there were no records of such incidents, but they were common knowledge. At the time, no African American with any sense would have reported a missing person to the local authorities, much less complain about the known lynchings, because of the dangers inherent in such a step. But the stories had been passed down from generation to generation within both the white and black communities. "My daddy told me. Billy's daddy told him. Aubrey's daddy told him," Gray said.

"It's ironic," Gray reflected, "that in 1998 I'm the DA and Billy's the sher-iff, and Aubrey Cole is working as my jury consultant. All three of us had fa-thers who were very close to one of these old incidents of racial violence and were haunted by it. They did not participate, but neither did they take an ac-tive role in stopping it. Nor did they go to the law or anything else. But they passed that down to us, what had happened in the old days," Gray said heavily. "It created more of a passion, a drive for us here in Jasper in 1998. We didn't want to be haunted the rest of our lives by what had happened here."

WITH THAT KIND OF DRIVE fueling his every waking moment, Gray fo-cused his sights on Bill King. While an army of FBI and local law enforce-ment officers were working up evidence and interviewing anyone who might have something useful to contribute to the prosecution of the case against King, Gray spent countless hours conferring with his prosecution team on what trial strategy might be most effective. FBI agents were also working the case nationwide, interviewing everyone with whom King had been associated while imprisoned at the Beto I Unit, where King had joined the Confederate Knights of America.

The results of these interviews sat in neat, labeled folders in Gray's office, along with such varied and potentially random documents as King's correspondence with various girlfriends over the years. There were countless documents, histories, and photographs, all of which gradually formed an enormous collection of evidence or potential evidence, stacked in piles on every surface in Gray's office. Somewhere in all of those files and folders was Gray's case against King and the others. Like a sculptor's block of granite, they lay there awaiting the prosecutor's creative imagination to give them contour and definition. It all had to be fashioned somehow, orchestrated, conceived.

The Jasper district attorney spent hour after hour reading and rereading material. There was so much powerful and dramatic evidence to draw from, but how to bring it to life? The tattoos covering King's and Brewer's bodies, for example, were not admissible as evidence unless they could be used to establish motive and intent. Otherwise, telling as they might be, they were constitutionally protected as acts of free speech. Much of the Klan and white supremacist literature found in King's apartment was similarly protected. The fact that King was an avowed racist was not, on the face of it, admissible as proof that he had participated in the murder of James Byrd Jr. This was Gray's most significant challenge, one he confronted virtually every waking minute as he prepared for what would be the biggest trial of his career: How to translate those abhorrent beliefs into useful devices that showed intent and motive?

Then one afternoon Gray suddenly had the insight that he had been waiting for. On the floor across from his desk that day were arrayed the jail photographs of King, Brewer, and Berry. The three men's tattoos had been photographed from every possible angle, and some of them had been blown up so that their details were clearly visible. Berry's tattoos were unremarkable, the kind of stuff that half the kids in Jasper were sporting on their bodies. There were only four of them, and none with racial content. King's and Brewer's tattoos were another matter altogether. Gray knew, intuitively, that the tattoos were important evidence. To show these to any jury would be exceedingly powerful. Just sitting there looking at them, as he had countless times already, still stirred deep feelings in Gray. There was something prim-

itive, deeply unsettling, and repulsive about these tattoos. Gray believed that they represented one of his most effective tools in helping the jury conceive of the unthinkable. He felt certain that to see these tattoos would be to know that these men were capable of committing an act as gruesome and haunting as the torture to which Byrd had been subjected.

As he sat there, staring at the assembled photographs, Gray suddenly re-membered one of the thousands of pages of materials that the FBI had for-warded to him: the cover of a photo album that Bill King had signed while serving time at the Beto I Unit. Inmates tended to pass these albums around as they neared release, much like graduating high school seniors do. The owner of the album, an ex-con named Matthew Hoover, now lived in Mis-souri, which is where the FBI had tracked him down and interviewed him. The FBI had also taken possession of the photo album, in which King had invited Hoover to come to Jasper to attend a "wood gathering" and "bash-ing" on the Fourth of July, 1998. Bashing, Hoover had volunteered in his in-terview, was a reference to an assault on one or more African Americans. It took Gray almost half a day to locate the FBI report and a copy of Hoover's photo album. When he finally had Hoover's materials in front of him, the DA believed he'd found the key that would allow the prosecution to show how King's tattoos, racist writings, and ideology formed part of a specific conspiracy to commit violence against blacks. It was the link that Gray had been looking for; he felt he had finally solved the puzzle.

Prison Kites

THE AUBREY COLE LAW ENFORCEMENT Center, where Bill King, Russell Brewer, and Shawn Berry were held following their arrests on the night of June 7, 1998, is situated just a few blocks from the house where Bill King had grown up. The building, a one-story cement-and-brick structure with a parking lot in front, serves as the administrative headquarters for the sheriff's operations in the county while also housing the county jail. Chain-link fences topped with concertina wire circle open areas on either side of the building where prisoners take their outdoor recreation. The center is festooned with the state and national flags, not to mention numerous antennae protruding from its roof.

On a typical day it is not unusual to see a number of "trustees" in black-and-white-striped prison garb, some of them sweeping and mopping, but mostly smoking cigarettes while sitting out on the benches at the entrance to the Aubrey Cole Center. There is an unlikely casualness about the prisoners as they walk in and out, and there is nothing to indicate that they are monitored in any way. Immediately inside the building is a modest waiting area with plastic chairs along the wall for the inmates' visitors and for individuals waiting to give statements or to be questioned by an officer.

Beyond the waiting area is the jail itself. An imposing steel door marks the entry into the U-shaped cellblock where everything is painted a light coffee-cream color. There is a distinctly foreboding feeling inside the jail, which has two long hallways, each lined with individual and multi-person cells. The lighting in the cellblock is dim, as if the fluorescent lights lack the requisite wattage to illuminate the area properly, creating a dull and heavy atmosphere that exudes a sense of desperation. Though clean, the entire cellblock feels sticky, gloomy, and dank.

Bill King occupied the individual cell nearest the entrance to the cellblock. It was also closest to the administrative office, where officers sat and drank coffee, read newspapers, and made phone calls when not otherwise occupied. Presumably, this meant that King could be monitored more easily. Russell Brewer and Shawn Berry were kept in individual cells along the second hallway that forms the other leg of the U. They were separated by the length of the hall, an attempt to keep communication between them to a minimum. Despite the fact that the cells were separated by solid walls and steel doors, inmates could still shout from cell to cell.

In the weeks following his arrest, King languished in his small, cramped cell, waiting for the wheels of the criminal justice system to turn. His cell contained a bed, parallel to the hallway, and at its foot was a metal shelf where a prisoner could keep a radio or a small television, although the electrical power in this particular cell was out during the initial weeks of his incarceration. Next to the shelf were a stainless steel washbasin and toilet. There was barely enough space to stand between the bed and the cell door, with its thick, milky plastic window, food-tray slot, and intercom. The cell was inadequately lit by a recessed fixture in the ceiling whose light bulb was on twenty-four hours a day, requiring inmates to cover their heads with a blanket if they wished to sleep. With its dim lighting, its stainless steel appointments, and its cramped quarters, a pall hung over the cell.

Having spent only fourteen months out of jail since his first arrest at the age of seventeen, King, now twenty-three, had long ago become acclimated to the aesthetics of prison life and thus did not find his present circumstances particularly oppressive. On the contrary, he was on familiar ground, home territory. Not long after his arrest, King had noticed a white trustee at the jail who appeared to be a fellow gang member. Like King and Brewer, Spiderman, as he was nicknamed, was covered with tattoos, the telltale signs of a "peckerwood," or "wood." Spiderman (the nickname came from the prominent spiderweb tattooed on his bald head) had obviously served hard time. Prison trustees' duties at the jail primarily revolved around delivering and retrieving meal trays and endlessly sweeping and mopping the floors. Standing at the milky window to his cell, King saw Spiderman cross his line of sight all day long, and King and Spiderman often exchanged small talk when the latter delivered or retrieved King's meal trays.

King and Brewer had been entirely uncooperative with law enforcement and had refused to answer questions during their interviews. However, through their court-appointed attorneys, they had learned the details of Shawn Berry's statements to local law enforcement and the FBI. Because King and Brewer were at opposite ends of the jail, they had no contact with one another and limited contact with prisoners in the cells adjoining theirs. Information traveled by word of mouth through the jail, but this form of communication was completely useless for exchanging anything of substance about their cases, which was essential if the two men were going to align their stories. One obvious mechanism for achieving this aim involved mutual visitors. A second involved correspondence, since prisoners are permitted to send and to receive mail. While such correspondence was subject to inspection and monitoring by prison authorities, it was possible to circumvent such surveillance to some extent by writing in code and allusion.

None of these mechanisms, however, could substitute for direct communication between King and Brewer. Perhaps born out of the desperate necessity of his situation, King gradually became convinced that he could confide in Spiderman. In exchange for a few considerations, such as cigarettes, chocolates, and other conventional prison barter, he thought Spiderman might help him communicate with Brewer. Spiderman was apparently a willing collaborator, and less than two weeks after their arrest, King and Brewer started using Spiderman as a go-between. King handed his newfound courier a small tin of Skoal chewing tobacco containing a neatly folded note that had been written on plain lined paper. In what would be the beginning a series of important written exchanges between the two men, Spiderman delivered the note, called a "kite" in prison lingo, to Brewer. Unbeknownst to either prisoner, however, Spiderman was first passing the kites to one of the jail administrators, who carefully unfolded the kites, photocopied them, and then returned them to the Skoal tin so that Spiderman could take them on to the intended recipient. Thus, for several weeks, jail personnel were able to intercept and closely monitor the communications between King and Brewer.

King sent his first kite to Brewer on June 18, 1998, a mere eleven days after their arrest. He included a note to Spiderman as well, thanking him for the "considerations" he had received thus far. The note also explained how to contact Kylie Greeney, who was to put together a small package containing three or four packs of cigarettes, several lighters, and the "fuck books" that were next to King's bed at the apartment. Spiderman was to instruct Greeney on when and where to drop off the contraband to avoid detection. King told Spiderman that if the arrangement worked, he'd have her make similar drops twice a week. Greeney was apparently an ambivalent "mule." While King in his kites would make repeated reference to his efforts to get Kylie to deliver these "care packages" to Spiderman, it is not clear that she did so consistently, if at all.

King's first kite to Brewer asked what Brewer had learned from his attorney about Berry's statement to the authorities. King also sketched in "the truth" about what had happened that night—namely, that after picking up "Toby Boy,"[1] Berry had taken King and Brewer back to the apartment before heading off on his own with Byrd, implying that Berry had killed Byrd on his own. King also outlined a possible motive: that Berry had wanted to join the Confederate Knights of America so that he could have a "patch," like the one that King and Brewer sported, and that since Berry was on steroids and had a terrible temper, he was "more than capable" of committing this crime to "earn our respect." King then provided a timeline of events, beginning with the trio's search for a party after leaving the Timbers Apartments earlier that night and ending with King and Brewer being dropped off at the apartment before Berry and Byrd headed off. The note closed with "Aryan Love, Honor & Respect" and was signed "PoZZum" with "Death Before Dishonor!!!" as a postscript.[2]

Suggesting that Berry had acted alone was an implausible scenario. For one thing, even if a believable motive could be fashioned, Berry had broken his right hand while playing Ping-Pong (having smashed it against a wall in a cramped room), and the cast had been removed just a couple of days before the murder because the break was not healing properly. However, King and Brewer had to come up with some sort of an account of what had transpired on the night of June 6 and early-morning hours of June 7 if they were to have any chance of a successful defense.

"Aryan greetings my long lost 'faithful' little fat bro! Man I almost shit on myself to when I saw the police report," is the way Brewer opened his response to King.[3] Brewer's kites, like King's, have to be read with an eye toward the circumstances in which they were written—two men whose chances of being exonerated of murder charges depended, in part, on their ability to coordinate their stories. The kites contain details about the crime, about their activities the day preceding it, and about their fraternal feelings for one another. However, given their context and purpose, it is evident that the kites contain a mixture of facts and "facts." The latter were conveyed as if with a wink, or like a stage whisper delivered to a fellow actor en scene. Brewer's kite continued:

> That back stabbin trader did sign saying that me & you did assault & you chained & druged his friend while he was forced to watch after King stated "Shut up niger lover or you'll be next!" HA! Bro Shawn is one scared piece of lying shit. I also seen & read with my eyes statements from evidence found on or around crime scene, broken and unbroken beer bottels, "Kiss" CD holder, cigerretes, Zippo lighter with a triangle symbol on top and possum on the bottom, tools with the word "Berry" ingraved on them, shoes, wallet containing victims I.D., I believe that was it bro. Kyle [Kylie Greeney] stated on some form that when shown the Zippo she stated "That's Bills that's what they called him in prison." The chick [Keisha Atkins] that came over Sat. night stated she was over at Bill's with Bill until 1:45–2:00 when she left *after* meeting Shawn and a guy named Russell she had never seen. Kyle also stated she came over Sun. around 1 or 2 (I can't remember which one) & seen Russell & Shawn over at Bill's all 3 asleep. *Some* lawabiden citazen lit there nuts while and stated they seen 2 possible 3 white males in a blue or gray stepside truck with (whatever the victims name was) in the back of the truck at a certain time (I think it was between 2–3 (I think)). The statement went on sayin that eye witness was later called down to

identify Shawn's truck & claimed that it was dark but it did resemble
the one seen Sat late night. You got me bro. Comon "say you swear"!
I ask my lawyer how any one could at 2:30–2:45 in the dark mornin
see a truck & remember how many occupied the front — the color of
them — the color of the vehicle and on top of that see a toby & rec-
ognize him by name in pitch black! My lawyer said maybe there
street lights in the area. I also seen where Shawn had told that you &
me went to Tom's [Tommy Faulk] The Feds I guess on 2–3 days after
bein here called me in that little room where on the table sat a white
plastic bag. The crack head lookin guy said open the bag & see if you
reconize that. It was a chain (simular to the one we used to clear the
land at Wildwood with) with pine needels all inside the bag too. I
told them Yea — it's a chain so. He got a little loose & said it's the
chain you and Bill took out to Tommy Folks to hide after yall used
it the night before. I told them what ever man just take me back to
my cell. I aint got shit to say. So they did. They took leg hairs —
chest — arm, pubic, and head hairs from me. Even drew blood from
me bro! . . . I don't touch nothin in his sack so [they] can't blame that
one on noone.

Brewer then proceeded to detail for King what he had told his lawyer in reference to their activities on the day preceding the murder as well as on the night of the murder. It is a long passage describing their adventures, including playing horseshoes, riding dirt bikes, and going to the river "to chase girls," and organizing a barbecue to cook the stolen steaks. The account of the barbecue offers a window into their social life as well as the men's mercurial, rather adolescent petulance. Brewer describes a contretemps when an African American shows up:

Well then this black man showes up & now I'm ready to go. So me
& Bill both told Tommy "Fuck this man, you did us——[illegible]
be back later to eat when the foods ready. We're goin back home." So
we left for about 3 hours to go take a power nap. Lewis [Louis Berry]
called wakin me up to say that he was getting "The" drums & for
me and Bill to come on back out there to party. After Bill got up we
went back out to this same house we just left in Kyle's car. No one

was there no beer no food no nothin—except 2–3 pieces of meat in the frige wraped in foil. . . . We me & Bill left & went to where Lewis was over at some Blacks house playin over there. Well the whole damn party was moved over there. I didn't know about Bill but I wasn't goin in there to party with some Black or blacks with my tats showin. Hell one of those blacks sees some Bolts [Aryan light-ning bolts] or other racial tat on me I probably wouldn't make it out alive. Bill either. I was just goin to sit in the car until it was over. Well when we pulled up Lewis girl (corny)[4] was outside & told me & Bill to get out & come in. Simutansuly we both said Hell No! . . . Lewis stated that there was food & drinks over at Tobys well Lewis knows me & Bill don't associate with blacks that often. After a few words were passed Bill told Lewis that he was goin to use the house tonight.

Brewer now attempted to account for the fact that at the time of his arrest his toe was broken or badly bruised. After they left King's apartment that night, they went in search of a party out in the country to which some girls had invited Brewer.

Keep in mind Shawn was buzzin pretty good at the Apt. Now he's slamin 1 after the other. We get out there & cant find the house. So Shawn lost the cooler we went back to get it & it was broke on the road. Beers everywhere. I had a few beers, I was stumbling through the grass with my sore ankel from jumpin over balcony cause "no key for door" & kicked I thought was a beer but since it was dark & it didn't move I soppose it was a stump or fence post that been there.[5] I don't know what I kicked it was just sure solid! Then I joined Bill & Shawn pickin up beer & we left back home. (Now Bro that's where you need to say you were laughin at me & callin me a pussy for cryin over my toe then when I injured it. You know the truth will set you free). On the way home Shawn was upset I guess because he couldn't find the house & started hitten stop signs & mailboxes. (Ha! The same damn thing you said!) I started getting scared because I knew we was either goin to jail or end up dead the way Shawn was actin drunk. I told him "Shawn" just to take my ass home that I'm on parole & I don't need no B.S. like this. & he did after we tried & callin the girls back 1 more time.

Brewer went on to describe a scene that he said took place the next day. While back at the apartment, he and King had supposedly become aware that it was Berry who had committed the brutal murder, an insight that "dawned" on them once they realized Berry's "motive," a desire to prove himself so that he could join the CKA. Brewer feigned shock upon learning of the murder. (A year later, however, when he took the stand at his own trial, Brewer told a very different story of what transpired that night, a story that placed Bill King at the center of the crime while minimizing his own involvement.)

After sittin there (me & you alone) stunned that's when you informed *me* (on my patch Bro) that Shawn had been asking a lot lately about getting the same tat as we had.[6] Bill told him he was in no position to do that. I knew right then that Shawn knew that I (one of Bill's Bro) was getting close to leaving goin back home & wanted to "join" so bad & was fucked up enough & mad enough the night before I knew it had to have something to do with it.

At this juncture in the kite Brewer drew a thick perpendicular line to demarcate the prior narrative from the kite's concluding comments. Here Brewer describes his experience of having his tattoos extensively photographed and his awareness of the district attorney's interest in their racist content. He also discusses the prosecution's interest in establishing kidnapping as a component to the murder, which would make this a capital murder case punishable by death.

Now Bro this was like I said my story. I told my lawyer. He only jotted a few notes down. I have not talked to any detective cop FBI or sign shit. That's all *any one* "mostly my lawyer" knows. On my patch. Now on your patch you run me down whats up on your end. O, my lawyer did read me some reprt statin the head & right arm was found in the front yard of ? house! Also \ $ (the word they use for blood) was found on the under pinnen of Shawn truck also in *or* on the rear leave of axle! I'm sure your lawyer read you that by now?

Today they took more photos of me nude up against the wall for at
least 20–30 min. My lawyer was present with about 4 city slickers.
Yea Bro the fucker started zero-ing in on ol tat after a few seconds
he raised up from his tri-pot & said are they—are they all the way
around that?? Bro I couldn't help but laugh & held it so they could
view all directions!! If I get the death sen. It was damn sure worth it
Bro just to see these city folks face when they see Your Name![7] Any
way Bro, my lawyer said these folks are tryin to see if any of my tats
can be linked to any racial organization. He also informed earlier in
the——[illegible] one thing. When its racially motivated any time
the feds FBI come in & can be pre moved to capital murder "death"
just for race words. Also he was sayin that "they" are lookin at kid-
nappen to—to put on us. There's a fine line in between all of it that
considers life sent. Or death sent. He hasn't come out & told me yet
but he dam sure it doesn't look good. Bro, you know whats goin to
get us, me & you? Prison records & tats on top of believs. The public
has got there little pantys in a uproar & I do mean uproar & *you*
know just like *I* know, they "the public" will be out to get what they
thinks fair. I've already came to REALITY Bro. I'm history. Fuck it,
John.[8] You can bet your white ass the world or USA knows that some
crazy down woods have gotton all the way loose! As much as been
goin on as far as publicity I know years from now talk will still be in
the air (say you swear!). . . . Listen Bro. Lets not take our one & only
mule [Spiderman] for granted or run the high risk of getting roped
(caught). Unless its "absolutly" nesasary lets stay off the internet. I
do want to hear from you soon maybe tomoro or this weekend, after
that only when something majors shakin. YEA! Bro the trustee
[Spiderman] damn sure been getting all the way loose on this end
☺. I drew him up a ᚻ on a piece of paper & wrote a thank you
note of theres still a few good woods out there. I told he would be
remember even after our "faithfull system" lies me to rest. & so on it
was bad ass how I made it like a 8 X 10. Signed autograph from a
accused MAD MAN dated & all. Hopefully he will keep it & it
may be worth something as the world progress! MAKE HIM ONE
TOO BRO Just be carefull not to get out of line in case he gets his
house shook down.[9] Basically I just thanked him for his small but

wonderfull blessins. Alright Bro I wut up be cool & like always Flush
this now—later
BRO'S FOREVER
LIKE IT WAS
INTENDED TO BE
Lawrence Russell Brewer

In the margin, next to his signature, Brewer drew the same triangular Klan symbol that was on King's cigarette lighter and wrote: "LIVED BY IT, AND WILL REST BY IT."

Through their attorneys and the prison grapevine, both King and Brewer were aware that neither had given statements to the authorities concerning the events of June 7. Brewer's prison kite was, in part, an attempt to coordinate the two men's stories. The kite is striking in its indifference to Byrd's fate (whose name Brewer doesn't even appear to remember). It also reveals a man who is neither anxious nor repentant. Brewer seems absolutely disdainful of the world's response to the brutal murder. Far from humble, he is almost gloating, covering himself with the glow of celebrity. He is clearly elated as he describes giving Spiderman his autograph which, he conjectures, "may be worth something" when the world finally realizes Brewer's and King's proper place in some imagined pantheon of heroes who have given their lives to the cause of racial purity.

King's response to Brewer's kite, delivered two days later, was short, reflecting the same caution regarding the security of their communications. King assured Brewer that he was attempting to obtain, via Greeney, some money for them, as well as some books, complaining that the romance novels and westerns available at the jail were "killin'" him. More to the point, however, was King's concern that the media interest in the murder meant that it was unlikely that they would get a "fair chance." King closed this kite by echoing Brewer's view of their circumstance as one in which they were noble martyrs for a cause: "We'll die knowing where our hearts were Bro," King said to Brewer. "At least we'll go out like Vikings of this day and age and be remember with the names of Robert Jay Mathews and David Lane."

The reference to Mathews and Lane underscored the extent to which Bill King was an adherent of the white supremacist movement. Robert Jay Mathews, who died in 1984 when his house burned to the ground while surrounded by federal agents, is considered a martyr by the movement. He wrote numerous treatises on what he perceived as the precarious status of the white race in America ("Has the cancer of racial masochism consumed our very will to exist?" he once asked). He founded the Order, a right-wing extremist group whose activities have included the murder of Denver radio talk-show host Alan Berg in the 1980s.

Like Mathews, David Lane is an icon of the white supremacist movement and a vocal member of the Order. Lane coined the slogan "We must secure the existence of our people and a future for white children," referred to as "14 words." The number 14 is also a reference to Lane's "14 codes," his rules for living one's life. A number of these planks also invoked a darker theme of racial supremacy ("Love, protect, reproduce and advance your folk. As natural instinct prohibits miscegenation and self-destruction," "Live in harmony with nature and the fold and compromise not with evil. As racial survival is your perpetual struggle"). It is in reference to these codes that "14" appeared repeatedly at the end of King's and Brewer's kites.

Spiderman delivered King's kite and retrieved the following kite from Brewer for delivery to King. It is evident that Brewer was concerned about the security of these communications, writing "AFTER SUPPER TIME *SEALED* FRIDAY NIGHT IS WHEN I SHOT THIS OFF" across the top of the page. Brewer made an astonishing offer to Bill King in this kite, telling King that he was willing to take the fall for the murder in order to save King's life. It is likely that the offer stemmed from their growing, shared pessimism about avoiding conviction. Brewer's offer also illustrated the depth of his attachment and loyalty to King. Despite being ten years older, Brewer was under the sway of a powerful allegiance, and he clearly looked up to King. Their gang affiliation obviously defined their lives, their very identities. Brewer's willingness to sacrifice himself came out of that mind-set.

> Greetings once more Bro! You know I've been thinking a lot lately and to make a long story short—on my skin & patch Bro the only safe & sure way to win this Hoe, is for 1 of us to go down with the perpatrayer. On my "scales" you're the youngest (plus a big plus) 90% chance of a youngster headin to earth [eventually being freed from prison]. Theres a little more to it, but that's the main course cut short Bro. I'm not goin to tell or sign any thing with lawyer until I

shot you another kite first—so don't panic. *I need* to know *where* me
& Shawn dropped you off the night me & him went grocery shoppin.
   Also Bro send shit important in sealed envolope. That way we
can see foul play if any. Don't wory about nothin Bro. That's what
true Bros are there for—Remember always remember "Organized
in prison 'only' to be brought to the world." . . . I'm not pissed or
holdin nothin over your head Bro—This is just history in the
makin—88![10] Lets let the games begin ! ! I'll jump back on the enter-
net sometime this weekend.
With much pride
Respect & courage
For the game . . .
Love you Bro—Russ

The phrase "Organized *in prison* 'only' to be brought to the world" would
be seized upon by the prosecution to bolster their argument during the subsequent trials that King and Brewer were intent on forming a chapter of the
Confederate Klan of American outside of prison. In addition, Brewer was
clearly feeling what might best be described as a delusion of grandeur, seeing himself as a warrior for a noble cause. His life might be lost, he seemed
to be saying, but that was a small price to pay because "This is just history in
the makin." Brewer also appeared to be forgiving of King, presumably because he was responsible for the predicament in which they now found themselves, when he reassured King that "I'm not pissed or holdin nothin over
your head."
   Brewer wrote a second kite the next day, which Spiderman delivered to
King along with the previous kite. In his second kite, Brewer's account of his
most recent conversation with his attorney shed light on the extent to which
Jasper law enforcement and the FBI were testing the theory of a possible link
between the CKA and such right-wing extremists as Timothy McVey (convicted of the 1995 Oklahoma City bombing). When Brewer was asked if he
knew McVey, he replied snidely, "Not on a personal basis." Brewer also acknowledged reading *The Turner Diaries,* the well-known white supremacist
book written, under the pseudonym Andrew Macdonald, by William Pierce,
leader of the neo-Nazi group National Alliance. The fictional account describes a racist, anti-Semitic underground that gains power in the United

States through a series of violent acts that precipitate a race war. Pierce was an assistant to George Lincoln Rockwell, founder and head of the American Nazi Party. In the 1980s he was the mentor of Robert Mathews, who purportedly used *The Turner Diaries* as a blueprint for the Order's activities.

Finally, Brewer closed out this lengthy, rambling kite with a postscript in which he reiterated his willingness to take the fall for "everything" in an attempt to save King. "Let me know Bro," Brewer said to King. "I'll go out for a cause on everything. I love King. All you got to do is say Jump. I'm ready to be rembed in the U.S. of A."

Brewer and King both repeatedly invoked the solidarity of their Confederate Knights of America identities in these kites ("Much Aryan love, Honor, and Respect Bro") as well as a more intimate relationship: "Daddy loves you," King wrote to Brewer, while Brewer, in one of his kites, had referred to King as "my long lost 'faithful' little fat bro." However, there were notable differences between the kites as well. King appeared more confident and adopted a more knowledgeable posture regarding their legal strategies. He was partly cheerleader to Brewer ("We're still sittin' good"), partly a source of reassurance ("They just don't have much evidence at all to use against us Bro."). In addition, King appeared to have control of the resources that might give Brewer some comfort. King was corresponding directly with mutual friends back at Planet Beto and sent letters from friends on to Brewer, and it was King who sent Brewer care packages. King also arranged for Greeney and another friend to visit Brewer.

While both King and Brewer were high school dropouts, it is readily apparent that King was considerably brighter and more articulate than Brewer. For the most part, King wrote in clear, properly punctuated sentences using a more ample vocabulary with words that were spelled correctly. Brewer, by comparison, was hard pressed to formulate a coherent sentence, and his spelling was like that of the average third or fourth grader learning phonics.

Perhaps one of the most striking elements of these exchanges is that nowhere in them is there even a faint thread of remorse. In fact, James Byrd is rarely mentioned by name. Instead, he is simply referred to as "toby" or "toby boy." King and Brewer are clearly indifferent to the powerful reactions within Jasper and the rest of the world for what has been done to James Byrd Jr. If anything, the widespread outrage is simply denigrated ("The public has got there little pantys in a uproar").

King had settled into a familiar modus operandi: in addition to his attorney, he had regular visits with his girlfriend, Kylie, his father and his sister, and others. He also kept up an active correspondence with fellow inmates from Beto as well as former girlfriends and friends. However, King's forte was analyzing all facets of his legal situation. He asked his attorney to get him copies of the jail's rules and regulations, which he studied closely to insure that his full rights as a prisoner were respected; he knew how to use such documents to good effect against prison authorities. King also reviewed copies of Berry's statements and other legal papers, searching for inconsistencies or any opening that might be exploited for their legal case. It was precisely his penchant for this kind of tenacious and incisive analysis that made King a thorn in the side of prison authorities in Jasper and, later, on death row. And it was this knack for legal detail that would later make King's death row attorney remark that he would have made a formidable lawyer.

On Friday, July 3, King wrote Brewer a kite containing a response to an extended *People* magazine story that had appeared in the June 29, 1998, issue. The story covered James Byrd's funeral and Jasper's response to the murder. In addition to interviews and photographs of the Byrd family, the story included quotations from Kylie, Shawn Berry's brother, Louis, and others. The story confirmed what King had been saying to Brewer all along: that one of the biggest problems they faced was the media.

> RuZZ 分 just got your lil ol kite out of the Skoal can bro. As you
> know by now. I shot you copies of a couple of those news articles
> (please return) And I know what People Magazine said that Kylie
> said this or that,[11] and they lied and misquoted her bro. Her and her
> mom are trying to sue them now for the shit. As for the giddy up
> cowboy,[12] yo! Me and Shawn were getting ready to go ride a cow. A
> cow girl that is. . . . Did you read that one where Louis was getting
> loose on a wood?[13] Man, that's some ho-ass shit bro! After I put
> myself out to help that ho when he had no place to live nor job. I
> just don't think some of these ho's would make it in Planet Beto bro.
> I do know that wherever Shawn goes, he'll be a hoe or in P.C. [pro-
> tective custody] HA! HA! Anyway, yeah we're suppose to a different
> lawyer if this shit goes capital. . . . [I]f they don't find us guilty of
> kidnapping but do find us guilty of murder, it will be a simple first

degree murder bro. No death sentence! Still though, we will be found "not guilty" of it all bro. I truly believe that! As for the clothes they took from the apt. I do know that one pair of shoes they took were Shawns dress boots with blood on em, as well as his pants with blood on em. As far as the clothes I had on, I don't think any blood was on my pants or sweatshirt, but I think my sandles may have had some dark brown substance on the bottom of em. Anyway, my lawyer will get me a copy of everything that seized in the search as well as test results when the D.A. release em to him. And we'll know how to handle those things by time we go to trial, which may be 3–6 months or more! . . . Anyway, I'll back with ya Bro Monday. Take care suck my dick, and lick my nuts. Send my shit back for bitch. Seriously though bro, regardless of the outcome of this, we have made history and shall die proudly remembered if need be. If not, we sure will get a hell of a lot of set offs,[14] huh ☺ Gotta go. Much Aryan Love, Respect and Honor my brother in Arms.
SEIG HEIL
(HAIL VICTORY) 14 & 88
[卐 "C K A"]
Death before what?
Say you swear.
PoZZum.

Notwithstanding the bravado at the end of this kite—with the claim that, whatever the outcome of their trials, King and Brewer have "made history"— it is clear that King could see that the position that he and Brewer had so carefully constructed was teetering. The national media was not letting go of the story, thereby keeping the spotlight, and hence the pressure, on them, and—what was worse—the evidence emerging was increasingly difficult, if not impossible, to explain away. Specifically, the identification of Byrd's blood on their clothing potentially posed an insurmountable hurdle to their defense, making it much more difficult to convincingly argue that King and Brewer had been dropped off at the apartment while Shawn Berry had gone off alone to murder Byrd.

King's final kite to Brewer announced that he suspected there was something "fishy" going on with Spiderman. Spiderman had apparently told King that he had delivered some kites to Kylie Greeney, but King had learned from her that Spiderman had called her to ask her to come to the jail, which would have been unnecessary had she received the kites. "Its beginning to smell like Jack Smack around this cannery," King declared to Brewer, noting also that he found it suspicious that several of the trustees had disappeared from the jail the day that the grand jury was meeting.

The discovery that they had been betrayed by Spiderman must have been a crushing blow to King and Brewer. Their kites formed a paper trail, in which they attempted to construct a serviceable narrative for their upcoming trials. Thus they had provided the prosecution with more potentially damaging evidence. King's prison kites could certainly be read as a kind of coded admission that King and Brewer were both implicated in the murder. King and Brewer could be shown to be trying to fashion a story that would conceal their involvement and counter the eyewitness report placing Byrd in Berry's truck with three whites riding in the cab. The kites also convincingly and disturbingly revealed the depth of King's and Brewer's white supremacist ties and allegiances.

As savvy as he was about legal matters, King must have immediately recognized the implications of Spiderman's betrayal. King had felt in command in the county jail; it was home territory. In addition, compared with Beto, the county jail was definitely in the minor leagues. How quickly King had found a "confederate" to carry kites and care packages to Brewer. For a few weeks it must have seemed to King that he was on top of things. His propensity for grandiosity and narcissism had led him to underestimate the authorities. Now, that bubble of illusion had abruptly popped, and he was facing the dire reality of his circumstances. The cocky, self-assured attitude that pervaded King's kites was profoundly shaken. He had lost control of his situation and of Russell Brewer as well. As long as the two were yoked together, Brewer could perhaps be kept in line. But who knew what would happen when that tie was broken, as it now was?

Within a few weeks, King was transferred to the Terrell Unit in Livingston, the same maximum-security prison to which he would return as a death row inmate. In his newly vacated Jasper County jail cell authorities found that King had scratched "Shawn Berry is a snitch ass traitor" into the cell door's cream-colored paint. At his new home at the Terrell Unit (subsequently renamed Polunsky Unit), King was kept in isolation, or "administrative segregation," in the corrections vernacular. Not long after his arrival he wrote his father, Ronald, a desperate, panicked letter in which he said he feared for his life. He said that he was not sure "how much time" he had left and that he believed that his and Brewer's safety were "in grave danger," implying that he had received threats from an unnamed high-ranking prison official. He was "scared to death," he said. He went on to implore Ronald to contact his lawyer, judges, the mayor of Jasper, and state representatives to voice concern over his son's and Brewer's safety. He also asked his father to press for them to be immediately "bench warranted" back to the county jail "where we 'were safe' and out of harms way from other inmates and officers."

Gone was the bravado and the smiley faces that King previously used to punctuate the text of his communications. As he awaited his trial, which was set to take place in Jasper at the end of February 1999, King was now alone, isolated and scared.

NOTES

1. In their correspondence, King and Brewer both refer to African Americans as "tobys." The term alludes to the slave Kunta Kinte, the main character in Alex Haley's *Roots*. Kunta Kinte refused to let his master call him by his slave name, Toby, and insisted on the use of his African name.

2. When writing "Possum" and "Russ," their respective nicknames, King and Brewer substituted lightning bolts for the two letters *ss*.

3. Like most of the kites, this one has an occasional word that is illegible either because of the poor handwriting or, more typically, because of the poor quality of the photocopy due to the note's multiple folds. And in some instances, a note has been photocopied through so many generations that a word or, rarely, phrase is unreadable. The kites also contain numerous spelling and grammatical errors.

4. Louis Berry's girlfriend's name was Courtney.

5. According to Shawn Berry's statement, Brewer had kicked James Byrd in the head ("the motion was like that of someone kicking a field goal") when Byrd was initially assaulted in the clearing on the logging road.

6. Brewer may be acknowledging King's "theory" that membership in the CKA was a possible motive for Berry to have committed the murder. The phrase "on my patch" is obviously intended to convey a solemn oath or vow.

7. Here Brewer drew a smiley face. He is describing the photographer's re-action to the tattoo on his penis, which bore the words "YOUR NAME." The tattoo had been the object of much interest and discussion since Brew-er's arrival in Jasper. He allegedly told a woman at a bar that he had "her name" tattooed on his penis, presumably making her curious to see it for herself.

8. Brewer sometimes referred to Bill King (John William King) by his first name.

9. "House" is a term that prisoners use to refer to their cells.

10. According to the Anti-Defamation League, the "88" slogan is short-hand for the Nazi greeting "Heil Hitler." *H* is the eighth letter of the al-phabet, so "HH" is rendered as "88." This number is often found on flyers of hate groups, particularly in the salutation and close of letters written by neo-Nazis.

11. Greeney's statements implied that King had racist feelings toward Jews and African Americans.

12. The magazine had published a photograph of King dressed in a cow-boy hat, vest, chaps, and boots and holding a rope with a cow bell on the end of it.

13. The article quoted statements of Louis Berry that exonerated his brother ("He was in the wrong place at the wrong time"). Louis was critical of King ("When he came back [from prison], he was a person I'd never seen") and observed that, after his release, King could speak of little other than the racist dogma he had picked up in prison.

14. "Setoff" is prison lingo for additional prison time for bad behavior while incarcerated.

The Prosecution's Case

THE ADVENT OF BILL KING'S TRIAL transformed the usually sleepy Jasper County courthouse into an armed encampment. In addition to the Jasper Police Department and the Sheriff's Department, there were officers from the Texas Rangers and the Texas Department of Public Safety. Hundreds of officers were arrayed around the courthouse. The officers were heavily armed, many toting shotguns and most wearing bulletproof vests. Because of the high-profile nature of the crime, underscored by the Klan and Black Panther marches that had taken place since Byrd's murder, law enforcement was prepared for any eventuality. It was anyone's guess what some deranged individual might think to do under these circumstances, and the authorities were not going to chance a mishap.

In addition to law enforcement personnel, the courthouse lawn was full of radio, television, and print journalists, as well as a good number of gawkers hoping to get a glimpse of King as he was spirited in or out of the courthouse. Others were simply there to take in the strangeness of it all. An area adjacent to the gazebo had been set aside for press conferences. There prosecution and defense attorneys, as well as anyone else giving a formal statement, could step up to a bank of a dozen or more microphones and face a phalanx of cameras, recorders, and lights as members of the assembled press corps asked questions. In addition, when newsworthy people arrived or departed from the day's proceedings, television anchors and crews toting cameras and microphone booms huddled around them, asking questions in hopes of obtaining something fresh or novel that might be aired during the next news cycle.

Bill King's trial started on Monday, February 17, 1999, eight months after the murder. The defendant was brought from the Jasper County jail for each day's proceedings under tight security in a caravan of vehicles. His hands were handcuffed in front of him, and a chain linked the cuffs to leg irons that permitted King to take only small strides. He was outfitted with a thick, heavy bulletproof vest. In addition, he wore a stun gun device beneath his shirt that could deliver sufficient voltage to disable him immediately, if temporarily, should he try to escape or act in a threatening manner. King was escorted in and out of the courthouse through a second-floor door with an external staircase. Each arrival and departure of the now notorious defendant brought camera crews to this side of the courthouse, where journalists shouted questions and spectators sometimes shouted taunts, although King rarely acknowledged any of these efforts to get his attention.

Entry into the courthouse itself was tightly monitored, and only individuals with an approved pass were permitted access. In addition to armed officers, a metal detector stood guard at the entry to the courthouse, where no cell phones or other electronic devices were allowed. The courtroom was on the second floor. It was an ample room, with exceedingly high ceilings from which six fans, attached to long metal extensions, whirred silently in *To Kill a Mockingbird* style. High on the north and south walls at either end of the courtroom were sets of beautiful crimson, forest green, and royal blue stained-glass windows, reminiscent of a church. The courtroom was divided nearly in half. Along the south wall were the judge's chair and desk. The jury box was to the left. The prosecution and the defense teams' tables occupied a space in the center of the room, with the prosecution's table closest to the jury box. The presiding judge was a veteran of the bench, the Honorable Joe Bob Golden. A gruff, no-nonsense man, Golden was large, over six feet, and the traces of a former athlete—he had attended college on a golf scholarship—were still discernible even though his shoulders were now a bit stooped. The judge was nearing retirement. Next to the judge's chair was the witness booth, in front of which the court stenographer occupied a small table.

An aisle with a short wood railing separated this side of the courtroom from the north side of the room. At either end of this aisle were sets of windowed doors where armed officers were posted to monitor entry. The gallery had two seating sections, each with ten rows of aging, dark wooden benches that resembled pews. James Byrd Sr. and Stella Byrd, along with James Byrd's siblings and children and the family's immediate friends, occupied the first two rows of seats in the gallery section on the left side of the courtroom. Byrd's mother and father were aging and had clearly endured an enormous amount of anguish over the fate of their son; yet they carried themselves with poise and dignity. The same was true of Byrd's siblings, who had frequently been called upon, as they would continue to be throughout the upcoming trials, to render their opinions about the proceedings. With a single voice the family had placed their faith in the judicial process.

The seats behind the Byrd family were mostly reserved for the media. Across from the Byrds' seats, on the right side of the gallery, sat Ronald King, Bill King's father, his wheelchair parked in the aisle. Next to him sat Father Ron Foshage, a Catholic priest who had volunteered to sit with the elder King when it had become clear that neither of the defendant's sisters (one of whom lived in town, the other an hour's drive away) nor his brother (who lived in Indiana) would attend the proceedings. Guy James Gray's wife, an appealing dark-haired woman, occasionally sat in one of these first two rows of seats, as well as a mysterious, attractive woman named Misty. Misty was rumored to be from Houston, perhaps the daughter of a judge. She had begun a correspondence with King not long after his arrest, and it had apparently blossomed into something more. It was yet another illustration of King's force of personality that he had somehow succeeded in engaging her faithful allegiance. Kylie Greeney, who had recently delivered the couple's child, was not permitted to sit in the courtroom because she was a potential witness. Lum Hawthorn, Shawn Berry's attorney, also sat in these seats, hoping to learn something about the strategy that the state would deploy against his client in Berry's subsequent trial. Behind Father Foshage a gaggle of courtroom artists sketched the proceedings every day for the evening news. The seats behind these two rows were mostly reserved for Jasper residents who had managed to obtain a pass as well as spillover from the media section.

The atmosphere within the courtroom, like the atmosphere on the court- The
house lawn, was tense. People spoke in quiet tones and tended to avoid eye Prosecution's
contact with those around them. The gravity of the proceedings created an Case
air of solemnity.

In addition to Guy James Gray, three other attorneys were seated at the
prosecution table: Jasper's assistant DA, a man named Pat Hardy, and two
federal attorneys with the Justice Department, John Stevens and Jim Mid-
dleton. The bulk of the trial would be carried on Gray's and Hardy's shoulders. Hardy cut a striking figure. His head was clean-shaven, and his boom-
ing voice matched the military bearing of a man who had served in the
Special Forces and seen more than his share of action in the Vietnam War.
Hardy dressed with a distinct flair, preferring bolo ties, ostrich-skin boots,
and a belt with a prominent western buckle instead of more conventional
lawyer attire. He also favored a white sports coat that had the cut of a formal
dinner jacket. Hardy was a study in prosecutorial flamboyance.

Guy James Gray, by way of contrast, dressed conservatively and tended to
eschew the kind of theatrical posturing that is the hallmark of many a trial
lawyer. Gray preferred to delegate those dramatic moments to Hardy. Gray
was not inclined toward grandstanding flourishes, for they ran counter to
his rather reticent personality. Instead, Gray's defining characteristic was a
steady, methodical, unrelenting approach to his work. The DA had a way of
appearing cool and unflappable, even when worries might be eating away at
his insides. Many a defendant had felt like a rat in a python's pet-store tank
when Gray was at the prosecutor's table. He tended to take careful stock of
his prey, calmly constructing the case against them. He was widely regarded
as an effective prosecutor, accounting for his perennial reelection to the post.
Gray had also earned the respect and loyalty of people like Speedy Drake and
Mike Wilson, his trusted investigators.

Sitting at the defense table, King looked collegiate in his khaki pants and
blue sport shirt. Indeed, he exuded innocence, almost a sweet bearing, which
was precisely the kind of contradiction that had often confounded people
about Bill, as if the visual cues did not match up with how he behaved. King's
shirt revealed the contours of the stun gun strapped around his waist, and the
tattoos on his arms were entirely covered by his shirt's long sleeves. King was
flanked by his two attorneys, Sonny Cribbs and another Beaumont attorney
named Brack Jones, who was assisting with the case. By the time of the trial,

FATHER RON FOSHAGE

the tension between King and Cribbs was plainly evident. The two rarely spoke as they sat at the defense table.

Notwithstanding popular conceptions, trials are only partly about evidence. They are also about the creation of plausible narratives that compete for the hearts and minds of the jurors. The evidence merely provides convenient places to anchor such narratives, functioning as devices to make stories more or less compelling. While it is true that during a trial evidence often lends itself more effectively to one of the competing stories, the congruence is most often, and at best, but an approximation of the truth. In view of this, every fact of a case need not be accounted for during a trial; every piece of evidence need not be unambiguous. Trials, in other words, are something of an interpretive exercise. The rules of evidence, the conventions and procedures that guide what jurors may hear and what attorneys may argue, are, simply put, the allowable parameters that dictate how each side will go about creating a plausible story for the benefit of the jury. Beyond them, it is a matter of craft, theater, and wit, a matter of who can create, out of the fragments of evidence, a vision of the "truth" that the jury might share.

ON THE OPENING DAY OF KING'S TRIAL before bringing in the jury, Judge Golden asked if there were any announcements in case no. 8869, *State of Texas v. John William King.* The prosecution indicated that they were ready to proceed. Sonny Cribbs, however, asked for reconsideration of the defense's motion for a change of venue. The press was giving the case extraordinary coverage. Cribbs was especially concerned about the regional coverage in the *Jasper Newsboy,* the *Beaumont Enterprise,* and the *Houston Chronicle,* where the Byrd story was receiving consistent front-page play. All were readily accessible and widely read. Judge Golden had already instructed the jury to avoid such coverage, however, and Cribbs had no evidence that anyone had violated those instructions. Judge Golden ruled against the motion. Following a little more pre-trial wrangling over procedures and admissibility of evidence, the jurors finally marched in, single file, from a door immediately adjoining the jury box.

King was instructed to stand as Guy James Gray read the indictment against him. It accused the defendant of "intentionally, while acting together with Lawrence Russell Brewer and Shawn Allen Berry and while in the course of committing or attempting to commit kidnapping of James Byrd, Jr., did cause the death of James Byrd, Jr., by dragging him on a road with a motor vehicle against the peace and dignity of the state."

Judge Golden turned to King: "Mr. King, how do you plead to that indictment?"

King was still standing. In a clear and unemotional voice, he replied with the only words he would speak for the remainder of the trial: "Not guilty, your Honor."

King sat down. There was a strange stoicism about him, as if this were the point toward which the trajectory of his life had been moving inexorably since the childhood moment in which he had first experienced a glimmer of awareness about himself and his world. From that initial consciousness, he had sensed that something was out of kilter about his life, as if a grand and sardonic error had been committed. Yet he could not even give words to that feeling. It hung there, nameless, a kind of unthought but known reality that seemed to govern everything. His role now, as silent observer to these grave proceedings that would determine his fate, was an oddly familiar one. In any case, he was a person of few words. Thus, flanked by his two defense attorneys, both of whom, for all intents and purposes, he had already dismissed, King simply sat there at the defense table, staring blankly at the judge, already convinced that the trial's outcome was a foregone conclusion.

In his opening statement Gray laid out an outline of the case against Bill King. He described the fact that King, Brewer, and Berry were roommates at the time of the murder and how a witness had seen them leave the Timbers Apartments together early on the morning of June 7. He then told them how an hour later Steven Scott had seen Byrd riding in Berry's pickup on Martin Luther King Boulevard. The District Attorney now turned to the specific evidence against King. He noted that King's Zippo lighter, with its Ku Klux Klan symbol, had been found at the crime scene, along with Berry's tools, and that cigarette butts with DNA matching the defendants had been found there as well. Gray also told the jury that "tiny specs of blood on the three pairs of shoes that belonged to these three guys" had been identified as Byrd's blood.

Gray spoke in a calm, evenly cadenced tone as he looked each juror in the eye, attempting to convey the impression that the case against King was overwhelming and incontrovertible. "Now you come to the motive. Why the

three did it; and in particular why this one did it," Gray said, pointing directly at an expressionless King. Motive, Gray asserted, would be established
from statements that King had made to friends in letters and in conversation.
King's tattoos would also help them understand his motives. "He's what they
call a full-sleeve," Gray told the jury. "He has tattoos all the way down exactly to where the end of the cuff is. There are a lot of racial tattoos," he said.
Gray then noted that King was a member of a gang called the Confederate
Knights of America and that his side was tattooed with a large gang patch
acquired in prison. "It has a burning cross, a Confederate flag, and a particular Klan symbol. Underneath it, it has the words, 'Aryan Pride,'" Gray
said. "This young man is full of hate," Gray told the jury, his voice for the
first time rising for emphasis. It was as emotional as the prosecutor would
get throughout the trial. "He has devil figures on his body, and all kinds
of tattoos that will show you the deep-seated anger and hatred that this
man has."

Gray indicated that it was King's intention to form a hate group in Jasper,
noting that in the apartment, in his own handwriting and under his own signature, King had developed the constitution and bylaws, code of ethics,
membership applications, and letters to potential new members for a group
called the Texas Rebel Soldier Division of the Confederate Knights of America. "And the evidence presented to you during this week will include evidence that Bill King needed to do something dramatic that would attract media attention in order to gain, in their warped world, respect for this newly
formed gang, to attract new members. And that's the way of it," Gray said
with emphasis.

Finally, Gray addressed the pivotal question that would make or break
this as a capital murder case. "I've got one more thing to say before I sit
down. For this to be a capital offense, it's got to have the kidnapping in it . . .
I'm going to introduce 12 or 13 pictures of the body and they're pretty
rough to handle, particularly for some of you ladies, but they have a specific
evidentiary purpose. And I must ask you not only just to look at them, but
I must ask you to study them some. And it's a little hard to do, but we
can do it." Gray then described what he thought the photographs would
prove, namely, that Byrd was not only alive when he was dragged, but that
he was also conscious. "Alive and somebody tying you up to restrict your
movement, that's kidnapping," Gray said emphatically. He told the jurors

that this would be clear from the photographs, which was why it was crucial that the prosecution burden the jury with such gruesome and disturbing evidence. "It will be a little rough on you," Gray said with a tone of fatherly understanding, "but you can do it. In this courtroom, we need to do our jobs."

The latter comment appeared to be aimed at eliciting and reinforcing a feeling of solidarity and joint purpose between the prosecution team and the members of the jury. The prospect of graphic images of Byrd's torn and shredded body created an almost palpable sensation in the courtroom. There was an approach-avoidance feeling; everyone in the room was at once curious and horrified at the thought of what those photographs might contain. It was emotionally powerful stuff, and the Jasper DA had the jurors' rapt attention even though Gray had delivered his remarks with characteristic steadiness. With that, he simply concluded his opening remarks by saying "Thank you" before slowly walking back to his chair at the prosecution table.

The courtroom was absolutely silent for a moment, a silence not broken until Judge Golden turned to the defense table. "Mr. Cribbs?" he said.

Sonny Cribbs stood up. "We have no opening statement. We reserve the right to make an opening statement later," he said.

It is not unusual for defense attorneys to defer making a statement until it is their turn to present arguments. A few top-drawer, high-profile defense attorneys choose to respond to the prosecution's opening statement, but many do not. There are risks inherent in making an immediate rebuttal, especially if, as in this case, there are thousands of pieces of evidence and the prosecution may approach them via a hundred different strategies. When the defense team responds to an opening statement in an impromptu manner, they risk making statements or revealing assumptions that might be proven erroneous, with a resultant loss of credibility with the jury. Nevertheless, to a jury uninitiated in these courtroom conventions, the defense's silence was hard to ignore. The failure of Cribbs to respond to Gray's strong opening remarks could not help but leave the impression that perhaps King's attorneys had no clearly formulated strategy. Almost any statement, no matter how formulaic, might have been preferable to the defense counsel's muteness. There was an odd symmetry between the strategy of King's defense attorneys and King's own silent, enigmatic demeanor.

JASPER COUNTY SHERIFF BILLY ROWLES was the prosecution's first witness. Gray used Rowles to describe what had transpired out on Huff Creek Road and what the Jasper law enforcement team had done in the twenty-four-hour interval between the discovery of Byrd's remains on Sunday morning and the sheriff's Monday morning visit to the FBI offices in Beaumont. The sheriff also reviewed the evidence collection procedures, the condition of the victim, and the subsequent investigation.

For all the bristling that the DA would later do regarding the media's devaluation of Jasper and Jasper law enforcement as unsophisticated country bumpkins, the sheriff at times appeared to play this very card, possibly in an attempt to establish an alliance with the jury. For example, when asked if Curtis Frame's positive finding for human blood under Berry's truck had raised his concern, the sheriff responded: "Yes, sir. I knew this country boy's in trouble." Similarly, Rowles seemed to suggest that he was in over his head with this case when describing his thought processes early on in the investigation. "I'm a brand new sheriff and I didn't even know the definition of a hate crime," he recalled. "But I knew somebody had been murdered because he was black, and it was a bad murder." When Gray asked the sheriff if, in hindsight, he thought his decision to go to the FBI had been a good one, the sheriff replied: "You bet you, smartest thing Billy Rowles ever did."

Rowles was a compelling witness. Paradoxically, despite his self-effacing, I'm-just-country manner, Rowles immediately dispelled the stereotype of the good-old-boy sheriff who might be indifferent to the fate of an unemployed African American man with a criminal record. The appealing Rowles came across as sensitive and compassionate, a man deeply affected by this unspeakable murder and a man determined to bring the perpetrators to justice.

In his cross-examination, Cribbs looked for holes in the sheriff's account or lapses in the evidence collection process that might undermine the viability of testimony he knew would be coming, especially testimony regarding DNA evidence. He emphasized, for example, that several patrol cars had driven up and down Huff Creek Road before the area was sealed off, the implication being that the sheriff's own people might have corrupted the crime scene. He inquired hard about the logging road: "I believe it is your testimony on that road [that] you found various articles of evidence, you think?" Cribbs asked Rowles.

SHERIFF BILLY ROWLES

"Yes, sir, we did."

A moment later, Cribbs came on strong: "You don't *know* who actually made the individual recovery of each piece of evidence, do you?" he said in accusatory tones. The implication was that the evidence recovery had been improperly supervised, though obviously it would have been impossible for the sheriff to be present when every single piece of evidence within the three-mile-long crime scene was found and logged.

The Jasper district attorney now turned to some of the most powerful and dramatic evidence. The prosecution team had selected a dozen or so photographs of Byrd's remains, as found on Huff Creek Road and from the autopsy, and put them into booklets. The booklets permitted each juror to view the gory pictures, obviating the need to project these onto a screen where the victim's family and others in the gallery would have to see them.

The introduction of the photographs drew strong objections from the defense table. Citing the Rules of Evidence, Cribbs's associate, Brack Jones, argued strenuously that the photographs were irrelevant, inflammatory, and overly gruesome. The photographs lacked probative value, he said, and might unfairly prejudice the jury. However, in another key decision for the prosecution, Judge Golden ruled that the photographs could be introduced.

Keenly aware of their emotional power, the DA and his team had made the tactical decision to enter the pictures of the victim's remains in the opening moments of the trial. They knew that even the most hardened member of the jury would find the images highly disturbing as seasoned law enforcement veterans like Tommy Robinson had been deeply unsettled by the victim's condition. Thus, presenting the pictures at this juncture served two functions. First, it helped to underscore the raw barbarity of what had happened to Byrd. Without actually seeing it, the imagination faltered in its efforts to conjure a mental image of that horror. Second, showing the pictures at the outset was a kind of planned inoculation. The prosecutor knew that he would show the photographs to the jury again at the end of the trial when he put a forensic pathologist on the stand. He hoped that when the jurors saw the photographs the second time, it would be easier for them to attend and concentrate. They would still be horrified, but after overcoming the initial shock of seeing so much gore, they would be able to absorb what the forensic pathologist had to say about them.

There was a strange and uneasy feeling in the courtroom as the people seated in the gallery observed the jurors opening the booklets containing the photographs. It was apparent from some of the juror's pained and disconcerted expressions that the contents of the booklets were quite powerful. Thus, as if refracted through the expressions of the twelve men and women seated in the jury box, those in the gallery got a hint of the booklets' nightmarish contents. The air of secrecy surrounding the distribution and retrieval of the booklets only added to the sense of drama regarding what those images actually depicted, which in turn only deepened the sense that the man at the center of these proceedings, the silent and unapproachable Bill King, was a figure whose alleged actions belied comprehension.

As the booklets were being collected, Judge Golden announced that it was time for the twenty-minute morning recess. The timing and tempo of the proceedings was a closely orchestrated affair. The sheriff's testimony that morning had moved quickly and had clearly held the jurors' attention. During cross-examination, Cribbs's line of inquiry tended to flatten the emotional intensity of the testimony by focusing on the comparatively boring issues of evidence acquisition and chain of possession. From Gray's point of view, that was fine. He knew that a jury could assimilate only so much information and could tolerate only so much emotional intensity. He didn't want the jury to be emotionally spent, and he knew that the sheriff's testimony, while engaging, was also draining because it invoked, step by step, the actions that had unfolded on Huff Creek Road. The photographs, on the other hand, had once again ratcheted up the emotional tension in the courtroom. Thus, the timing of the recess, was as if it had been scripted by Gray and his team. It gave the jurors a chance to digest what they had seen in the photographs while providing needed relief from their distressing content.

Following the morning's recess, Gray put an attractive young woman named Michelle Chapman on the stand. Chapman was asked to identify King, which she did by pointing at him. She had known King for five years, having met him at a party when she was thirteen years old. While King was serving time at Beto between 1995 and 1997, he had maintained an active correspondence with Chapman. For the benefit of the jury, Gray emphasized the fact that King was older than the young woman. It was a means of suggesting that King had a predatory nature. Gray hoped that the image of a ten-

der, vulnerable adolescent girl courted by King from prison would strike an
unsettling chord in the juror's hearts.

The prosecution was interested in presenting King's letters to Chapman because they contained statements that established his racist attitudes, which presumably formed the basis for his actions. The letters were potentially quite damaging, and King's defense team did what they could to squelch Chapman's testimony and the introduction of the letters in court, arguing that their content was extraneous and therefore inadmissible. Cribbs's co-counsel, Brack Jones, also cited chapter and verse from the Texas Constitution and from the U.S. Constitution, arguing that the correspondence was protected under the due process clause of the Fifth Amendment as well as the equal protection and due process clauses of the 14th Amendment to the Constitution. However, Judge Golden overruled the defense on every point, accepting the prosecution's argument that the letters served to demonstrate the defendant's "state of mind, his intent, and motive for actions that were taken in the murder of Mr. Byrd."

Having been repeatedly overruled all morning, the defense already appeared to be on the run. In frustration, Jones insisted that the defense's objections be duly noted: "Your Honor, so I'm clear on the Record, may we have a running objection to each of the exhibits that were offered?"

John Stevens, the head of the U.S. Department of Justice's Criminal Division for the Eastern Region, was assigned the task of leading Chapman through the letters. He was a slim man of average stature with the typical dark-suited look that one might expect from a federal attorney. Stevens asked the witness to read the identified segments out loud. In one, King bragged about his prison tattoos: "So far, I've gotten Woody Woodpecker (pecker-wood) wearing a clans man uniform, flipping off"—and in parenthesis—"niggers, of course, with 100% loco wood under it." Chapman testified that she had seen this and other tattoos after King had returned home from the Beto Unit, including "one with a black man hanging."

In another letter from Beto, King had written: "The niggers have this muslim shit, blood, and crips and Black Panthers. These ho ass spics have the Mexican Mafia, T.C.B., E.P.T., Texas Syndicate, and hometown clicks. Us Aryans have the Aryan Brotherhood, Aryan Circle, Confederate Knights of America, K.K.K., Aryan Legion, White Knights, Confederate Hammer

Skins, Skin Heads, and the Texas Mafia and thousands more." This letter was dated February 20, 1996, only some eight or nine months after his arrival at Beto.

"How old were you when you received this letter?" Stevens asked.

"Fifteen," Chapman responded.

In this same letter King had gone on to say: "What do you think about niggers and spics? Would you date one, fuck one, and become a race trader like a lot of those whores in Jasper? It's my opinion that any race trading bitch should be hung alongside the niger she fucked. White is right."

A few months later, in September 1996, King wrote Chapman: "What do I have to look forward too returning to Jasper? A town full of race traitoring, nigger loveing whores? Bitches that are so fucken stupid and blind to the pride of their race and heritage that they should be hung on the limb adjacent to their niger loveing man." And then, "Who knows, maybe the Jews and niggers will kill one another before long."

It was powerful stuff and quite effective in making the state's point that Bill King was a virulent racist. King's letter was decorated with the same triangular Klan symbol that was on his Zippo lighter. Chapman then described how King had seemed proud when he came over to her house to show off his tattoos shortly after his release from prison.

"Was that when you saw the tattoo of the black man hanging?" Stevens asked.

"Yes, sir," Chapman replied.

"Where is it located?"

"On his arm."

"Did he seem proud of that?"

"Yes," she said convincingly.

On cross-examination Cribbs did what he could to neutralize this powerful testimony that put his client in the worst light possible. His strategy was to emphasize the fact that King had changed while imprisoned at Beto. Chapman testified that before his incarceration King did not have racist tattoos.

"How many letters did he write you while he was in the penitentiary?" Cribbs asked.

"Nineteen," Chapman answered.

"Did he talk to you about being abused or beat up in the penitentiary?" he asked.

"No," she responded.

"Did the tone of these letters change from more racist to more racist the longer they went?"

"Yes, sir."

"The first letters you got from him while he was in the penitentiary weren't like the last ones, were they? . . . Did he sign the name 'Possum' on the first letters? . . . Didn't he sign them 'Bill'?"

"Yes, sir."

"So, this nickname that you're talking about, this racial hatred in these letters, that developed over the time in the penitentiary, didn't it?"

"I believe so."

Chapman's testimony was compelling and effective in depicting King as a hard-core racist. The best Cribbs could do with it was to plant the suggestion that perhaps King had been harassed or beaten up while in prison, implying that he had joined a prison gang for protection and emphasizing that it was only within prison that these racist views had taken hold.

The state next put Tommy Robinson on the stand, the officer with the Sheriff's Department who, along with Joe Sterling, had been drinking coffee at the Ramada Inn when the initial call came from the dispatcher. The flamboyant Pat Hardy handled Robinson's testimony, some of which duplicated what the sheriff had described earlier that morning. Stylistically, Robinson wasn't a riveting witness. He tended to talk slowly, with deliberation, and his overall demeanor was country through and through. It made him appear less sharp than he actually was. Robinson thus set a sleepy tone as a follow-up to Chapman's gripping testimony. However, Gray and his team had set a trap for the defense to spice things up. While describing an evidence photograph, Robinson said, "Those are a ring of keys I photographed along the Huff Creek Road that belonged to the victim, James Byrd Jr."

As Hardy went to enter the keys into evidence, Brack Jones jumped to his feet. "Your Honor, may I take him on *voir dire*?" he asked.

"Yes, sir," the judge said.

"Officer, how do you *know* they belonged to Mr. Byrd?" Jones asked.

"Because myself and Investigator Mike Wilson from the DA's office took this set of keys, we went to the apartment where Mr. Byrd was living at the time of his murder. I tried one key into his mailbox. It opened the lock on his mailbox. The other key opened the lock on the apartment he was renting at the time," Robinson replied.

The successful trap was a point in favor of the prosecution team, which looked sharp and thorough in the exchange, and a defeat for King's lawyers, who were made to appear nitpicky and defensive. Not long thereafter, the trial was recessed for lunch.

The highlight of the afternoon's testimony was Steven Scott, the eighteen-year-old African American who, in the early hours of June 7, had been returning home from a Beaumont nightclub. Scott described seeing James Byrd walking along Martin Luther King Boulevard. It was apparent to Scott that Byrd was drunk: "He was wobbling around the road," Scott said. Scott described his fateful decision not to pick Byrd up, a decision that would no doubt haunt him for the rest of his life. Instead, he drove past him and pulled into his driveway farther up the street. Scott exited his car and walked up the steps to the front door. "As my mother opened the door," he said, "I turned around and I seen him passing by on the back of a truck. . . . He was sitting with his back facing the front of the truck." Scott could not offer much information about the identities of the three individuals riding in the cab of the truck: "Only thing I could recognize was they were white. That's it," he said.

The best that King's defense team could do was to probe in hopes of revealing some inconsistency or contradiction. Cribbs tried to shorten the time frame during which Scott claimed that this incident had taken place. Scott had testified that he had seen Byrd sometime around two-thirty in the morning. "You said that was at 2:00?" Cribbs asked impatiently, as if ready to move on to other questions. "2:30," Scott corrected him. Cribbs then zeroed in on the fact that Scott had seen no signs of protest or distress as Byrd rode by:

"Did you see any indication that Mr. Byrd was hollering for help or anything?" he asked.

"No, sir. I did not," Scott replied.

This was an important point, given that the prosecution was alleging that Byrd had been kidnapped. Cribbs emphasized the fact that Byrd appeared calm, giving Scott no reason to believe that he was in danger or in a state of distress. He then extracted another key admission from Scott:

"You can't say that this boy was in that truck?" Cribbs asked sternly, pointing toward a taciturn Bill King sitting at the defense table.

"No, sir. I cannot," Scott responded.

Following the afternoon recess the prosecution put one of James Byrd's sisters, Mary Verrett, on the stand. She described the fact that Byrd had attended a family bridal shower on that Saturday afternoon. She then verified that various articles of clothing found on the victim or on the logging road belonged to Byrd, some of which she had given him as a present the previous day. Her appearance was emotional for the members of the jury and those in the gallery, even though Verrett handled the difficult testimony steadily.

Brack Jones was left with the delicate task of cross-examining Mary Verrett. He had a fine line to walk. On the one hand, this was an opportunity to paint a portrait of Byrd as an unsavory, irresponsible ne'er-do-well, a common defense tactic to make the jurors feel less sympathy toward the victim. On the other hand, the defense was well aware of the national and international abhorrence for what had happened to Byrd. There was only so far Jones could go in impugning the victim's character without risk of arousing the antipathy of the jury.

Jones's line of inquiry centered around the idea that Byrd was a known drinker, which Verrett acknowledged, and the fact that Byrd was on disability. He repeatedly probed into the nature of this disability (Verrett said he had hurt his arm, but she did not know the details) and his purported seizure disorder (Verrett did not know what kind it was and had never seen him have a seizure). Jones seemed to press the witness hard on this point:

"And you don't know anything more about these seizures other than what you told us? Do you know if he passed out from these seizures or anything? . . . What does a seizure mean to you?"

The implication was that perhaps Byrd had no such ailment, that he was simply a malingerer living off the taxpayer. In a community where poverty was rampant and people worked hard to scratch a living out of meager opportunities, this kind of questioning, the defense team hoped, might pay dividends.

The prosecution wrapped up this first day of testimony with some of the routine, bread-and-butter issues that had to be covered, including King's consent to having his apartment searched and an inventory of what was found there. The defense strenuously objected to the introduction of this

evidence, such as a book on the history of the Ku Klux Klan and other photographs, drawings, and papers containing materials related to white supremacist beliefs and organizations. They argued that such materials were
constitutionally protected and that the probative value of the evidence was
outweighed by the danger of unfair prejudice. As he had done repeatedly
throughout the day, Judge Golden ruled in favor of the prosecution, although he issued a specific instruction to the jury: "Ladies and gentlemen,"
he said, "you may consider that [evidence] for the intent, motive, and state
of mind and for no other purpose."

THE MATERIALS RETRIEVED from King's apartment were too numerous
to present in court. Some of these materials, though interesting and important, were not necessarily effective in developing the prosecution's case. In
the interest of maintaining a clear focus and a streamlined argument, the
prosecutors employed a disciplined eye in their selection of documents and
quotations, identifying those that most succinctly made their point, short
segments that could invoke the essence of those writings, parts that could effectively stand for the whole corpus of the materials. From these Gray and
his team could fashion their presentation to the jury under the imperative
that an effective trial presentation was one that kept things moving, striv-
ing at all costs to prevent the jury from getting bogged down. However,
the broader set of materials painted an even more unsettling picture about
King and his aspirations than the prosecution could succinctly convey in the
courtroom.

Other documents found at the apartment included a constitution for the
Confederate Knights of America, Texas Rebel Soldiers, as well as treatises, es-
says, and pronouncements about the plight of the Aryan peoples, the dangers
of the government, and the intent of others to destroy the Aryan race. "We
believe that the voluntary separation of the races is in the best interest of the
American Republic," one document declared. Another directed members to
avoid contact with non-Aryans: "Aside from business and job oriented matters, members will not, at any given time, engage in indepth personal socialization with individuals nor groups of minorities and Jewish races."

The documents left no question about the racist ideology behind the
Texas Rebel Soldiers, which presumably was intended to be a "free world"

offshoot of the CKA. In addition, these polemics were infused with more conventional right-wing views, such as "We believe that restrictions, regulations, and taxations of American businesses have virtually destroyed the free enterprise system of this country." Another plank in this same document declared: "We do not seek to discriminate against any race or creed but at the same time we strongly and activily oppose all programs of the government that give preferential treatment to so-called minorities in employment, promotions, housing, scholarships and in dozens upon dozens of other ways. We feel that every man and women should only be given the right to compete, but 'No One' should be guarenteed the right to suceed or any certain standard of living."

The documents retrieved from the Timbers Apartments were a mix of political posturing and a kind of *volks* guide to good living. They were also punctuated with comments and statements that could be read as expressions of more personal, psychological preoccupations and issues in King's life. "We do not choose to be common men," King wrote in one place, adding multiple exclamation points for emphasis. Elsewhere in the same document he announced that CKA members "should strive to . . . be tolerant [and] control their temper and not take everything personally," an issue with which King was himself known to have difficulty.

Mixed in among the oaths, codes of conduct, codes of ethics, and ambling statements about the plight of the Aryan race was a telling sheet of paper on which King had written only the following:

JOHN: English form of Latin Johann.
JOHANN: Common German form of John, representing a more
    learned form than Hans.
WILLIAM: English: The most successful of all Germanic names intro-
    duced to England by the Normans. It is composed of the elements
    Will, desire, and Helmet, protection.
WILHELM: German form of William.

Both the content of what Bill King had written on this slip of paper as well as its location—nestled in the very heart of his collection of polemical writings and musings about his endangered and embattled race—reflected a profound psychological truth. It formed part of a silent, unacknowledged undergirding to his search to understand his own identity.

Sandals and Tattoos

KEISHA ATKINS WAS THE MOST COMPELLING witness of Bill King's second day in court. Atkins was quite nervous on the stand, her voice periodically fading and quivering. The judge had to ask her to speak into the microphone, and Guy James Gray attempted to settle her down: "Are you pregnant right now?" he asked. (She was.) "And you're very, very nervous?" (Very, she replied.) "Just relax," Gray said in a fatherly tone. "It will be all right."

Atkins testified that King had written to her from prison but she had not received the letters. The young woman's mother, who did not approve of the relationship, had intercepted King's correspondence and destroyed it. Atkins acknowledged that she had seen King's tattoos on the night of Byrd's murder, when she had had her tryst with King. She also recounted that Kylie Greeney had shown up at the apartment but been barred from entering by Russell Brewer. It was a scene that the prosecution hoped would underscore King's duplicitous nature, with his pregnant girlfriend demanding entry at the door while King and Atkins were off in the bedroom behind closed doors. All of this line of inquiry was a mere prelude, however, to one of the most important questions that Gray asked her:

"That night when you were over there, did you see what he had on his feet? What kind of shoes was he wearing?"

"Sandals" was her reply. Atkins then positively identified a photograph of a pair of chocolate brown Outback sandals taken from the apartment as belonging to Bill King. The sandals had been found to have a drop of Byrd's blood on them, although Gray did not mention this fact. Atkins had already given the FBI a statement about the sandals; however, when Gray attempted to get Atkins to say that King was wearing the sandals when he left the apartment later that night, her testimony faltered: "I don't think I said when he left. He had them on at one point that night" is all that Atkins would affirm. It was enough, however, to link King to the sandals in question.

The next line of questioning was equally essential. Bill had tried to talk Keisha into staying, she said, but she just couldn't. King had walked her to her car. In the meantime, Berry had arrived home from work at the Twin Cinema, and he and Brewer had gotten into Berry's truck and pulled around to pick King up. Atkins testified that she saw the three of them leave the apartment's parking lot just ahead of her sometime between 1:30 and 1:45 that Sunday morning. She said that Berry was behind the wheel, Brewer in the middle, and King on the passenger side.

While Cribbs seemed intent on shortening the time frame when cross-examining Steve Scott the previous day, Gray was now equally intent on lengthening it. "That would be at approximately 1:30 in the morning?" he asked. "Yes, sir," she replied.

Like Steve Scott, who had unknowingly been in a position to intervene in the fate that befell Byrd by giving him a ride home, so Keisha Atkins, too, might have changed the course of events. "He asked me if I'd stay there," she said softly into the microphone, trying not to look directly at Bill King. "He said he wouldn't go if I'd stay there." The implication was clear to everyone in the courtroom.

In his cross-examination Cribbs attempted to capitalize on the fact that Atkins was a sympathetic witness and that if she had had a romantic relationship with King, he must have been "a pretty nice guy during that period of time." He also returned to the theme that he had emphasized the previous day when questioning Michelle Chapman:

"Before he went to prison, did he espouse any racial comments at all?" Cribbs asked.

"No, sir," Atkins replied.

Cribbs also asked her about her phone conversations with King in the weeks before the night of June 6:

"Did you talk about any racial activities? Did he espouse or talk about what he was going to do to somebody?" Atkins responded to all in the negative.

"And I believe you indicated at a point you left between 1:45 and 2:00 o'clock, was when y'all go out?" Cribbs asked, again attempting to truncate the timeline between when the three men left the Timbers Apartments and when a witness had placed Byrd in the back of Berry's pickup. Atkins corrected him: "It was closer to 1:30, 1:45."

Atkins had initially told the FBI that she had left the apartment between 1:45 and 2:00. Cribbs zeroed in on this contradiction. "Do you remember making a statement, or telling anyone else that you left the apartment between 1:45 and 2:00 a.m.?"

"Yes, sir. That's what I said," she replied.

"Okay. But now you're changing—now you believe it was closer to 1:30?"

"Well, whenever I left I had seen a policeman had a car pulled over in one place and then in a different place. They said it was around 1:30 or 1:45," Atkins replied.

"Who said?" Cribbs asked sharply.

"Whoever checked on that," she said. Atkins indicated that the FBI had corrected her time frame, having verified the time when the patrol car had pulled someone over on the highway near the Timbers Apartments. "I didn't honestly know what time it was," Atkins acknowledged. "I was just estimating."

This was the first real point scored for the defense. If it could be established that King and the others had not left the apartment until later, then there would not have been enough time for the trio to go out of town looking for a party, run over some country mailboxes on their way back into town (as they had contended), and pick up James Byrd close to two-thirty, which is what Scott had testified.

Cribbs now took aim at the question of the sandals. There were actually two pairs of identical Outback sandals found at King's apartment, one size 9½, the other size 10. It was one of the latter sandals that had a drop of the victim's blood on it. Cribbs continued:

"How did you know that these sandals that you identified as Bill King's were, in fact, Bill King's?"

"He had them on at one time while I was there," she responded.

"How do you know it was Bill King's?"

"They looked like the ones that he had on," she said.

"But your statement says they are the ones he had on. You positively identified them as the ones Bill King had on."

"Just like them," Atkins replied, reeling from the intense questioning. The unrelenting barrage from Cribbs finally yielded what he was hoping for, an acknowledgment from Atkins that she was not certain that the sandals she had identified were, in fact, those belonging to Bill King.

Atkins also testified that King was wearing a white shirt and white shorts when he left the apartment that night and that he had subsequently called her that morning around 5:00 or 5:30. He seemed "normal" in that conversation, she said. She had not noticed anything different about his demeanor or tone of voice. However, King called her again Sunday night, and in this conversation he seemed pressured and anxious. "He kept saying he needed to see me, needed to talk to me. Sounded different," she said.

Under redirect examination, Gray attempted to repair some of the damage caused by Cribbs's line of questioning. Calmly Gray asked Atkins to examine a series of statements that she had made, some of which were typed out, others in her own handwriting. All had been signed by Keisha Atkins and notarized. When Gray asked her to read from one of the documents, Brack Jones jumped to his feet and protested that the instruments had not been entered into evidence and that they were being used inadmissably to bolster oral statements from the witness.

Gray fired back that the defense had attempted to impeach the witness by portions of her statement. "We have a right to enter these statements for the correct and accurate version," he maintained.

Once again Judge Golden overruled the defense. Atkins read from one of these statements. It was evident that she was unsure of the exact time and that she had volunteered the information about seeing the patrol car stop a vehicle as a way of helping authorities establish an accurate timeline. Police logs indicated that the time was somewhere between 1:30 and 1:45 a.m. Gray used the opportunity to rebut another point scored by the defense. He had Atkins read further from her statement: "When I left, Bill was wearing a white shirt, white shorts, and sandals." Finally, Gray asked her if King was smoking cigarettes that night. (He had been.) "Did you see a lighter?" he asked. (She had.) "Did you see one that had the word 'Possum' on it?" "Yes," she answered.

In recross-examination Jones attempted to use Atkins to set up an explanation for evidence he knew would soon be presented, namely, the presence of King's DNA on a cigarette butt found at the crime scene. He asked her about the kind of cigarettes she smoked and whether Bill had been smoking hers or his own that night. "And if the boys were smoking in the truck, where would they put the cigarette butt when they finished with it? Did you see an ashtray?" he asked.

"I don't know," she replied. "I wasn't inside the truck."

"Where do you put yours when you smoke in your car?" he continued.

"Out the window," she said.

"Out the window?" Jones asked incredulously.

"Uh-huh," Keisha replied.

"Ever use your ashtray?"

"No, sir," Atkins said. It was not the response Jones had been looking for. Jones passed the witness.

THE OTHER KEY WITNESS on the second day of the trial was Detective Rich Ford of the Jasper Police Department. Ford had been present at Shawn Berry's arrest and had assisted Curtis Frame with the inspection of Berry's truck and, later, with the interviews of Berry, King, and Brewer in the Jasper County jail. Ford was in his late thirties, somewhat bulky, and olive-skinned. He had a serious, no-nonsense style that suggested more than just a professional demeanor. Smiles did not appear to come easy to the detective.

It was Ford who had photographed King and the others in jail. The prosecution's present attempt to enter these photographs into evidence drew sharp fireworks from the defense table. In addition to objecting to their admissibility, the defense also argued that the images had been "coerced" because the suspects had been asked to remove their shirts so that Ford could photograph them. Judge Golden overruled the objections.

Ford's photographs of King, clad only in boxer shorts, were projected onto a screen; some photographs were up close and detailed while others were nearly fullbody shots. Prominent on King's left arm in one of the photographs was what he called his "peckerwood" tattoo, the one described in his letter to Michelle Chapman. It covered a substantial portion of his forearm and consisted of a Woody Woodpecker figure dressed in Ku Klux Klan robes. The woodpecker's eyeballs were lightning bolt symbols, and the figure was pointing to an image of a man hanging from a tree. Numerous witnesses testified that King was quite proud of this tattoo and that he had drawn their attention to his "little hanging nigger."

Ford attempted an exegesis of the different tattoos and their meanings, referring to what he knew about gangs and what he had learned from his study of prison body art. In reference to a tattoo depicting the Virgin Mary and the infant Jesus with horns coming out of his head, Ford stated that "One of the big things in satanic type worshipping rituals, [is] to take something that's of the Christian value and sacred and make it look evil or destroy it." There is no indication, however, that King's attachment to satanic themes included actual religious practices or worship. Ford also asserted that the numerous pairs of lightning bolts tattooed on King's body had several meanings: "It's been used in Hitler's reign as the signs of the S.S.," testified Ford. "It can also be interpreted as 'Soldiers or Sons of Satan.'"

To what extent the jurors may have felt informed by the detective's interpretations of the defendant's tattoos (his credentials as an expert on this subject were somewhat dubious), they could not help but find the tattoos themselves powerful and absorbing. Few, if any, of the jurors were likely to have ever seen these kinds of tattoos or an individual so extensively covered with body art, regardless of its content. This, too, had been part of Gray's strategy. By design, there had been relatively little said about the defendants' tattoos in pre-trial publicity, except to acknowledge that King and the others had "some racial tattoos" on their bodies. Thus, when the jury was shown the actual images, there was a scripted shock value inherent in the presentation.

Despite a flurry of objections from the defense, Judge Golden admitted the tattoos into evidence, just as he had King's books, writings, and drawings. However, the judge duly instructed the jury that "the defendant is on trial solely for the offense contained in the indictment." He also cautioned that the tattoo evidence was being admitted solely "for the limited purpose of determining motive, intent, and state of mind." King had had no inkling in his Beto days, as he let Dirtball work on him between head counts, that his skin was being indelibly stained with evidence that would later help convict him of capital murder. No doubt the images had also left a permanent mark in the minds of the jurors as the riveting tattoo testimony brought the second day of the proceedings to a close.

DURING THE FIRST TWO DAYS of the trial the prosecutors succeeded in entering every single piece of evidence that they brought to the courtroom. With few exceptions, most of the defense's objections were overruled. According to Guy James Gray, these successes helped foster a conviction within the prosecution team that they could prevail without Shawn Berry's testimony for which, presumably, an eleventh-hour deal could still have been struck. Had the judge disallowed King's writings and tattoos as evidence of motive and intent, prosecutors believe they would have had an uphill battle convincing the jury of King's culpability "beyond a reasonable doubt."

"Scared, scared to death" is the way the Jasper DA had described his feelings going into the trial. He was acutely aware that when it came to material evidence, his case against Bill King was the weakest. This reality dictated the prosecution's approach to the entire trial. "If you can show the jury that the defendant is a no-good-scum-ball-piece-of-trash, a small amount of evidence gets huge," he later remarked. "If they want to believe that this person is guilty and did it, they will magnify little pieces of evidence into overwhelming evidence. On the other hand, if the defendant is a good solid citizen, married, church-going, never been in trouble, then the jury doesn't want to believe that he's committed this crime. They'll nitpick at all the evidence and become a detective for weaknesses in the case." It had been apparent to Gray from the outset that he was going to have to do a good job of painting King as negatively as possible. He would have been the first to admit that his evidence was not strong enough to stand up to much nit-picking.

This philosophy governed the prosecution's tactics in the case. "If you begin a case with your facts proving the crime, they'd better be good because the jury is expecting overwhelming volumes of evidence. If you tantalize a jury a day or two, it's like foreplay. If you hint at proof, hint at evidence but don't give it to them, they're waiting for it. They want you to give them this proof, and if you can get the jury to where they want to hear this proof, then they accept it quicker and a lot better." Those two fundamentals were driving Gray's strategy: spend the first day and a large part of the second day trashing the defendant—"This man's got these racist tattoos, a tattoo of a black man hanging and this devil stuff. He's got these books about the Klan. He's in the penitentiary writing to these fourteen-year-old girls about a black guy with a white girl and how they should both be hung from the same tree." The prosecution had now firmly established King's racist credentials and painted a portrait of the defendant as someone with the dark emotions and dark ideology that could explain his participation in the savage random killing of a black man he had never met. It was now time to see whether the jury was sufficiently primed. Would they be receptive to the available evidence that Bill King had committed this heinous crime?

RONALD KING HAD SAT THROUGH the first two days of his son's capital murder trial, but it was nothing short of an ordeal for him. Bill King rarely made eye contact with his father when entering or exiting the deliberations. For Ronald, the portrait of his son as a vicious, hateful person was quite difficult to take. Never, not even in his worst nightmares, would Ronald and his wife have imagined that it would end like this, with their prized and beloved child on trial for a crime whose barbarity defied description.

The elder King, infirm and upset, sat in the aisle in his wheelchair, only an arm's length away from James Byrd's family. Ronald, dressed in his signature navy blue Dickie jumpsuit, gazed at his son, the judge, and the jury through weary, pale blue eyes. Father Ron Foshage sat with Ronald most days, occupying a seat at the end of the row immediately adjacent to Ronald. Between his emphysema and the osteoporosis afflicting his back, Ronald at times struggled to stay alert during the trial. He was on high levels of pain medication that sometimes, perhaps mercifully, made him fall asleep. More than once, Father Ron had to shake Ronald to wake him.

Halfway through Rich Ford's detailed interpretation of the satanic symbolism of the Virgin Mary tattoo, as the implication of the testimony sank in, Ronald suddenly shifted in his wheelchair with a startle and grabbed Father Ron's leg. "Father, I'm so sorry," he said. "I didn't know that was there. I know you have a great respect for the Blessed Virgin Mary." Ronald was losing his hearing and had a tendency to speak rather loudly, so his words, in a deep voice whose resonances were now also rendered rather hoarse by the ravages of emphysema, carried easily. Everyone in the immediate vicinity of the two men heard the exchange.

There were days when the elder King was simply overwhelmed by the testimony. More than once during the trial he would have to be whisked from the courtroom at the end of the day and taken to Jasper Memorial Hospital for a breathing treatment. There were also days when Guy James Gray would alert him that the evidence presented during this or that segment of the trial might be difficult for the old man to bear. Once or twice Ronald King simply stayed home from a morning or an afternoon session. He wanted to be present, but there was just so much that he could take.

As Ronald King sat through the trial, he kept thinking about the fact that Bill had always appeared to be a happy, easy-to-please child who seemed outgoing and who liked people. As Ronald privately remembered images from his son's life, the short interval between Bill's childhood and his first arrest at the age of seventeen represented an entire lifetime of puzzlement. It was a puzzle that Ronald King ruminated about, a conundrum he tried over and over again to disentangle and resolve. Yet, for all his efforts, the solution remained elusive to the father. He had notions, theories, speculations, and hunches but nothing that really explained the why of it all. How was it possible that the boy he had so cherished had ended up at that defense table, accused of such a brutal crime? Bill's mother, Ronald thought to himself, would have been absolutely devastated.

For several years there had been a curious denial at work in Ronald. When Michelle Chapman read her letters on the first day of the trial, Ronald King immediately recognized the transformation in their content from benign reports to increasingly racist comments and observations. Bill's correspondence with Ronald had undergone the very same evolution until the elder King finally felt compelled to write Bill and tell him that he was not interested "in that kind of talk." Bill's subsequent letters omitted references to his emerging racial ideology or relations between whites and blacks in prison or on the outside. His letters reverted to what they had been initially: inquiries about family, hopes for the future, and day counting. While Bill's correspondence to others in the "free world" continued along the vein of the excerpts read from Chapman's letters, his correspondence with his family ceased to invoke such notions. Ronald had allowed himself to believe that perhaps all the

racist talk was but a phase, a transient manifestation of prison bravado that
perhaps had already begun to wane.

Curiously, though Bill's tattoos were impossible to ignore, Ronald never
really engaged Bill about them after his son's release from Beto. He claims
that he never saw them up close and was unaware of their specific content.
He was shocked when the troubling images were projected in the courtroom,
revealing a dark world indeed. Perhaps the elder King had been too anxious,
fearful that exploring these topics with his son might rupture their relationship. Bill King could be temperamental in that way. If he didn't like something someone said or did, he could cut the person out of his life for weeks
at a time, if not permanently. Bill had a low threshold for things not going
his way, and he did not respond well when challenged or questioned. It was
another version of Bill's my-way-or-no-way approach to life. More than
likely Ronald had simply hoped that the peculiar mind-set of a person living
caged up in prison, where terror and predatory behavior governed nearly
every waking moment, would give way to the ordinariness of a job, or perhaps even marriage and a family. Whatever Ronald's hopes had been for Bill,
as he sat through the trial those hopes became reduced to a single wish: that
his son be spared the death penalty.

The Verdict

THROUGHOUT THE FIRST TWO DAYS of Bill King's trial the prosecution's timing was flawless. The months of preparation and the neatly choreographed approach to the trial were paying big dividends. The previous day's testimony, for example, had ended with Rich Ford's description of King's tattoos, giving the defense no opportunity to cross-examine the state's witness. This left the imagery of the frightening, primitive tattoos burned into the juror's minds, fresh and uncontested.

The third day of the trial started with Brack Jones's cross-examination of the Jasper detective. His initial tack was to emphasize that King's tattoos were the product of the harsh, nightmarish Beto environment that forced prisoners into gangs in order to protect themselves. For example, he got Ford to acknowledge that a "peckerwood" was a prison term for a white person who stood up for himself. "Did you know that to become a wood, you either stand up for your rights or you have sexual things done to you or you pay for protection? Either one of the two, you become a wood or you become what they term a 'ho'?" Ford indicated that, indeed, he knew that to be the case.

Jones next called into question Ford's analysis of the meaning of the tattoos. "Really, these symbols are, in a way, what they are to the eye of the beholder; would you agree with that? Somebody equally qualified as you could have a different interpretation, couldn't they?" Ford had to concede this possibility. Jones pointed out, for example, that the Oakland Raider football team's logo was a skull and crossbones and that the old jolly roger was intended to strike terror in the hearts of opponents. It was a way of saying that seemingly frightening images could be perfectly ordinary in some contexts.

The questioning was combative and tension-filled, as if the defense sensed that it had now become essential to break down or at least explain the picture of King that the prosecution had so far meticulously constructed.

"Let's talk about full-sleeved tattoos, for example," Jones said at one point. Ford testily shot back, "Okay. What do you want to know about them?"

"If I'm 5 foot 7—do you know what the ratio of whites to blacks is in the penitentiary?"

"Quite a few more black than white," Ford conceded.

"Roughly 70/30, 70/20?"

"Sounds good," Ford said.

"If I'm 5 foot 7 and white and have tattoos and another individual is 5 foot 7, white, without tattoos, which one is going to make an impression on the rest of the population in the penitentiary?" Jones asked.

"I don't know that that necessarily will—I don't know if that has anything to do with it," Ford said rather awkwardly. He knew where Jones was going and did not want to acknowledge that King had gotten these tattoos, at least in part, to protect himself.

"I thought you said the symbols have a meaning, don't they intimidate?" Jones asked, scoring points by forcing the obviously uncomfortable Ford to concur.

"These symbols are not only a motivation for intimidation, they're motivation for survival aren't they?" Jones asked, his voice rising to a crescendo like that of a Southern preacher.

Ford had to agree.

"Without tattoos a 5 foot 7 person is more likely to have a problem, a lot more likely to be approached and tested to be determined whether he's going to be a ho or whether he's going to be a wood?"

"Could be," Ford answered feebly.

Jones next hammered on the fact that King's tattoos were a matter of freedom of expression that was constitutionally protected. Bill King had a right to worship any religion he pleased and to tattoo his body with expressions of any belief and opinion he wanted to, Jones stated emphatically. The implication was clear that, in the defense's view, the entire fabric of the prosecution's case was constructed from King's ideological beliefs rather than facts proving that he was a participant in the murder.

Under redirect examination, Guy James Gray sought to get Ford to establish a link between satanic beliefs and hate groups in what was a rather confusing and questionable association. Ford could muster little to back up what was, at best, a tenuous connection. However, Gray had a final point that he wanted the detective to make so that the prosecution could knit together the strands of the case against Bill King. Gray set out to show that King had intended to form a free-world chapter of the Confederate Knights of America following his release from prison. He hoped that this testimony would make it clear to the jury that, unlike countless convicts who join gangs in the penitentiary only to leave them behind when they return home to their communities, King returned to Jasper with his racist ideology intact. Gray asked Ford to read a letter that King had written while in the penitentiary to "Weed," a friend on the outside.

"Dear Kinsmen and fellow Aryan warrior," the letter began. "It is my hopes to be released from this prison with the knowledge so needed to benefit my precious race and begin a chapter of the Confederate Knights of America in the Jasper area." The handwritten letter was signed "John William King, president" and listed King's Jasper address. Gray also had Ford identify another document that had been found in King's apartment as an "application for citizenship with the Confederate Knights of America," also in King's writing.

This testimony paved the way for another compelling witness, a man named Matthew Hoover. Hoover had served time at Beto for aggravated robbery, and his tenure had overlapped with King's. The two had taken a college-level computer drafting class together and had become good friends, a friendship in part founded upon their shared white-supremacist beliefs. One afternoon just before his release from prison, Hoover had asked King to sign his photo album. The book contained girly photographs and other mementos of prison life. King had taken the album, inscribed it, and returned it a

day or two later. Gray set the stage for Hoover's testimony by asking him
to describe his relationship with King. However, Hoover's account of what
King had actually written in the album was left for after the morning recess,
like a promise of things to come, thereby leaving the jury in expectant suspense during the break.

The late-morning proceedings started with Hoover reading King's inscription in the prison album:

> To a true and tried wood who represents our Aryan race the way it
> should be, with power. I write these words with the utmost love
> and respect for you bro. We Aryan warriors are a relative handful of
> Aryans dedicated to fighting on behalf of a world that often fears and
> hates us. It would be dishonest if I did not concede the truth that
> relations between the Aryan kindred have been deteriorating. So,
> why do we do it? Why do we dare to dream a dream of a better
> world? Why are we willing to sacrifice any semblance of a normal life
> to make that dream a reality? Why do we seek, against seemingly
> impossible odds, to change a cold, often indifferent society into one
> that is a better place, more tolerant place for the Aryan race? Because
> we, bro, are the few, the proud, the peckerwoods, the Aryan race,
> a gifted race, a misunderstood race, a hated and persecuted race;
> but Aryans, true Aryans, nonetheless. And as Aryans, we believe we
> have a responsibility to shepherd the change. A change where all the
> branches of the white movement live together as one. We, my Aryan
> brother in arms, will rightfully claim what's ours, and in the end we'll
> wash our feet in the blood of the Jews. Stay proud, my brother, be
> as cool as you can and as cold as you must. And don't forget a huge
> wood gathering, barbecue, and bashing on July the 4th, 1998.
>
> Destroy, Erase, Improve. Your Bro, PoZZum, 1997, John W. (Bill)
> King.

It was this inscription that Gray had remembered one pre-trial evening when
he suddenly realized how all of the case's themes could be linked together.
Gray considered Hoover's photo album the case's Rosetta Stone.

"What was your understanding of 'bashing' . . . what did you think
that meant?" Gray asked, although he already knew what Hoover's response
would be. The answer wasn't for Gray's edification but for the jury's.

"Beating maybe, something like that," Hoover said.

"Did you discuss with Bill, during your time in the penitentiary, his feelings about the blacks and Jews?" Gray now asked.

"Yeah, just felt that we was being, I don't know how to put it. That the interracial couples and that our race would deteriorate and that Jews and blacks and television and everything—I don't know how to put it," Hoover said awkwardly, throwing out vague and unrelated notions that didn't add up to a coherent statement. That wasn't going to cut it as far as the Jasper DA was concerned. He hadn't arranged to have Hoover travel all the way from Missouri for this kind of testimony.

"Well, I think you just need to put it as honest and direct as you know how," Gray said sternly. The DA clarified that Hoover had been subpoenaed to be there; he was not testifying of his own free will. Hoover proceeded to live up to billing, with spellbinding testimony that described the stark realities of prison life as well as the ingenuity with which prisoners subverted the rule of the corrections system. Hoover also described prison gang initiations and the "blood in, blood out" code whereby a prospective member had to attack or kill another person to gain gang membership. "Blood out" meant that there was no option for leaving the organization voluntarily—once a gang member, the only way out was to shed one's own blood.

It was evident that the prosecution was attempting to situate King at the center of a vicious, racist gang whose members routinely resorted to violence. The cornerstone to their ideology was hatred against blacks, Jews, and other minorities. Hoover testified to frequent discussions about race wars and how they might be ignited. "Everybody talked about that in there," Hoover said, almost casually. "Everybody predicts a racial war between whites and blacks or between whites and Jews." Such racial warfare might be fomented by blowing up housing projects or by racial attacks, he suggested, "to where that race will turn in the street and go rioting, kind of like Rodney King, and the military come in and put them down." Hoover was referring to the riots following the acquittal of the police officers that had assaulted Rodney King in Los Angeles, igniting days of looting and rioting. The scenario was hauntingly similar to that depicted in the infamous book *The Turner Diaries*. In his statement to authorities, Shawn Berry claimed that, as Byrd was being dragged, King had shouted, "This is the beginning of the Turner Diaries."

Hoover made an important clarification about the dynamics at Beto. The notion that prisoners join gangs for protection had been bandied about by different witnesses for two days, becoming something of an accepted axiom. The reality was otherwise, Hoover noted, in that a prisoner did not get to join a gang unless he first proved himself. When prisoners arrived at the unit, they were tested—assaulted—without exception. Only those who proved their mettle, on their own, facing off against their assailants in the day room, the hallways, or the showers, became candidates for gang membership. This was the origin of the term "gladiator unit" as a descriptor of penal institutions like Planet Beto. Those who failed to stand up, those too weak or too scared, became the victims of a continued and merciless terror, either giving themselves over to be used at will by others or paying for protection or both. "Not really a matter of protection," Hoover concluded. "I mean, to be quite honest, they're not even going to approach you and ask you to be a member of their organization if there is any doubt in their mind that you're not a wood. You are already established, more than likely, when you join." Only then, when the prisoner had proven himself, might the gang membership afford a measure of protection: "After that, it helps to have close buddies," Hoover concluded.

Curiously, at moments it appeared that both the prosecution and the defense, in its cross-examination, were making the very same point. Both were arguing that Bill King's experience at Beto, a well-known "gladiator unit," had been traumatizing. It was a barbaric world in which King, like other inmates, had been subjected to unusual brutality at the hands of other prisoners, a brutality all too often governed by racial allegiances and identities that formed the organizing principles for the gangs. But the prosecution was using these experiences to focus on King's motive, whereas the defense was clearly hoping to suggest that they were a possible mitigating factor that might make the jury less inclined to administer the ultimate penalty.

Hoover's disturbing testimony was capped with one last observation:

"Do you feel that you have placed your life in jeopardy by coming here to testify?" Gray asked the former convict.

"Yes," Hoover replied flatly.

THE FINAL DAY AND A HALF of the prosecution's case in *State v. King* centered on the material evidence that supported the view that King had been present at the murder and that he had participated in it. The state also hoped to show that the victim had been chained against his will, thereby providing a firm basis for the capital murder charge.

There were several key pieces of evidence linking King to the murder. One was his Zippo lighter, with its triangular Klan symbol and "Possum" boldly written on its side. In his "Logical Reasoning" letter to the *Dallas Morning News,* King had implied that the lighter had been lost. He later gave me a similar account. However, Shawn Berry's brother, Louis, would shortly testify that he had used King's lighter to light a cigarette on the day of the murder. Similarly, Keisha Atkins had testified that King had been in posses-sion of the lighter that Saturday night before King, Brewer, and Berry had headed off in the pickup truck to find a party. Though not incontrovertible (someone other than King might have been in possession of the lighter after Atkins saw it that night), the presence of the lighter at the crime scene was strong support for the argument that King was a participant.

In addition, a box of Marlboro cigarettes had been found at the scuffle scene with one of its cigarettes turned upside down inside the box. Witnesses would testify that King often turned a cigarette in a pack upside down, sav-ing this "good luck" cigarette to be smoked last. Finally, a DNA expert from the FBI's laboratory in Quantico, Virginia, Dr. Frank Baechtel, testified that a cigarette butt found on the logging road contained King's DNA, although the cigarette also contained another person's DNA as a "secondary" contrib-utor. Berry and Brewer were specifically excluded as possible contributors to that secondary DNA, but Byrd could not be confirmed or excluded, prompt-ing Gray to say, in closing arguments, that perhaps the victim had asked for a puff from the cigarette as a last request. It was an unlikely scenario, and it was not the prosecution's finest moment. It seemed more likely, for example, that another person contributed the secondary DNA, someone who might have been riding in the truck with King in the days before the murder. How-ever, this scenario would have nullified the value of the cigarette butt as a means of placing King at the crime scene that night.

More to the point was a sandal print found in the sand on the logging road near where Byrd was first assaulted. A FBI expert on shoe print and tire tread analysis testified that the print was made by the right shoe from one of the two pairs of Outback sandals found at the Timbers Apartments. Ac-cording to court testimony, one pair belonged to Shawn Berry, the other

to Bill King. Sandy Wersema, the FBI analyst, testified that the shoe print
matched that of an Outback sandal, but she could not say unequivocally
which of the two right shoes had left it. Both pairs had been tested and compared with the impression in the sand at the scuffle scene, but the two shoes
differed in size only by about a quarter of an inch (Berry typically wore a
size 9, King a size 9½), and Wersema was of the opinion that either one
could have left the impression. Obtaining a definitive identification of a
sandy impression was usually difficult, she said, and determining an *exact*
shoe size from a sandy impression was all but impossible. However, Russell
Brewer's and Shawn Berry's shoes were accounted for. Berry had been wearing Polo-brand boots that night, not sandals, while Brewer, whose shoe size
was a 7, had been wearing Nike tennis shoes. That left King's sandals as the
most plausible source of the footprint in the sand. In addition, Atkins had
identified a photograph of a pair of Outback sandals as "just like" the sandals
King was wearing when he left the apartment that night.

That determination led directly to another significant piece of evidence: a
small speck of blood on the top strap of one of the Outback sandals that presumably belonged to King. The drop was minuscule, only about two millimeters in diameter—less than a single drop from an ordinary eyedropper.
However, Baechtel testified that the DNA from that drop matched James
Byrd's. The other sandal from the pair also had "human biological material,"
but the sample was too small to ascertain its DNA composition. Baechtel
also reviewed his findings for Berry's Polo boots and Brewer's Nike tennis
shoes. Both had been found to have blood on them with DNA matching
James Byrd's. Furthermore, DNA on other cigarette butts and on beer bottles
found on the logging road matched Brewer's and Berry's. The DNA findings
clearly contradicted King's account in "Logical Reasoning" that Berry had
dropped him and Brewer off at the apartment and then headed off on his
own with Byrd.

The prosecution's case against King ended on three powerful notes. The
first was a classic bit of trial theater scripted for Pat Hardy. The flamboyant
attorney, in his striking white dinner jacket and ostrich boots, was given the
assignment of entering into evidence the chain that had been used in the
murder. The instrument of Byrd's torture and ultimate death was taken from
a box and then allowed to crash loudly onto the courtroom's wooden floor.
There was an audible gasp as those in attendance instinctively recoiled. The

chain was dark and heavy, its metal links corpulent and coldly ominous in appearance. With assistance, Hardy then stretched the chain to its full length—twenty-four and a half feet—as he stood before the jury, ceremoniously, so that they and those in the gallery, all gazing with rapt interest, could see for themselves how far behind the pickup truck the victim had been dragged. It was as dramatic and potent a display as one would ever see in a court of law.

The second part of the prosecution's end game featured its final witness, Dr. Tommy Brown, a forensic pathologist at the Jefferson County morgue, where Byrd's autopsy had been performed. The booklets containing the dozen photographs of Byrd's dismembered body were once again distributed to the jury so that the pathologist could explain their forensic implications. Guy James Gray had alerted the members of the Byrd family that this would be a particularly troubling part of the trial, giving them the option of leaving the courtroom temporarily, which some did. The pathologist testified that Byrd was alive until his body struck the culvert on the side of the road, after being dragged over both dirt and asphalt for approximately two miles. That blow, which had severed the victim's head and right shoulder from the rest of his body, killed him. In agonizing detail, Brown described the condition of Byrd's remains. The victim's body had severe lacerations, scrapes, and "massive brush burns" throughout. There were gaping wounds and abrasions along both sides of Byrd's face; his left cheek had a large five-and-one-half-inch area that had been ground down to bone. Some of his teeth were missing. All of Byrd's right anterior ribs had been fractured, and his penis had been completely shredded by the grinding action of the asphalt road. The scrotum was present, but "both testicles had been traumatically removed." Brown had found gravel in the victim's scrotal sac.

Gray next led the pathologist through a series of questions that addressed the pivotal issue of whether James Byrd had been conscious during the interval between the initial assault on the logging road and the moment when his body struck the culvert, ending his life. He asked Brown to describe the victim's wounds around the buttocks, which appeared different from some of the other wounds. The pathologist stated that it was his opinion that James Byrd was not only alive but also conscious during a significant portion of his ordeal. The state of the victim's elbows and heels formed an important basis for this conclusion. Byrd's taluses, or heel bones, had been so severely ground

LOGGING CHAIN

down that they were perfectly flat. The pathologist believed that those wounds indicated that the victim was trying to hold his back and head up off the ground by pressing his heels against the road as he was being pulled by the ankles. His elbows had been so severely traumatized that both bones were exposed, although his left elbow had sustained greater injuries. Finally, Brown noted the relative absence of trauma to the back of the victim's head. There were some abrasions, but they were relatively small except by the victim's neck and upper back. There were also no underlying skull fractures. If a person were limp and unconscious while being dragged a mile over a hard surface such as asphalt, one would have expected to see more severe drag marks and related trauma about the head, Brown opined. "In my opinion he was attempting to keep his head off of the pavement. There's no drag marks. He was conscious, I think, during a portion of this distance, from up at the end of the logging road to where [he hit] the culvert," Brown concluded.

Perhaps Sonny Cribbs, King's defense lawyer, was affected by the testimony, although he had previously read the autopsy report and had seen the photographs. Whatever the reason, the defense's cross-examination did nothing more than draw attention to the fact that the official report, filed days after the autopsy was completed, made no mention of whether James Byrd was conscious as he was being dragged. That report had indicated only that James Byrd was alive until hitting the culvert. Brown's current testimony clearly added a new and very significant dimension; it was the pivotal issue in determining whether Bill King could be sentenced to death were the jury to find him guilty. The stakes were high, in other words. Yet, after Brown acknowledged that the official report did not address the issue of Byrd's state of consciousness, Cribbs appeared to have run out of ideas. "I have no other questions, Your Honor," he said before sitting down. His cross-examination of this key witness had lasted only two or three minutes.

The state was now ready for its closing presentation—a videotape of the segment of Huff Creek Road along which James Byrd had been dragged to death. Brack Jones objected to the screening of the video, arguing that it might create unfair prejudice in the jury and that the video had no probative value, but he was overruled.

An unusual hush fell over the gallery. Huff Creek Road had already been invoked repeatedly, beginning with Gray's opening remarks. Many witnesses had made reference to this heretofore little-known country lane, noting the evidence they had found along it, for example. However, few of the jurors and few of the people in the gallery had actually seen the road or knew its location with certainty.

The image that appeared on the screen had all the telltale signs of a home movie—shaky camera work and scenes that at times came in and out of focus. The video had obviously not been shot professionally, which only added to its gritty, true-crime feel. The opening scene was a collection of law enforcement vehicles at the intersection where the logging road met the pavement on Huff Creek Road. In the upper right corner the date, "June 8, 1998," indicated that the video had been made the day following the discovery of Byrd's remains. Slowly, the vehicle in which the person filming the video was riding made its way up Huff Creek Road from this point. The drag marks, the dark and ominous stains along the center of the gray pavement, were immediately visible. It was those stains that had led Tommy Robinson to believe, that Sunday morning when he and Joe Sterling had been called to check on the report of a dead person, that he was following the traces of an animal's carcass. The world now had a very different understanding of what those dark traces represented.

Like the courtroom itself, the video was silent. As the videographer moved up the road, following the trail of James Byrd's torture, viewers were left to imagine what this man had endured. Occasionally there were bright orange circles painted in the pavement. The circles indicated the location of evidence, and they were numerous: the place where Byrd's dentures had fallen or been knocked from his mouth, the site where his keys had worked their way out of the pocket of his pants, which had been wrapped around his ankles to prevent the chain from sliding free, or places where tissue or blood had been swabbed for subsequent DNA testing.

The video simultaneously captured the depravity of what had occurred while also depicting the striking and incongruent beauty of the country road. Tall majestic pines and stands of oak and mulberry trees nearly enveloped the ribbon of asphalt that meandered through them. At one point, a long, white wooden fence ran alongside the road, marking the home of a relatively wealthy rancher or farmer. More frequently the homes along the road were modest wood frame structures or run-down trailers. The stains left by the victim's body at times undulated in slow, almost graceful arcs back and forth across the asphalt. They suggested that the perpetrators had toyed with their

victim, sending his body careening first this way and then that. This impression amplified the viewers' awareness that they were witnessing the manifestations of a most disturbing, unbridled form of cruelty, one that instilled
horror.

In the silence viewers also began to comprehend just how far Byrd had actually been dragged. The notion of two miles (the distance Byrd had been
dragged over asphalt), as a spoken phrase from a sheriff's deputy or a prosecutor, could quickly became a mere abstraction. But two miles as rendered
by a video that followed the trail of a man's torture was agonizingly long. The
video brought the courtroom audience closer to the nightmare, making it
immediate. It was as close as the prosecution could get to actually showing
the jury, firsthand, what had transpired out on Huff Creek Road.

The video was eleven minutes and thirty-two seconds long. It ended at the
Huff Creek Church, where the headless body, like a monstrous apparition,
had been left that Sunday morning. A dark stain still marked the spot, seeming to almost outline the form of the torn and fractured remains. The stain
had been created by the collective wounds—the scrapes and tears and abrasions—that had left virtually no portion of Byrd's body intact. There was no
pool of blood because, as the forensic pathologist had explained, there was
no longer a living heart to pump the precious fluid out through the body's
wounds. Instead, the stain was left by the residual blood and other bodily
fluids in his tissues, drawn out through the tears and gashes in the flesh.
Here, a day later, the stain still bore witness to the unspeakable fate that had
befallen James Byrd.

The video that concluded the state's case against John William King was
a powerful tool for capturing the hearts and minds of the jury. As on the previous days, the prosecution's timing was flawless. The midday lunch break, it
was announced, would precede the opening of the defense's case. This meant
that once again the jurors would leave the courtroom with the prosecution's
uncontested evidence seared into their minds. It was likely that, for years to
come, few in that courtroom would find it possible to forget the gritty images captured on the Huff Creek Road video.

BILL KING'S ATTORNEYS made no opening statement after the lunch
break, an unusual step and the second time they had elected this option.

They mustered but three witnesses in their defense of King. The first was John Mosely, a convict tattoo artist who went by the nickname of Big Mo and had known King at Beto, where he was still serving time for burglary and sexual assault. The source of his nickname was readily apparent: he was a large, imposing individual, whose hard-core convict status only added to an aura of mystery and incipient menace. It was also evident that Big Mo was not awed or cowered in the least by the ceremonial trappings of a court of law. Instead, as he stepped into the witness box, Mosely cast a friendly wink at King. Most in the courtroom could not help but see the gesture as a sign of disdain for the whole affair.

Mosely's assignment was to put a dent in the prosecution's interpretation of King's tattoos. He was also to make the point that Beto was a place in which white inmates were terrorized. Convicts who, like King, were not physically large were constant victims of assault and other predatory behavior. While Mosely's testimony was interesting, the State's witnesses had already covered much of this ground either under cross-examination or under direct examination. Furthermore, Mosely's effort to downplay the racial meanings of King's tattoos or the disturbing implications of the satanic images fell short of convincing. "It's prison," Big Mo declared at one point. "Ain't too many people going to ask for butterflies and roses and stuff. . . . That's kind of gay sounding, ain't it? In Beto I?" he said, with a tone of incredulity at the thought that anyone would even suggest it.

Mosely's utility as a defense witness was further undermined when, under cross-examination, Gray read from a recent letter that Mosely had written to Kylie Greeney, King's girlfriend. In the letter Mosely seemed to imply that he had told another convict who had agreed to testify for the prosecution that he would be "jammed" if he went through with his testimony. This amounted to tampering with a State's witness, Gray reminded Big Mo.

The second defense witness was a former roommate of King's named Allen Cunningham. In some of his prison kites to Brewer, King had indicated that Cunningham was trying to line up some friends who might have some "shit" on Shawn Berry and might therefore be of some assistance to King and Brewer. Cunningham testified that he had known King for two years and that during part of this time Cunningham had had a black girlfriend. Cunningham said that King had "teased" him about the relationship, without elaborating on the specifics. Cunningham testified that although

King's racial views were apparent, he never spoke about them at length and he never made mention of wanting to hurt black people. In response to a question regarding whether Cunningham had ever heard King make racial slurs against blacks, Cunningham responded: "In a personal setting, not in public." When Cribbs asked Cunningham if King appeared to be "proud of the white race," the witness responded, "Shouldn't we all be?" Cunningham also said that King had not seemed to take unusual pride in his racist tattoos or affiliations. Under cross-examination, however, Hardy produced a signed affidavit in which Cunningham had said, under oath, that in fact King and Brewer "seemed proud to be in the [Aryan Brotherhood]." As a defense of King, it was less than compelling.

Finally, a former employer named Dennis Simmack was put on the stand to testify that King was a hard worker while employed in the man's construction company. The work involved weatherizing homes, 65 to 70 percent of which belonged to African Americans. Simmack testified that King never said or acted in ways that suggested a negative attitude toward working in those homes. However, when traveling to work sites King and Simmack had occasionally engaged in more philosophical conversations, some of which drifted into discussions about topics such as who the Aryan people were and how they had come to be. King had also talked about the Klan. Still, Simmack reported that he had never had the impression that King was attempting to start anything in Jasper. King's views simply seemed personal, he said, although they also seemed deeply studied. On one occasion Simmack had even come home and said to his wife, "Man, this guy knows a lot. He must have done a lot of reading."

Under cross-examination, Simmack revealed a behavior pattern similar to what had emerged in Cunningham's testimony. "Isn't it true that the defendant often made racial comments about how he did not like black people?" Stevens asked.

"One on one on a ride to work, yes," Simmack responded.

And a few moments later:

"He was intensely bitter toward black people, isn't that true?"

"Yes, sir."

Those were the last words of testimony heard in Bill King's capital murder trial. Stevens indicated that he had no further questions on the part of the prosecution. When Judge Golden turned to the defense table and said, "Your

next witness," Sonny Cribbs stood and announced: "We have no other witnesses at this time, Your Honor. The defendant rests."

The prosecution offered no rebuttal; none appeared necessary.

THE NEXT MORNING, WHEN THE JURORS filed in to hear the closing arguments, Judge Golden read them the formal charge and defined the terms that would govern their deliberations. He also told them that there would be three options in deciding a verdict: they could find the defendant not guilty; guilty of the offense of capital murder; or not guilty of capital murder but guilty of the lesser charge of murder.

The closing arguments followed closely the issues that had been mapped out during the trial. The prosecution's arguments centered on the evidence linking Bill King to the scene of the crime—the cigarette butt, King's lighter, the shoe print, and the sandal with Byrd's blood. As for motive, Gray and his team once again argued that King's racist ideology both revealed a deep-seated hatred of African Americans and formed the motivational basis for the murder itself. Perhaps the murder had even been some sort of initiation, it was argued, although they conceded that that point had not been established conclusively. What could be said definitively, they argued, was that King was a leader of the Confederate Knights of America and that he had intended to form a chapter of this group in Jasper. Byrd's murder, Hardy suggested to the jury, was a modern-day lynching. Referring to one of King's tattoos with a similar image, Hardy argued that King, Brewer, and Berry were the three "robed riders coming straight out of hell. Instead of a rope, they used a chain, instead of horses, they were using a pickup truck."

Brack Jones sat in the witness box as he spoke to the jury for the defense. He argued that there was more than reasonable doubt regarding the kidnapping charge. Byrd had gotten into the pickup truck willingly and had drunk beer with the three accused men. As abhorrent as this murder was, the fact that Byrd had been killed or chained to the back of the truck did not prove kidnapping. For example, an altercation in which two individuals are fighting and one tries to get away and is grabbed and brought down does not constitute kidnapping, Jones argued. This was closer to what had transpired that night, and it meant that the kidnapping charge could not be supported. "Tattoos, writings, the infamous K.K.K. book do not prove kidnapping. Beliefs don't prove kidnapping. Byrd voluntarily got in the pickup," Jones said in his remarks.

Sonny Cribbs preferred to address the jury while pacing before them. "I get a little nervous, and I think a little better walking and talking," he said. Cribbs emphasized that a defendant is under no obligation to prove anything at all. That is the state's burden. He emphasized that no witnesses had directly testified that King had attempted to induct them into any racist organization. "He may have had racial beliefs," Cribbs said, "he may have made racial slurs, but that's his right. You have a right to be a racist; right or wrong, you still have that right. You have a right to be a satanist."

Cribbs argued that the cigarette with King's DNA could readily have fallen out of the ashtray after being there for days. King had ridden to work in that truck three or four days a week, he reminded the jurors. Similarly, "A drop of two millimeters of blood could also have gotten on that sandal because there's none any place else." He noted that in his view the prosecution had not clearly established that the Outback sandal with Byrd's DNA was actually King's. Cribbs also read from the definitions the judge had given the jury earlier: " 'Mere presence alone at the scene of the alleged offense if any, will not constitute one a party to the offense.' Presence doesn't make it," Cribbs asserted.

In conclusion, Cribbs argued that King was a victim of posttraumatic stress disorder, much like many Vietnam veterans had suffered after the war. "This boy had something happen to him in the penitentiary, he became a racist, he became a hater. The penitentiary created him, he was a normal kid from Jasper until then."

Finally it was Gray's turn. The DA reviewed the definition of kidnapping, arguing that chaining a man against his will clearly fell under the definition. After reviewing some of the other evidence that had been mustered to support the view that King had been present and that King had the motive for committing such a crime, Gray concluded with the following reflection: "We'd all be a lot more comfortable if this was what we originally thought it was; and that is some kind of drug deal that went bad, or three drunks out there on Saturday night and it just got out of hand. But that's not what the facts show. Whether we like it or whether we don't like it, the facts show that we've got two gang guys here; and we've got one look-out. And Bill King is not just a gang guy, but he is a radical gang guy."

Gray continued, "The degree of anger and hate that has to be in some-body's heart and soul and mind, not only to kill somebody, not only to drag somebody, but even after the head is severed from the body . . . drive another mile to mutilate that body more . . . that is a virus. That's something that's very, very dangerous in our community; and we've all got a job to do and a responsibility that rests on our shoulders. . . . We hate that it happened here. We wish we didn't have this responsibility, but it's our job to do it." The job to which Gray was referring, of course, was the job of sentencing Bill King to be executed.

It took only a few hours for the jury to arrive at its verdict, which was an-nounced in the courtroom: "We the jury find the defendant guilty of the of-fense of capital murder as alleged in the indictment."

THE NEXT DAY THE JURY HEARD both sides argue why Bill King should or should not be put to death. The prosecution's witnesses emphasized that King had been given every opportunity over the years to change the course of his life and had failed to do so. A psychiatrist testified that King would pose an ongoing threat of committing violence were he ever to be released from prison. The defense presented a psychologist who argued that by the time King might be eligible for parole, he would be in his sixties and very un-likely to pose a threat to anyone.

Knowing that his father was going to take the stand to plead for his life, Bill King requested, via his attorneys, permission to leave the courtroom. It was a gesture that no doubt surprised many, suggesting that, despite the crime for which he was on trial and his stoic demeanor, he was a man capable of emotion. King was removed to an adjoining room where he could watch his father's testimony on closed circuit television. Ronald King, a grayed and elderly man, his voice full of gravel and sadness, gave very emotional testi-mony that concluded with this tearful declaration: "I love him, really do. You don't have to love what they do, but . . . . We've invested a lot of love in that boy. You hate to think you're going to lose him, and I guess as a daddy I'll never be able to resign myself to that."

The jurors returned to the courtroom after a short deliberation, filing in one by one, like somber acolytes, and the courtroom was absolutely quiet ex-cept for Ronald King's emphysemic breathing and the slow, steady whir of

the six ceiling fans that gently moved the air in the room. Every seat was occupied, including the defendant's—Bill King had been brought back to hear
the jury's verdict. The Byrd family huddled together, their arms around one
another. Ronald King sat in his wheelchair across the aisle from them, with
Father Foshage at his side offering a supportive presence, as well as Carol,
Bill's sister, who was making her first appearance in the courtroom that day.
None present could ignore the gravity of the circumstance or the enormity
of the responsibility carried by those twelve men and women. The abstrac-
tions of the legal system, with its odd conventions and ritualized encounters,
had yielded to this moment: a jury's decision between life and death. This
brute fact, inescapable and raw, seemed to saturate the emotional tenor of the
room. At the outset of the trial, his peers had elected as foreman the sole
black juror. He now handed the bailiff the envelope containing the jury's
decision.

"Mr. King will you stand up, please, sir," Judge Golden said somberly after reading the contents of the envelope. "Based on the jury's findings, I
hereby sentence you to death by lethal injection."

There were no shouts of joy or other celebratory outbursts in the courtroom. Instead, there seemed to be a profound awareness of the gravity of
what had just transpired: a society's encounter with evil and a quiet, unacknowledged desperation at its own impotence. Perhaps for some there was a
sense of horror in recognizing not only that there is evil in our midst but also
that the young man sitting before them at the defense table, the one staring
vacantly into some infinite space, was now considered beyond reach, beyond
redemption. It had come down to this, the ultimate penalty. The men and
women sitting in the jury box were merely proxies for us all, instruments of
the nation's Old Testament self-understanding. The air felt thick in the
room, burdened by the weight of the moment, as Bill King slowly rose from
the defense table and was escorted from the courtroom, enveloped in an eerie
silence.

Blood Ties

THE FIRST TIME I VISITED BILL KING on death row I was accompanied by his father, Ronald. On subsequent visits, every time I made my way down the Polunsky Unit's main walkway, I thought of Ronald King whizzing down it in his motorized wheelchair. The cobalt blue wheelchair is testimony to the wizardry of modern engineering; it can be assembled quickly into a solid machine that runs on two electric batteries and is controlled with a joystick that allows it to turn on a dime. Once we were cleared to enter the prison, Ronald led the way, moving at a good clip, bantering with every inmate we encountered (they were from the prison's general-population blocks). The first prisoner was a tall, middle-aged black man standing immediately inside the fence. "You going to take the bus on in to town this mornin'?" Ronald asked him. The prisoner, disarmed and surprised by the comment, let out a laugh. "No, don't think I'm gonna be doing *that* today," he retorted. About halfway down the walkway we encountered a group of three prisoners weeding around the base of one of the rose bushes, which were in full bloom. "Lookee here," Ronald exclaimed loudly as we approached them. "Got three new Japanese gardeners to tend the roses." One of the convicts bent all the way down as if he were about to touch his toes and then slowly raised himself up to a three-quarters position, clasping his hands in front of him, imitating some imagined Asian prayer ritual. He proceeded to rise up and down several times, all the while uttering a series of incomprehensible phrases in pseudo Japanese. The other two convicts broke into laughter as Ronald whirred by in his strange motorized transport, breathing through the clear plastic tube attached to the green oxygen tank that rested like a ceremonial pole in a rack at the back of his wheelchair. Finally, as we neared the end of the walkway, another prisoner was working alone, weeding with a three-pronged implement. "You're going to have one helluva time tunneling out with that thing," Ronald said. This man broke into a smile as we cruised by.

Ronald King is Bill King's strongest and most reliable supporter. Though he is seriously ill and lacking in financial resources, his very existence seems to revolve around his son. Bill has repeatedly described his relationship with his father as distant and strained, although that had begun to change when Ronald was hospitalized in Mississippi not long after Bill's first arrest at the age of seventeen. Since the murder of James Byrd, however, Ronald has become Bill's primary lifeline, and something appears to have changed in Ronald, mobilizing him to do whatever he can to save his son's life. Taking care of Bill's needs has become a full-time job for the ailing elder King.

Ronald wavers in his views regarding his son's guilt or innocence. "Why did all of this come down, and actually what *did* come down? You know, why? It's hard for me to picture a child of mine being involved in something like this," he said when I first met him. The whole incident is something that Ronald finds difficult to fathom. The closest he can come to acknowledging his son's involvement in the murder is to say, "I can love him and hate what he did. But as far as loving him, I love him as much as I ever did."

Ronald once gave me a sheaf of letters to read that Bill had written to him since the Byrd murder. What stood out about them were the incessant requests. Every letter was about what Bill needed. For example, Ronald was to round up all the extended family and have each deposit a prescribed amount every month into Bill's fund so that he could purchase stamps, envelopes, snacks, and other items from the commissary. Then there were the materials he needed to have copied, letters sent, phone calls made, and people to be contacted. Bill's list was endless, and all of it seemed to fall on the shoulders of an infirm seventy-year-old man who hardly has enough money to pay his medical bills, let alone subsidize the legal and personal needs of a man on death row. Nevertheless, Ronald does what he can afford—and sometimes more: "I try to do everything I can," he told me, "because I'm the last thing he's got as far as family is concerned."

There is a powerful paternal force at work in this relationship. It has come to absorb virtually every spare dime in Ronald's bank account and virtually all of his emotional resources as well. "Even if he'd come out and said to me, 'Look, Daddy, I did it.' I still couldn't say, 'I don't love you, son.' I would still love my boy. And I hate like hell what he did! You get my point? But nothing is going to stop me from loving my son. . . . The fact is that I always wanted him, right from the beginning. I've always loved that boy. . . . I'd just like to see his sentence commuted to life," Ronald said.

Notwithstanding his father's tireless efforts, Bill often feels that Ronald is not doing enough, which leads to conflicts between them in which Bill resorts to a kind of emotional brinkmanship. If he feels that Ronald has not come through in some way, there is always hell to pay. The basis for such conflicts ranges from the petty to the substantive. One squabble revolved around Ronald's refusal to forward some pornographic material to a friend of Bill's. Another involved Ronald's refusal to sue for grandparent visitation rights when Kylie wasn't bringing Blayne to see Bill (Ronald couldn't afford to hire a lawyer). Bill's strategy is always the same: a blistering letter or two followed by weeks of cold silence when Ronald hears nothing at all from his son. It is the same counterphobic strategy—precipitating precisely what makes him most anxious—that Bill deploys with everyone who cares for him. While he feels an enormous fear of emotional abandonment, that is what he most often puts into play when he chooses to throw down the gauntlet. It is as if he dares those close to him to leave him or shut him out. Fear of abandonment constantly lurks behind King's bravado and posturing. This fear, which King keeps well hidden, fuels his relentless need to control others, which seems to assure him that he can stave off that moment when he might again be left alone.

.BILL KING IS LIVING IN A UNIVERSE where time has its own trajectory, governed by laws that fundamentally alter one's consciousness. The acute and peculiar awareness that time is limited, that one has reached a prescribed end

RONALD KING

game of sorts, takes an enormous toll. King spends his days in a six-foot-by-ten-foot cell, which has no bars. Like all death row cells, his is sealed off from the adjoining cells by solid walls; his door has small holes through which he may peer out and a slot through which food trays are passed. The doors are electronically controlled from a central command center, and when opened, they slide back into the wall, pocket style. Inside his cell is a cot, a permanent surface jutting out from a wall that can be used either as a desktop or as a table, and a stainless steel toilet and washbasin. A single narrow shaft of natural light enters the cell through a window that is three inches tall by four feet wide. There was a time when King was in a cell pod whose back side faced out onto the open fields along which visitors walk on their way to the prison's visitation area. King could roll up his mattress tightly and, by standing on it, peer out the window slit and watch the people approaching along the long, rose-bordered walk. However, prisoners are periodically rotated to different cells, and King's current view is of the concrete back side of another pod of cells.

Like other death row prisoners, King is allowed out of his cell for one hour a day and escorted to a nearby recreation area where, typically, another prisoner is in the adjacent recreation area. Those two prisoners are able to talk to one another, but a wire-mesh fence prevents physical contact. Prisoners are also allowed periodic excursions to the prison commissary, to the prison barber ("Haircuts for male offenders are a requirement, not a privilege," read the TDCJ regulations), and, when necessary, to the prison's infirmary. Beyond these contacts and the occasional visit, King has very little opportunity to interact with other people. Prison staff conduct bed checks every few hours, and inmates are able to communicate with others in the same eight-cell pod using creatively fashioned "fishing lines" with which they exchange notes, books, newspapers, and other material. Otherwise, King spends much of his time trying to figure out what to do with himself within the confines of his cramped cell. There are no televisions on death row, although prisoners who are not disciplinary problems are permitted to listen to radios through headphones. With the exception of crashing cell doors and the episodic shouts of fellow prisoners, death row is much quieter than the prisons with which these men were familiar before coming to the Polunsky Unit.

The isolation of death row quickly erodes many men's psyches. For example, during one visit, King pointed out an older African American death row inmate who was being interviewed in a nearby visitor cubicle by a group of law students from the University of Texas. According to King, the man had been a high school principal, "a pretty smart guy," before coming to death row, where he had now been for twelve or thirteen years. The word on the row was that two or three years ago the man "just snapped." Indeed, the prisoner had a crazed, faraway look in his eyes, and he seemed to be incoherent, judging from the way the students were struggling to make sense of what he was saying.

The man in the cell next to King's has a peculiar water fixation. He spends his days pushing the flush buttons on the toilet and on the sink. The latter tends to make a whistling noise, as water coming up the pipes forces air through the faucet. The prisoner has developed this into something of an art form, "playing" the whistling air as if it were an instrument. The sounds are an ongoing irritant to King, whose cell shares the same plumbing. One morning King's neighbor had been unusually persistent in his toilet flushing. It had been going on for hours. King happened to have an appointment in the prison infirmary that day, and as he was being escorted down the hall, he turned to look into his neighbor's cell. He was startled by what he saw: the inmate was standing on top of the toilet, naked except for a white sheet, which he had fashioned into a cape that was tied around his head and flowing behind him. He was making strange motions, thrusting his arms out in front of him, while occasionally reaching back and pushing the flush button. "What are you doing in there?" the guard who was escorting King asked. "I'm surfing," the man replied with absolute sincerity. King attributed the man's behavior to the fact that he smoked anything he could get his hands on in his cell (TDCJ prohibits smoking by death row inmates), including the stuffing from his mattress, which King claimed the prisoner rolled in toilet paper. He then lit the smoking material using a "stinger," a makeshift heating element fashioned out of wire and plugged into the electrical outlet.

The school principal and the "surfer" are examples of the impact of that strange and altered sense of time. However, not everyone is similarly affected by the death row experience. Ironically, for some the routine and structure of death row actually produces a level of psychological cohesion that eluded them in the "free world." Bill King is one of these people. While he would be the first to choose to be elsewhere, prison is not a particularly noxious experience for him. On the contrary, despite evident mood swings and periods of depression, he is able to muster a degree of focus that he finds empowering and that allows engagement with a wide variety of ideas and projects. King can devote hours of study and research to his legal defense, for example, or carry out extended correspondence with people on the outside. He also reads a great deal and has recently discovered jazz and opera. Whereas King's former life was characterized by persistent chaos, inside the Polunsky Unit's walls he is shored up somehow. It is as if those walls have reinforced him, like a prosthetic device for an otherwise faltering ego structure, sharpening his attention and his ability to use his faculties effectively.

Most prisoners on death row do not talk about the fate that awaits them. A peculiar collusion of silence seems to operate among them when it comes to acknowledging the place they occupy in that dark queue. King disdains the fact that so many of his fellow death row prisoners seem impervious to their collective circumstance, blindly awaiting their turn to be slaughtered, more interested in football statistics and pornography than mobilizing against their shared predicament. He also claims that the unique stresses of death row dissolve the kinds of grievances and factionalism that in ordinary prisons create irreconcilable enmities. For example, he said that the African American man who shares his recreation time is his best friend "on the row," although I found no way to confirm this.

Weeks may pass at the Polunsky Unit without a single inmate being transported to the Death House in Huntsville for his execution, or a spate of executions may be carried out within just a few days. There is an appearance of randomness to the process, but in actuality a variety of factors play a role in the timing of executions. Some death row inmates obtain more substantive reviews of their cases than others. Then there are the vagaries with which local communities, prosecutors, and judges embrace the death penalty. Through one or more of these strategies and circumstances, some inmates succeed in buying themselves time, but few succeed in their ultimate goal of securing freedom. The efforts represent a desperate grasping for a few more months or, with luck, a few more years. Ultimately, there is a dull inevitability to it all, as inmates leave "the row" one by one.

When the last appeal has been turned down and an execution date has been set, death row inmates are moved to what is known as "A Pod." Inmates on A Pod receive closer scrutiny because, paradoxically, their proximity to death ushers in an increased potential for suicide. For most, the time eventually arrives for the final walk down those lonely halls, the "dead man walking," the last meals, the last notes, the final visits, all part of an inexorable flow that ends with toxic chemicals bringing permanent rest. Many prisoners seem to delude themselves into believing that perhaps they may be the exception, the ones plucked from the abyss at the last moment. It keeps them going. It distracts them from the nightmarish acts they have committed and the nightmarish fate that awaits them. It also distracts them from their own tragic failures, the haunting "what ifs" and "if onlys."

Bill King, too, works hard to keep himself distracted. He has a penchant for sleeping during the day and working on various projects all night, a habit that earned him his prison nickname, "Possum," at the Beto I Unit. It is easier to concentrate at night, he says, because it is quieter. However, he once asked me about sleep disorders, perhaps because he wondered whether there might be a less pragmatic reason for his sleeping patterns. Whatever its source, King has for years known the nighttime as his time, disdaining the daylight hours, much like the creature whose name he has taken on as if it were his personal totem.

ONE OF THE MOST STRIKING FEATURES of Bill King's psychology is his unsettling capacity to undermine one's sense of known coordinates. During many visits I experienced firsthand his ability to reshape, contort, and subvert my sense of reality. For example, the notion that a "lost" Zippo lighter might somehow accidentally end up at the logging road clearing was highly improbable, but this is what King argued convincingly when I visited him on December 1, 2000. King told me that the lighter had been stolen from him one night while he was at the hospital visiting Kylie, who was having pregnancy-related problems. Russell Brewer, he said, had invited some people over to the apartment and one of them had stolen it. He had told Brewer that "he'd better get it back," but when Brewer did retrieve it, the lighter was no longer working. According to King, Brewer purchased lighter fluid and a package of flints to repair the lighter but still couldn't get it to work, so Brewer placed the lighter, flints, and lighter fluid behind the seat in Berry's truck. "If you look at the evidence photographs," King said to me, "they took a picture of the truck with the seat back down and you see the package of flints and the lighter fluid right there."

King spoke in authoritative tones, as though any rational being could see that this account exonerated him. I sat across from the cherubic-looking King, staring at his visage through the smudged bulletproof glass of the prison's visitor cubicle as he told his version of events over the telephone line, and I found myself momentarily swayed. It was plausible, I thought to myself; perhaps the discovery of the Zippo lighter at the crime scene was not, as I'd assumed, conclusive proof that King was present at the murder.

King also dismissed the DNA evidence. The cigarette butt with his DNA also included the secondary contribution of someone else. "There are thirteen strands of DNA," King informed me with the air of an expert. "It takes seven to make a definitive match. One cigarette butt had seven strands of my DNA and three strands belonging to another person." At the trial the FBI's DNA expert had testified that those three secondary strands were not incompatible with those of James Byrd. "He could not *exclude* Byrd on the basis of them," King emphasized, noting that those three strands might just as easily have come from any number of *other* people. King said that the cigarette butt had no doubt been in the truck's ashtray, only to be strewn on the ground in the fray that ensued during Byrd's desperate resistance to the assault. "It's clear that he fought being pulled from the truck," King said. "There were fingerprints across the dashboard of the truck."

King's account again seemed quite plausible. I knew that he had spent a great deal of time in the truck in the days preceding the murder; no doubt he had smoked in the truck and may well have extinguished his cigarette butts in the ashtray. Only later did I realize, when examining a photograph of the logging road, that the cigarette butt with King's DNA had actually been found some sixty-one feet from the evidence-strewn clearing where the initial assault had occurred. At this location, the perpetrators had apparently stopped after the chain had slipped off Byrd's ankles. The cigarette butt in question had also been found next to two others, one of which contained Berry's DNA, the other Brewer's. That placement seemed to suggest that the three men had exited the truck and smoked a cigarette at that spot. Was it possible, I wondered, that King had lit up a stub, thereby accounting for the unidentified secondary DNA?

Similarly, King's claim that he was dropped off at the Timbers Apartments while Shawn Berry—or Berry and Brewer, depending on the version—had gone off to murder Byrd did not square with the evidence. Berry and Brewer had both implicated him in the crime, Berry in a statement made shortly after his arrest and Brewer in testimony at his own trial. And yet somehow King had a way of placing his account within the realm of possibility. I found myself wondering if perhaps King had never been up that logging road at all. All of these and similar explanations of the evidence or of what had transpired that night became momentarily plausible under the sway of King's telling. King's talent for silver-tongued talk, for apparent eye-to-eye sincerity, had a deconstructive effect on my notion of reality. In the moment, he could readily plunge me into doubt, making me question my understanding of what was true.

Louis Berry, Shawn Berry's brother, in describing his experience of sharing the apartment with King in the weeks before the murder, revealed something about King that I found to be an especially telling point. He was describing a treasured photo album of which King was quite proud. In it was a collection of photographs of girls with whom King had been involved since returning to Jasper from the Beto Unit, most of them posing nude and more than a few taken while the girls were performing sexual acts with King. I asked Louis how it was that King had managed to enlist these girls for this purpose, a query that drew a laugh from Berry. "Bill's always had that knack," he said, "all the way back to when he was in high school. Bill has a way with words, he can talk; if he called a girl and she didn't want to come over, or sneak out, he'd talk her into it. If she had a boyfriend, if she was married, he'd say 'come on over' and she'd end up doing it even if she didn't want to. He could talk them out of it or into it, it didn't matter. If you talk to him long enough, he's going to convince you. He could make you question yourself; he could make you second-guess what ever it is that you thought was in your head."

Such thoughts reminded me of something that Kylie Greeney had once told me. She found Bill to be very compelling when he outlined all the things that proved his innocence. She could find herself believing nearly all of it. And yet there was one thing that made it difficult for her to accept wholeheartedly Bill's claims of innocence. On the Sunday that Byrd's remains were discovered, as she was driving King and Brewer to the movie theater to meet up with Berry, they asked if she had heard about the murder, instructing her to tune the radio to the local news station. Greeney recalls that they mentioned that the victim had been left in front of a church, which, she later re-

SHAWN BERRY

alized, had not yet been disclosed. "How did they know that?" she had asked herself. It was a reality to which she clung, like to a buoy in a confusing storm that often left her unsure where the boundary between fact and fiction lay.

I knew the emotional vortex to which Louis Berry and Kylie Greeney were alluding, and I recognized its power. Months after my initial visit to the Polunsky Unit, when King had looked at me through the glass and said, "I know you don't believe me but I wish you'd just give me the benefit of the doubt," I knew that on numerous occasions I had done just that. I had felt myself pulled into the dark waters of uncertainty and doubt, pulled into this constructed notion of the plausible: Could it be? I would ask myself. Is it possible that Bill is telling the truth and the rest of the world has been served a monumental lie? Is it possible that a great injustice has been committed and Bill King is a victim of a strange governmental conspiracy or a community's need for a scapegoat?

These questions were deeply unsettling. It is not that I had concluded that King was telling the truth but rather that I realized I was experiencing a dark undertow whose power was enormous. At times it had taken all of my emotional strength to prevent that undertow from sucking me into the depths. It was a disturbing experience to recognize the strength of that emotionally subversive force. Ronald King, too, seemed familiar with it. "Bill can pretty much make anyone believe what he wants them to believe," he once told me. It was the same emotional force that compelled girls to pose for him in compromising positions, or Shawn Berry to let him use his truck at will, or a pregnant Kylie Greeney to plan ways to smuggle contraband to him, knowing a false step would send her to prison. It was this power of persuasion that could make Russell Brewer send a prison kite offering to take the fall for the whole mess: the murder, the burglaries, and the hatred. Bill King had a way of making people think what they might not otherwise think and do what they might not otherwise do. It was a profoundly unsettling trait. And it was also easy to be misled, to underestimate King. After all, his defining traits veered toward the quiet and taciturn. He was so disarming. It was another of those confusing contradictions about King, part of what made him so enigmatic. Moreover, he had a keen ability for reading people, an emotional radar that was finely honed to a razor's edge, although for the most part King tended to operate via psychological stealth rather than blunt coercion.

King was not unaware of some of these qualities within himself. He once described his first visit with one of his "pen pals," a woman who had made her way to Texas to meet him in person. He had been anxious, as he often was at such initial encounters, but he felt that the visit had gone well. She later wrote him to say that she found him to be "arrogant, conceited, cocky, stubborn & hard headed but sweet and charming, too." King was pleased with her summary of his attributes and thought she had captured him perfectly.

THERE WAS A DARKER COROLLARY to this psychology. During one of my early visits King remarked, almost offhandedly, that he believed some individuals possessed unusual psychic powers. The disclosure took me by surprise because King had initially struck me as someone much more linear and pragmatic in style, someone canny about the world and experienced beyond his years. Now, as he sat across from me in his white jumpsuit, on which "DR" was prominently stenciled, it seemed that he was revealing a very different side of himself.

I had asked him how he spent his time in his cell. His answer to this question suggested that at times he lived in a world of strange semimystical feelings and experiences. He said that he corresponded with people who were "into" psychic travel and things of that nature. Sometimes he could spend hours lying on his bunk trying to levitate by utilizing his psychic powers. He imagined himself leaving his cell through the long and narrow window and escaping from the Polunsky Unit, with its guards and razor wire, and meeting up with fellow psychic travelers somewhere out in the universe. So far the results had been disappointing: he hadn't managed to get much farther than the window and wondered if *that* was only because he was so familiar with every square inch of his cell. The unnamed correspondents suggested that perhaps his lack of success was an indication that he was holding himself back, that he was not opening himself up to them. Whatever the status of their mystical notions, the psychic travelers were right about King's holding himself back: he did that with everyone.

During a subsequent visit King explained that he could easily lose himself in fantasy. He described lying in his bunk and going through the "chambers in his mind," opening doors and closing others as if venturing through a complex labyrinth, exploring a mix of memories, feelings, and fantasies. It

Blood Ties

217

was an activity that could occupy him for hours on end. Perhaps this was simply the natural product of a life in which twenty-three hours of one's day is spent with very limited contact with other human beings, confined within a six-foot-by-ten-foot space. But it also reflects a proclivity within King toward magical thinking, the kind of thought process in which logical connections are easily dispensed with and where fantasy can readily substitute for reality. It means that King can seriously entertain the possibility of escaping his incarcerated circumstance via his imagination, even if only temporarily. I wonder if it might not also mean that he could have come to believe his own account of James Byrd's murder, willing it into being, displacing the inconvenient evidence and replacing it with what was congenial to his own explanations.

King told me that he believed that some of his girlfriends wrote about thoughts and feelings, even dreams, which he felt the two of them might have experienced simultaneously. He often found in these relationships some validation for his belief in a special kind of emotional fusion with them, as if they shared thoughts. One woman who took to visiting him on death row believed they had such a special mystical connection, and King, too, believed that they could read each other's minds. King had found himself imagining that the woman was standing around a group of friends next to a black motorcycle. In her next letter, King said that she described this exact scene and that it had occurred precisely when he had found himself thinking it. For King this kind of phenomenon was confirmation that a powerful mystical connection existed between the two of them. The woman had taken to signing her letters "Mrs. King" and introduced herself to prison authorities as his wife. However, this relationship ended abruptly when she stopped corresponding, leading King to believe that the FBI must have threatened some sort of reprisal for her involvement in his life.

When King spoke to me or wrote to me about such phenomena, they seemed to capture something essential about him. One of the functions served by King's penchant for the mystical is that, through it, he can finally feel profound connections with other people, especially some of the women with whom he has become involved over the years. The mysticism provides a peculiar and idiosyncratic intimacy, giving him the sense of a psychically intermingled closeness. King is also able to draw people to him via this sense of communion—especially young and naive women, to whom he seems to offer a special kind of intimacy that cannot be found elsewhere.

Yet there is a great paradox here. While King entertains these feelings of mystical closeness, simultaneously he is very clear that no one is permitted real access into his emotional world. He seems to pride himself in appearing to be an enigma, or, as he likes to say, "an enigma within an enigma," thereby exponentially amplifying his inaccessibility. He claims that it is not pride that makes him so but rather fear: a fear that drives him to constantly subvert efforts by others to reach him. For example, in describing one of the women with whom he was corresponding he once said, "No sooner does she think she has me figured out [than] I throw [her] a curve ball." Remaining elusive is King's standard defensive tactic. "I prefer that no one person know and understand me entirely," he says. He fears that such intimacy will give others control over him, a prospect that he finds unbearable, in part, because he is adept at controlling others by using his knack for reading emotions. "I know all about playing on people's emotions and manipulating them," he once said. "I'll be damned if I'm going to let the same happen to me." It is a strategy that King has finely tuned over the years; yet it is also a strategy that can only ensure his isolation and loneliness. King is thus caught in an irresolvable cycle of loneliness and paranoia: the barriers he creates between himself and others leave him feeling profoundly empty; yet incursions into his emotional interior produce deep anxieties and fears of being controlled by others. It is much safer to be "an enigma within an enigma," secure in the knowledge that no one can reach him.

At times, King finds evidence to bolster his farfetched beliefs in the type of literature that he reads. He is a voracious reader and his tastes run the gamut from Faulkner to Lovecraft and Rice. King described one such book with which he had become quite engaged, *The Spear of Destiny* by Trevor Ravenscroft. "The book sat here for months before I started to read it, just to pass time. To say the least, it has been the most interesting, intriguing, and enlightening book that I have ever read," King said.

Ravenscroft is a self-described White Magic practitioner of the occult magic arts. In the book in question, Ravenscroft argues that Hitler was a Black Magic practitioner. He claims that the "spear of Longinus," which according to occult legend was the actual spear used by a Roman soldier to pierce the side of Christ at the Crucifixion, possessed enormous powers to be used for good or evil, depending on who possessed it. Ravenscroft attempts to explain much of Hitler's behavior as well as that of the feared Nazi SS (which he describes as a "satanic coven") in terms of the enormous powers of this mystical spear.

"I had heard of Hitler's dabblings in the occult and his satanic interest," King once wrote to me. "But this book confirms it all and goes into great detail about his exploits. I have never been into Hitler, or Nazism, so to say. And until reading this book, I had no idea what 'schutzstaffeln' (the 'SS') really meant; or even knew much about the 'SS.' I wasn't particularly interested in a spear that supposedly pierced the side of Christ, either. But this book is *so* much more," King continued.

King found the book to be revelatory: "It brought everything together for me, and turned on a light where there's always been darkness." It spoke to him on many levels. For one thing, King credited it with helping him understand the true meaning of the lightning bolts that were so central a symbol among his white supremacist acquaintances in prison and the numerous designs that Dirtball had tattooed on him. "Now, after learning more about the 'SS' I want to put as much distance between myself and everything that has to do with Hitler," he said. "The first available opportunity that arises, I am covering up these 'SS' bolts with a fleur-de-lis (aka: the New Orleans Saints symbol)."

One passage in the book was of particular interest to King. Near the conclusion of the book, in a chapter titled "The Doppelgänger: Heinrich Himmler, the anti-man," Ravenscroft explains a key feature of the Doppelgänger, or the Double, in the context of the perennial battle between good and evil within each person's soul:

> This inhuman onslaught of the Double on the soul intensifies as we get older, and the conscious experience of resisting evil in order to achieve moral aims continues throughout our lives. But the Doppelgänger, a shadow Being of fear and darkness, is afraid of death, for it cannot face a confrontation with the Light of Spirit—existence beyond the grave. For this reason the Double quits the human soul exactly three days before death. Sensitive souls are aware of this moment when the Double departs

The notion of the Doppelgänger resonated with King's internal struggles between good and evil, between light and darkness. It was a battle that he experienced as familiar, immediate, and, at times, overpowering. King claimed that most of his tattoos, especially those of satanic symbols and figures that invoked the dark side were by and large randomly chosen from tattoo magazines or were artistic decisions made by his prison tattoo artist. However, there was clearly something more in them. They did, in fact, represent the dark side, celebrating the part of King's psychology that felt deeply drawn toward an inversion of categories and social conventions, a world in which evil might be viewed as good, and vice versa.

The struggle between good and evil, embodied by the concept of the Doppelgänger, spoke to King forcefully, and he could see it plainly within himself as an active, present reality. It dominated his thinking to such an extent that various family members found themselves inundated with letters from King that spoke in dark tones. His sister Carol received so many such letters that she finally asked him to stop writing about these dark themes, because she found them so unsettling (he also grew concerned that such writings might be "misconstrued" and used against him). King's drawings (he is quite talented artistically) are similarly foreboding.

During one of our visits, King told me that he was more prone to such dark imagery when feeling upset and depressed. At the time I was not sure what to make of the dark themes expressed in his writings, drawings, and fantasies. Over time, however, as I've come to know King better, I realize that he chooses to dwell on this kind of grim material because it provides an outlet for a troubled soul that feels rejected and betrayed by the universe. It is a way of discharging the tensions emanating from a deep place within him, tensions that he cannot master, subdue, or placate. King actively wrestles with his demons, with his own manifestations of the Doppelgänger, in the realm of fantasy. I suspect as well that such feelings are implicated in his own self-hatred.

The reference in Ravenscroft's book to the Doppelgänger's fear of light, and thus the idea that the Double leaves the soul "exactly three days before death," spoke to King as well. "I've seen that," King wrote to me, referring to his observation that as his mother lay dying in a Beaumont hospital, "mom seemed to finally be at peace." But because his brother Donald was at her bedside, King took her peace as a betrayal. "My brother had never done anything for the family, or even cared about anyone but himself. Why, then, was my mom so delighted to have him there?" King had felt crushed. "It seemed like we (meaning me, Carol, Linda, Dad and Grandma) didn't mean as much to mom as Donald did. I was especially angry and hated to see Donald there." At the time, Bill took Jean's transformation as proof of that which he most feared, that blood ties were stronger than the emotional connection between him and his adoptive mother.

Now, however, King believed that Ravenscroft's rendering of the Double clarified these observations. "I believe I misunderstood what had actually happened that day," he wrote. "Do you know what it's like to carry around the regret of being angry with your dying mother? She died before I could apologize for being upset. In fact, I was so angry, and hated Donald so much, that I refused to go to the hospital the day mom finally died." King now believes that Jean's peaceful state in those final days was actually a sign that the Doppelgänger was fleeing "the Light of Spirit" in anticipation of her death. Her equanimity, in other words, only coincided with Donald's arrival. Bill had simply misunderstood. The notion of the Double therefore served as a mystical palliative for an incident that for years had been the source of considerable guilt as well as resentment, bitterness, and rage. King found a degree of redemption in the concept of the Doppelgänger, for it allowed him to forgive Jean her seeming betrayal and use this insight to bring closure to an episode that had long haunted him.

If the notion of the Doppelgänger had found a powerful resonance within Bill King, it was because it spoke to the two deeply fractured templates around which his emotional life was organized. King was, on the one hand, Jean's prized child, the one who could do no wrong, the one for whom the word "no" did not exist. It was out of this pool of experience that King's malignant narcissism and grandiosity had bloomed like an overfertilized weed. The second template was an inverse of the first. I wondered if Bill King unconsciously identified with the role of pariah to which African Americans in his world had frequently been consigned. King had grown up in a region where "niggers" were the rejected and devalued ones. And yet King had himself been given up by Sylvia for reasons he had never understood, much less accepted. When Kylie Greeney first sent him pictures of Blayne, the newborn's images had a bluish hue because he had been born quite premature. Although the child later became the single most important tie in King's life, King initially rejected Blayne, according to Kylie, describing him as a "nigglet baby," apparently because of the infant's color. Beneath King's Aryan Warrior heroism and bravado lurked an unsettling feeling, a dark secret that he could scarcely bring himself to acknowledge. Unconsciously, King viewed himself as rejected, extruded, and discarded. This was the intolerable metaphor around which he had constructed his life—namely, that *he* was the "nigglet baby"—and he hated the world for it.

MY LAST VISIT WITH BILL KING, before he removed me from his visitor list, started out inauspiciously. It had rained all night, and the week before tropical storm Allison had dumped in excess of thirty-six inches of rain on East Texas, flooding hospitals in Houston and leaving fifteen people dead and billions of dollars in damages. The Polunsky Unit seemed to be enveloped in a fine, gray mist, and the parking lot was covered with puddles of rainwater that had settled in the pits and depressions. I was searched and scanned before walking through the gates and down the long walkway bordered with roses in full bloom, which provided a bright contrast to the otherwise drab, waterlogged landscape.

I hardly recognized King when he was brought to the "box." He had shaved his head and was now noticeably overweight. He volunteered that he had been quite depressed and described the telltale signs: he wasn't exercising; in fact, on many days he wasn't getting up from his bunk. At times he wasn't even motivated to retrieve his lunch tray from the door slot, choosing instead to simply eat the food he had in his "house," consisting mostly of cans of soup and roast beef purchased from the prison commissary.

King was wearing the usual prison-issue white jumpsuit; he had ripped the sleeves off entirely, thereby prominently displaying his tattoos from his shoulders to his wrists. He had gained thirty pounds since I'd last seen him and was now carrying about 225 pounds on his five-foot-seven frame. He had unbuttoned his jumpsuit halfway down the front, Elvis style, betraying a pudgy belly. His shaved head revealed a tattoo I had not seen before: a large pentagram within which a monklike figure was worshiping the devil. The spiderweb tattoo extending from his left armpit down the side of his arm was also prominently visible as King held the black phone in his hand.

He immediately sensed my reaction to his appearance. "It's my prison psycho look," he said, only half in jest. I felt that I was finally meeting a side of Bill King that, until now, I had supposed must exist but had never actually seen. The person before me looked capable of murder, whereas the Bill King I had met when I entered the Polunsky Unit for the first time seemed incapable of such a crime.

King blamed his altered state on "a bunch of issues" weighing heavily on him. Foremost among these was the fact that in the prior six months Kylie had brought Blayne to visit only once. He felt that she was just trying to hurt him by withholding contact with his son—that is, depriving him of what she knew he wanted and needed most. Blayne was, after all, his own flesh and blood. Their last visit had not gone well, either. They had gotten into an argument over it all, and impulsively he had said, "Why don't you just leave." When he looked up, that's exactly what she had done: Kylie was gone. King had a penchant for pushing away the people whom he most needed. Now, once again, they weren't speaking.

King was also upset with his father. He had managed to hire an investigator whose expenses were being underwritten by the same Dallas socialite who was paying for a top-drawer California death penalty attorney. The investigator had discovered evidence that supported King's timeline for what had transpired the night of the murder, and Ronald had said that this development made him more open to Bill's version of events. "Dad said he wanted to believe me all along, but felt that he couldn't because he didn't have anything to rest that belief on," Bill said angrily. Ronald's doubts about his son's claim of innocence dug into Bill. He felt entitled to blind faith from his father, no matter what evidence was presented to the contrary. "I expect Dad to believe in me," he said.

Bill experienced Ronald's hesitation as a form of betrayal, even though it was difficult to dispute the evidence that pointed to Bill's complicity. And Ronald had plenty of firsthand experience with Bill's penchant for distorting things to suit his needs. After all, Ronald had been clashing with Bill for years. It was the dilemma Ronald had been facing ever since he first learned of the murder: how much to believe Bill's version of reality and how much to discount his spin. "You can't believe him all the way," Ronald once said.

Yet he found himself frequently waffling back and forth. "You know he'll lie to you, but then you get back to how much of it am I going to believe?" he said. Ronald hypothesized that perhaps someone had planted Bill's Zippo lighter back up the logging road in an effort to frame him. Maybe that cigarette butt with Bill's DNA had simply been in the truck's ashtray from the previous days when they were clearing land, just as Bill said. These were questions that Ronald found himself debating endlessly, grasping for something to hold on to. But the very fact that Ronald could not simply accept Bill's account as the whole truth made Bill angry and depressed. He found little comfort in the likelihood that Ronald might now accept some of Bill's account if it had been verified.

I asked Bill how the investigator's findings, if true, really changed things; it was a minor point, this question of the timeline. If King was with Berry (which King wasn't contesting) and it could be established that they picked Byrd up later—if the eyewitness who saw Byrd in Berry's truck simply had the time wrong—what difference did it make? It meant only that the murder happened later than the prosecution claimed, but it didn't change the key evidence that had convicted King of capital murder. Nevertheless, King, his attorney, and the investigator were working feverishly on King's federal habeas corpus appeal. They were attempting to attack every possible point in the state's case against King, and *any* detail that might undermine the state's theory of events was useful for this purpose.

Bill's fury with his father stemmed from the kind of person he was—someone who needed hook-line-and-sinker acceptance of his views. Anything short of that was, to him, about as good as nothing at all. True, there was a great deal riding on the question of whether King was believed to be telling the truth: his life. However, his desperate circumstance was only part of what fueled his rigidity and unreasonable demands for allegiance. Those who knew him readily recognized this familiar trait; it was the way Bill was about many things. He did not find it easy to relinquish a position or to alter a point of view. There was a tenacity and bullheadedness about him that could drive people crazy. Whether the issue was his account of what had transpired on the night of a murder or how best to play mechanic, his way or no way was often how it had to be with Bill King.

Another topic occupying King's attention was his attempt, for the first time in his life, to engage the question of his adoption. He had written to his biological parents and siblings, in addition to Ronald and his adoptive sisters, and asked for the story of his adoption. Sylvia had not bothered to respond, and neither had one of his adoptive sisters, but the accounts by Ronald, Carol, Sammy Rae, his biological father, and his biological sisters, Samantha and Serena, all appeared to converge in their main themes. According to Sammy's account, Sylvia had been heavily into drugs and it was Sylvia who had abandoned Bill, Sammy, and the two girls. Samantha and Serena, on the other hand, indicated that Sammy had been doing drugs and behaving abusively. While the particulars differed, the accounts all confirmed that it was the chaos produced by a mixture of marital conflicts, drugs, and poverty that had led Sammy and Sylvia to hand their baby over to Ronald and Jean.

I have always believed that beneath the arrogance and the hubris, beneath his ability to charm and seduce, Bill King had self-loathing at his core. One of the questions he frequently asked himself, once he started exploring the fact of his adoption, was why it was that *he* was abandoned. Why had Sylvia chosen him, specifically, as the child she would relinquish? Sylvia already had two other children at the time, Serena and Samantha, but it was Bill that she had decided to give away. Eventually, Sylvia gave birth to half a dozen other children, all of which she kept. When Bill learned that he was adopted at the age of thirteen, the source of his profound feelings of estrangement had been given shape, if vaguely. Just weeks prior to the murder, during the ill-fated reunion with Sylvia on Easter weekend, she had told Bill that he was "the product of the devil." It was a disorienting revelation, and it confirmed his worst fears that perhaps he was, after all, a monster. A year later, following his arrest for the murder of James Byrd, Bill wrote to Ronald, in reference to Sylvia, "Thanks for saving me from *that* woman." But Bill King had been vulnerable to abandonment all his life, and it was due, in large part, to his feelings of being so fundamentally abandoned from the very beginning.

King's identity as a white supremacist must have been, for some time, a corrective to that feeling. Via this affiliation, for once he felt that he belonged. And it is no coincidence that notions of lineage and genetic belonging are so central to white supremacist ideology. His prison-library explorations and surreptitious reading of smuggled white supremacist literature while on Planet Beto revolved, to a great extent, around idiosyncratic ideas of racial purity: safeguarding the gene pool. With the vengeance of the true believer, King finally felt legitimate. But following his release from Beto, as he at- tempted to reintegrate himself into ordinary life in sleepy Jasper, those moor- ings became increasingly less reliable.

I did not know that this was my last visit with King. He gave me no indi- cation while we spoke that he was about to rupture the tie between us by tak- know of his decision, he claimed that it was necessary to drop me to add someone who could help get Blayne from Jasper to Livingston. I have won- dered since then whether he felt that during our last conversation he had in- advertently revealed too much—had the young man who preferred to re- main an enigma perhaps gone too far in our talks? Did he feel vulnerable, overexposed? King and I continued to correspond, but of course it was not the same. Whatever the cause of the break in our relationship, as it turned out, I was left with this "prison psycho" image of King as my last impression. It was a malignant stranger, not the more innocent-seeming Bill King I had first met, who said goodbye to me for the last time when the corrections officer informed us that the visit was over.

As I drove away from the Polunsky Unit, I felt discomfited by the en- counter. It had been difficult to see King this way—depressed, angry, dis- connected. It was as if the affable, engaging version of Bill King had taken refuge elsewhere, supplanted by Possum. This was the real tragedy in King's life. He had been a boy of such promise. And that old sparkle of possibility was still evident in almost every communication we had, in practically all of our visits and correspondence. The hard-won character of his accomplish- ments was evident as well: he was an autodidact, and he sometimes mispro- nounced words that he had discovered in his reading but had never heard anyone utter. Nearly every letter was laced with references to authors he had read, from Norman Vincent Peale (he pronounced the name PAY-LAY, like the renowned Brazilian soccer star Pele) to William James. He liked to ex- cerpt things he had read: musings, philosophical reflections, or simply inter- esting quotes. His tastes varied greatly, from the poetry of Emily Dickinson to the lyrics of the Dave Matthews Band. He read and quoted from film reviews. He had become something of a jazz and an opera buff, the latter un- der the tutelage of a gay school teacher from New York with whom he cor- responded. The school teacher sent him programs from the opera performances he had seen recently and explained the world of opera to him, encouraging King to tune his built-in prison radio to Houston's public radio station so that he could hear it for himself. And King did, at least for a while.

It was all too easy for me to see how the people closest to King—his adoptive mother and father, in particular—were blinded by all this promise and insensitive to his faults. I still puzzle over exactly why he was riddled with such fatal flaws. It may be that he had experienced more than his share of sadness and travail, although, by his own admission, he had been overly pampered as a child. Perhaps this excessive love proved as problematic as negligence and deprivation, for it seems to have led to a narcissistic pathology whereby grandiosity and omnipotence succeeded in holding sway most of the time over feelings of emptiness, impotence, and abandonment. Some might argue that the explanation for King's life was simply in his genes, that a chemical imbalance had set him on a life course that he had simply played out, without reflection or awareness, carrying to fruition some strange plan encoded deep within his genetics. I don't believe this. Whatever role his genetic makeup played in shaping his temperament and proclivities, the Bill King who participated in the murder of James Byrd was more made than born. Possum, the individual I glimpsed during that last visit, was a creature created out of sorry beginnings, a childhood disrupted by overindulgence and profound and overwhelming loss, and by prison. True, Bill King never divulged enough of his secrets to betray, ultimately, how he became someone capable of the worst crime in recent memory. In the end, he remained just what he wanted to be: an enigma.

THE MYSTERIES THAT PERSISTED in shrouding King were not dispelled by his final appeal for mercy. By August of 2002, having exhausted all of his state appeals, Bill King and Richard Ellis, his death row attorney, filed a habeas corpus brief in the federal court in Beaumont. With four hundred pages of argument and four hundred pages of supporting exhibits, the brief was one of the longest ever filed in a Texas death penalty proceeding. The brief argued that Bill King was innocent and that someone other than King had been the third perpetrator. It also claimed that the state had violated King's right to a fair trial, both by not disclosing the fact that a key witness had testified in exchange for a reduced sentence and by violating King's First and Fourteenth

Amendment rights. Finally, the appeal argued that King had been the victim
of ineffective counsel during his capital murder trial.

The contention that King was innocent of the murder was less than compelling. The thrust of King's claims of innocence revolved around the idea that he had never gone to Huff Creek Road that night with Brewer and Berry. His appeal argued that evidence linking him to the murder could be explained away. For example, perhaps Brewer or Berry had taken King's Zippo lighter to the crime scene, or else it could have dropped out of King's pocket while he was riding around in the truck earlier. Similarly, the cigarette butt with his DNA could have been in the ashtray and then knocked out when Byrd struggled for his life as he was dragged from the pickup's cab. As King had been doing all along, he and his attorney argued again that the presence of the cigarette butt and the lighter did not necessarily prove that King was at the crime scene that night.

They also argued that the bloodstained sandal found at the Timbers Apartments actually belonged to Louis Berry, not Bill King. Jasper authorities had made casts of three distinct footprints found in the sandy soil on the logging road: one from a boot, one from a tennis shoe, and one from a sandal with a print pattern that matched those made by Outback sandals. It was established that Berry was wearing boots, and Brewer tennis shoes, both of which had Byrd's blood on them. And, at King's trial, when shown a photograph of a pair of Outback sandals found at the apartment, Keisha Atkins had testified that King was wearing them when he left the apartment that night.

A central ambiguity lay in the two pairs of identical, chocolate-brown Outback sandals, one pair a size 9½, the other a size 10. Byrd's blood had been found on one of the size 10 sandals, but King's shoe size is 9½. Shawn Berry was serving a life sentence for the Byrd murder at the Ramsey Unit in Rosharon, Texas, when I interviewed him there. Berry told me that he had purchased both pairs of sandals at a two-for-the-price-of-one sale at Payless Shoes and given the size 10 pair to King, who was with him at the time. In court testimony Louis Berry had testified that one pair of the sandals had belonged to his brother and the other to King. Louis owned his own pair of sandals, but they were of a different brand. However, King and his attorney seized on this shoe-size discrepancy to argue that Louis Berry (who wore a size 10) was the third person at the murder scene, not Bill King. King had thrown Louis out of the apartment the day before the murder, but Louis had been in and out of the apartment for weeks and much of his clothing remained in the apartment.

For obvious reasons, the brief ignored other material that readily belied this contention. For example, in one of King's kites, he seems to acknowledge that he was wearing a sweatshirt and sandals that night. "As far as the clothes I had on, I don't think any blood was on my pants or sweatshirt, but I think my sandles may have had some dark brown substance on the bottom of em," he wrote to Brewer. King once told me that he assumed that the blood on his sandal had come from splatter when he was helping Berry wash the bloody chain the day after the murder. At the time he did not deny knowing what had taken place ("I knew that they were going to kill him"), and he acknowledged destroying evidence by helping wash the truck and chain the following day. Now, however, he was denying that they were his sandals altogether; in other words, he had changed his story. One plausible explanation for the shoe-size discrepancy is that Shawn and Bill may simply have been fitted with sandals that were a half size bigger than they typically wore. One Payless employee who was familiar with the Outback sandals told me that the sandals tended to run small.

To further support the contention that it was Louis Berry who had participated in the murder, King's attorney mustered a June 2001 letter that he had received from Russell Brewer. Brewer, like King, was on death row waiting for the courts to complete their automatic reviews before setting his execution date. In this correspondence Brewer recants his own trial testimony that he, Shawn Berry, and Bill King murdered James Byrd. Instead, Brewer was now alleging that Louis Berry was the third individual involved, not King. Brewer claimed that Louis returned to the apartment after learning that King and the others had been arrested and disposed of the bloodstained sweatshirts that Brewer claimed he and Louis had been wearing.

One couldn't help but wonder, recalling Brewer's kite offering to take the fall for the murder, whether the offer was now finally being put into play. It is true that the sweatshirts described by Russell Brewer (and noted in King's kite to Brewer after the murder) have never been found. However, one might also wonder why Louis would not have also disposed of his brother's boots and clothing (which were the most bloodstained of all) if he went back into the apartment to destroy evidence linking them to the crime. Shawn Berry's bloodstained clothing remained at the apartment for weeks until the FBI inspected it a second time. It is more likely that King and Brewer disposed of the sweatshirts. Brewer testified at his trial that he had not noticed the blood stains on his Nikes ("If I knew there was blood on my shoes, I sure wouldn't have left them"). And the exceedingly small drop of blood on the Outback sandals would have been easy to overlook. This would explain why King and Brewer neglected to dispose of the shoes along with the sweatshirts.

The effort to cast Louis Berry as a key participant in the murder also falters in other ways. In his statement to authorities, Shawn Berry said that Byrd had been sprayed in the face with black spray paint. In one of Brewer's kites to King, he voiced concern that investigators had checked under his fingernails for black paint residue. In his only mention of Louis Berry in his kites to Brewer, King reassures Brewer that fingerprints on the can of spray paint would not necessarily implicate Brewer: "Well, where's the can with your fingerprints, Huh?" King wrote to Brewer. "If it's the same can that was in Shawn's truck, hell, we all touched that damn thing; even Lewis."

Similarly, the only mention of Louis Berry in Brewer's kites to King is to complain about his apparent comfort with blacks: "Lewis was over at some Blacks house playin music over there. Well the whole damn party was moved over there." Thus there is a striking absence of any suggestion that Louis Berry was involved in Byrd's murder until after King is on death row.

The second issue raised by Richard Ellis in King's habeas corpus brief regarded the admissibility of King's tattoos, writings, books, and correspondence as a basis for establishing motive. King's trial attorneys had consistently objected to the admission of this evidence from the opening moments of the trial, arguing that the First and Fourteenth Amendments to the Constitution protected their client's freedom of expression. The habeas corpus brief built on those objections as another basis for arguing that King should be freed or, at the very least, retried.

Finally, the third major thrust of the brief, and perhaps the most substantive, was that King had been inadequately represented during his capital murder trial. The fact that Sonny Cribbs had not made an opening statement or a statement at the beginning of the defense phase of the trial suggested, at the very least, a lack of preparation. King's attorneys had presented few witnesses and no experts to rebut the prosecution's case, not even the argument that Byrd was conscious as he was dragged along the pavement. Cribbs's rebuttal of Brown's testimony had been surprisingly anemic, especially in light of the fact that his client's life depended on it.

Even without an expert witness, evidence was readily available to raise questions about the state's claim that Byrd was conscious during his ordeal. For example, Shawn Berry, hardly friendly to King's defense, told investigators that Brewer had kicked Byrd in the head during the initial assault, a blow that had purportedly dropped the victim to the ground. According to Berry, Byrd appeared to be unconscious at that point. Brewer's severely swollen and bruised toe lent support to this account.

Berry also said that the chain had slipped off Byrd's ankles some twenty yards down the logging road and that King, who, according to Berry, was driving, had backed up and actually run over Byrd. (It was at this location that the three cigarette butts containing DNA from the three suspects were also found.) This account was congruent with the blood-splatter evidence discovered by Curtis Frame on the underside of the truck. It was also supported by the presence of a pie-tin-size pool of blood at that location on the logging road, indicating that the victim had lain there long enough for his blood to collect. However, the defense mustered none of these arguments to create plausible support for the notion that Byrd might have already been unconscious at the time that he was chained to Berry's truck. In other words, King's attorneys did not make a pivotal argument that might have undermined the kidnapping charge—the charge on which the death penalty depended.

When I asked Cribbs why he had not obtained his own expert to counter the pathologist's testimony, he said that he had not been able to find an expert who could specifically refute Brown's conclusions. The best he could do, he said, was a pathologist who was willing to testify that the autopsy did not prove *conclusively* that Byrd was conscious. According to Cribbs, such testimony, especially given its tentative character, also had a downside: it would mean placing the autopsy photographs into the jurors' hands once again. Given their gore, Cribbs considered the photographs to be extremely prejudicial to his client. Thus, Cribbs claims that he weighed the pros and cons of allowing weak counter-testimony to stand versus reintroducing the disturbing autopsy photographs and concluded that the wiser course was not to bring in his expert. King's habeas corpus attorney argued further that Cribbs and Jones had done very little to pursue King's version of events, as reflected in the fact that a mere three witnesses (and no experts) had testified for the defense.

The most damaging accusation presented in King's habeas corpus appeal, however, was that Cribbs and Jones had acted unethically. To support this claim, Ellis submitted a copy of a document titled "Literary rights agreement between C. Haden Cribbs, Brack Jones, Jr. and John William King, February 25, 1999." The date was the eve of King's sentencing, after the Jasper jury had already found King guilty of Byrd's murder. As the jury deliberated between the death penalty or life imprisonment, King was presented with a seven-page, single-spaced contractual document, ostensibly "for and in consideration of the mutual benefits to the parties." In it, King granted Cribbs and Jones "irrevocable rights" to King's life story for a period of twenty-four months (the latter stipulation was in the form of a hand-written amendment inserted by King). The creative rights agreement specified that any financial consideration that might accrue from the commercial use of King's life story would be divided up into three equal parts. One third would go to Cribbs, one third to Jones, and one third to Ronald King ("and, upon his death, one third to Carol Spadaccini—my sister," King wrote in the margin). The contract, Ellis argued, suggested a conflict of interest because King's life story might be worth considerably less had he been found innocent. Indeed, the Texas State Bar Association appears to prohibit attorneys from entering into such arrangements with their clients.

When questioned about the ethics of the "creative rights agreement," Sonny Cribbs grew circumspect. He was hesitant to discuss the agreement but drew my attention to the fact that he had not actually signed it. While this was true—only Jones and King had signed the contract—it seems unlikely that Jones would have drafted the document without consultation with Cribbs, who was the lead attorney in the case.

Cribbs argued that he and Jones were much more active in pursuing King's defense than Ellis's brief or the trial transcript would indicate. For example, Cribbs maintains that he sent all of the FBI's DNA evidence to a reputable genetics lab in Dallas, but the lab's report replicated the FBI lab's findings. One of King's arguments was that someone saw him at the apartment later that night and might be able to provide an alibi. Cribbs maintained that his team interviewed "every single person in the apartment unit" but found no one who would corroborate King's story. Cribbs also said that of King's relatives, only King's father was willing to testify on his behalf. His adoptive sisters refused, as did his adoptive brother, who had actually written a strongly condemnatory letter about King, in essence disowning him. King's biological mother, Sylvia, also refused to testify on King's behalf, as did a number of King's friends, according to Cribbs. "I spent every night during the trial interviewing people," Cribbs maintained, but he could not turn up anyone willing to testify who would be helpful.

Cribbs also suggested that his defense was sometimes hampered by the fact that he and King had an on-again, off-again alliance. "He had mood swings," Cribbs remarked. He said he never knew what to expect when he showed up at the Jasper County jail or, later in Livingston, when King was transferred to the Terrell Unit to await trial. "King would say 'I'm not meeting with a fucking lawyer today!' And yet the next time I'd come he'd be fine," Cribbs recollected. He also cited King's "Logical Reasoning" statement, which King had sent to the *Dallas Morning News* over the strenuous objections of his lawyer. At one juncture Cribbs even filed a motion to have himself removed from the case because of these conflicts with his client, but Judge Golden refused to let him step aside.

PERHAPS THE MOST TELLING QUALITY about King's federal appeal is his continuing claim of innocence, despite all indications that he is not. It is not a terribly surprising stance—many of King's confederates on death row also cling to claims of innocence well past the point when reasonable bystanders would believe them. King is a desperate man trying to save his own life. Yet it is a posture that keeps King, in the end, mired in his role as Possum, incapable of finding his way out of the inner turmoil that has plagued him for most of his life.

Knowing King, having seen his capabilities, I find it terribly sad to see such wasted promise. Bill King is a flawed soul, a man who has spent his life acting on a fatal metaphor. And he is blind to or perhaps simply unwilling to face the truth: the truth about who he is, the truth about his crime. He also seems incapable of feeling remorse, although I have never quite relinquished the idea that perhaps, through the convoluted workings of his mental life, he has simply managed to convince himself of his innocence. To do

otherwise would mean to unravel. Yet the forgiveness he needs, and the tran-
scendence that it might offer, requires just such an acknowledgement.

Long after my visits with King came to an end, I find myself disturbed by the discontinuities in his identity. The most difficult to accept is that he can seem like such an ordinary character in so many ways, and yet apparently is capable of such an extraordinarily heinous act. Disturbing as it is, Bill King is all too human, a man driven by human needs and human anxieties. It would be much easier to think of him simply as a monster. However, while it is clear that his psychology is marked by significant character problems and strange idiosyncrasies, and while the murder of James Byrd is a monstrous act, in many respects King seems to be a man whose emotional life is defined mostly by concerns that are familiar enough. The kids that King grew up with never dreamed that he would end up on death row. His family, though aware of his self-centeredness and his penchant for manipulation and his inability to tolerate frustration, never imagined the course his life would take. The people who knew him following his release from the Beto Unit were surprised to learn that he had committed such an act. This is true even for those who knew of King's racist views, with the possible exception of Russell Brewer. Shawn Berry, I suspect, is one of the surprised ones, a miscalculation for which he will spend the remainder of his life in a maximum-security cell, isolated from the general population, a target, if for different reasons, of both white and black inmates.

I am reminded of the story recounted by Guy James Gray about the 1920s lynching in neighboring Newton County. The feature of it that kept intruding into his thoughts, that he found most disturbing, was that the lynching had been carried out by "upstanding" members of the community. "Normal people," in other words, are capable of doing the unspeakable. Though few if any in Jasper would have described Bill King as an "upstanding" citizen, King was not feared, and the trajectory of his life did not seem to point toward death row. On the contrary, people like Sparky, his probation officer, had bent over backwards to help him out precisely because they saw the promise in him and because he seemed reachable. In fact, Bill's father, Ronald, still clings to that hope, still believes in the possibility of Bill's innocence despite the trial and despite the fact that, in retrospect, one can see that Bill's life has been organized around a debilitating flaw. Like many others, I, too, did not want to believe that relatively ordinary people could commit such brutal acts. If "upstanding citizens" are capable of lynching people, if those around us whose lives are punctuated by simmering but not terribly obvious loss and rage can brutally torture and murder a black stranger who happens to cross their path, it means that, given the right alchemy, perhaps anyone might become capable of monstrous cruelty. After years of thinking about Bill King—his life, his motives, his world—I am haunted by the realization that the distance from Bill King to Possum may be shorter than we care to believe.